BRITISH STRATEGY IN THE FAR EAST

1919-1939

LOUIS, William Roger. **British strategy in the Far East, 1919-1939.**
Oxford, 1971. 284p map tab bibl 75-854550. 10.50. ISBN
0-19-822346-3

The story of the road to disaster for Great Britain's policy in East
Asia between World Wars. From ally Japan became enemy. Revolution in China swept out the British. Those who fashioned British policy
in this era were, of course, severely handicapped by their rapidly
ebbing power to shape events. The Victorian heritage of trade and investment remained but the British no longer had the means to protect
it. Moreover, the British faced a dilemma: the reconciliation of the
desire to support China for the sake of both fair play and Britain's
economic stake there with the wish to preserve friendship with Japan,
recognizing that Japan's desires for a special position on the Asian
mainland might have some legitimacy. Louis' book uses newly opened
British archival papers. He writes well, and it is a pity that he allows
copious use of quotation to interrupt at times the flow and grace of his
argument.

BRITISH STRATEGY IN THE FAR EAST
1919-1939

BY

Wm. ROGER LOUIS
University of Texas

CLARENDON PRESS · OXFORD

1971

Oxford University Press, Ely House, London W.1

GLASGOW   NEW YORK   TORONTO   MELBOURNE   WELLINGTON
CAPE TOWN   SALISBURY   IBADAN   NAIROBI   DAR ES SALAAM   LUSAKA   ADDIS ABABA
BOMBAY   CALCUTTA   MADRAS   KARACHI   LAHORE   DACCA
KUALA LUMPUR   SINGAPORE   HONG KONG   TOKYO

PRINTED IN GREAT BRITAIN BY
WILLIAM CLOWES & SONS, LIMITED
LONDON, BECCLES AND COLCHESTER

TO
Geoffrey Hudson
Kenneth Kirkwood
AND
Elizabeth Monroe

CONTENTS

The Far East and Foreign Concessions

INTRODUCTION

WITHIN the last three years, British documents on the Far East have become accessible for the entirety of the European inter-war years. This book tries to survey their content and meaning. Any historian audacious enough to attempt such a task needs to begin with several disclaimers. This volume is impressionistic and thematically selective, not systematic in treatment. Any number of the issues raised in the course of the argument deserve exhaustive investigation in the form of dissertations or monographs, and indeed many such works are already in progress. Nevertheless this general (but in some ways specific) study of these previously unavailable and quite voluminous sources does reveal several important themes that hang together and that deserve greater attention than they have received in the past. To name only the most controversial, the origin of the Pacific war might have been in part *racial*.

Like 'imperialism', the word 'racism' is difficult for scholars to manage. Both are vague and imprecise concepts. Perhaps ultimately their significance lies in psychological or cultural values, or in the techniques of asserting superiority and the reaction of the suppressed. This phenomenon in the Far East obviously is worth pursuing, though not, I think, in the context of this volume. Among other reasons, any author who employs the concept of race runs the risk of interpreting the problems of another era in the light of the troubles of his own times, and of distorting the issue of racism out of proportion to other central themes. In so far as I do attempt to deal with the question, I have tried to achieve some measure of exactitude by using the word 'race' as it was used by the protagonists of British statecraft. Basically, there were two ways in which they envisaged the concept. First, there strongly existed the idea of individual races. The British believed they saw the difference between the Japanese and Chinese races as distinctly as they saw the

difference between the Latin race and their own. Englishmen
spoke proudly of the 'British race' and more often than not
believed it to be superior to any other. Second, and perhaps
more important, the question of race in the Pacific basin meant
colour: Australia, New Zealand, the United States, and
Canada were white; Japan was yellow. British statesmen
referred to the Japanese—the 'yellow men'—as their loyal but
dangerous allies during the First World War, and to the
Americans as their 'kith and kin', at least those Americans 'of
old stock', meaning, of course, those of English descent.[1]

In 1921 Great Britain terminated the Alliance she had
maintained with Japan since 1902. As will be seen from chapter
II, the question of race figured prominently in the discussions of
the Prime Ministers of the Empire as they analysed the problem.
They assumed for economic and demographic reasons that
Japan as a growing and powerful nation had to expand. Where?
The white nations ringed off Japan from their own territories,
yet objected to her expansion on the Asian mainland. To some
extent these issues came to a head at the time of the Washington
Conference, when the Alliance was terminated. The Permanent Under-Secretary of State for Foreign Affairs for most of the
1930s, Sir Robert (Lord) Vansittart, once half ruefully com-

---

[1] Apart from a few notable exceptions such as Hannah Arendt, in *The Origins of
Totalitarianism*, scholars have only begun to examine the concepts of imperialism
and racism in their historiographical context. One outstanding recent pioneering
effort in the British field, written with grace and insight, is by Lewis P. Curtis, Jr.,
Anglo-Saxons and Celts: A Study of Anti-Irish Prejudice in Victorian England (Conference
on British Studies, University of Bridgeport, Conn., 1968). To give an example of
one of his major conclusions: 'If many educated Victorians actually believed in the
existence of a wide racial and cultural gap between themselves and Irish Celts,
then how much more profound a gulf must have separated them from the Indian,
African, and Asian peoples over whom they held formal or informal sway. The
ethnocentric ladder on which the races of the world had their assigned positions in
Anglo-Saxonist eyes must have been much longer than is usually assumed, if the
Irish occupied a position little more than half-way between the Anglo-Saxons at
the top and the Hottentots at the bottom. Since Anglo-Saxonists accused Irishmen
of being unstable, childish, violent, lazy, feckless, feminine, and primitive, and
since they likened them to Hottentots, Maoris, Chinese, pigs, apes, and chimpan-
zees, one may well wonder what epithets, adjectives, and similies were left in the
Anglo-Saxon vocabulary to characterize men of darker skin and more primitive
cultures' (p. 121). As will be seen from the quotations of this book, the Chinese and
Japanese were the exception that partly proves the rule: both were, at different
times and even simultaneously, admired and despised, the objects of British friendship but also fear and even hatred.

mented that Britain ended the Alliance 'to please America'. If one studies the minutes and memoranda of Vansittart and his colleagues, it becomes quite clear that he believed American fear of the 'Yellow Peril' to be at the heart of Britain's decision to terminate the Alliance. But it is also quite clear that he saw broader aspects of the question. If Great Britain wished to achieve the overriding goal of naval disarmament, she had to pay the price of severing her intimate relationship with Japan. To summarize the contention, he was fully aware that powerful strategic, political, and economic forces as well as the issue of race helped to bring about the end of the Alliance—an observation more or less in line with the traditional interpretation of the causes of the Pacific war. To modify his logic (as he and his colleagues often did), one could make out a strong case that Japan contributed to the causes of war by her quest for political domination over China and economic hegemony in the Far East, but that in an evaluation of Japanese motives the racial issue was perhaps crucial—a train of logic more or less in line with the so-called 'revisionist' school of historical thought.

To evaluate the causes of the Pacific war in relation to traditional and 'revisionist' theories is, to say the least, far from easy. Perhaps middle ground can be reached by posing a hypothesis of Professor Jean Stengers: if there is an important connection between historical truth and psychological truth, then it is important to comprehend how men understood the events of the time in order to understand the meaning of the events themselves. In dealing with such topics as the Chinese revolution, the Manchurian crisis, the economic problems of the 1930s, and, finally, the question of appeasement, I have tried to illuminate the preconceptions or set of often unstated assumptions about Asia that British statesmen brought with them as they tried to cope with Japan and China. So that the framework of the book and my approach to the topics will be clear, by way of introduction I shall attempt briefly to illustrate how Englishmen typical of their age viewed the general history of the Far East and how they broadly conceived of the political and economic problems of the 1920s and 1930s. For the sake of convenience and clarity, I choose as particularly representative the ideas of two men who probably contributed more than any others to the continuity of British Far Eastern policy in the

inter-war years, Sir Victor Wellesley,[2] and Sir John Pratt.[3] The
following quotations will illustrate, I hope, not only how they
understood the history of Asia and Britain's past experience
with Japan and China, but also the extent to which they
viewed the causes of possible war as political or economic, how
they conceived of the racial issue and how these variables in
time changed.

Wellesley frequently compared Japan with Great Britain or
Germany, and often noted the differences between Japan and
China.

On the one hand, you have an enormous country like China, almost
a continent in itself, with a teeming population of 400 millions and
untold natural resources, but with a Government which is corrupt,
incompetent and obstructive. On the other hand, you have, lying off
that continent, a small island empire, geographically situated very
much like the British Islands off Europe, with a population of some
60 millions, thrifty, industrious and enterprising people, disciplined
very much on the Prussian model, with a Government in full
authority and exercising efficient control (except so far as the army
and navy are concerned), but poor in natural resources, their chief
asset consisting almost exclusively in cheap labour.

Within a brief space of fifty years Japan has succeeded in con-
verting herself from a semi-barbarous State into one of the Great
Powers of the world. This rapid progress is inseparable from a great
expansion of her economic needs as a civilised nation. Like Great
Britain she has become more and more dependent on the outside
world for the supply of her raw materials and for her markets for
manufactured goods, but unlike Great Britain she has no great
Colonial Empire. Korea and Formosa are comparatively small
markets, and produce a still more limited range of raw materials. Her

[2] Victor Alexander Augustus Henry Wellesley, K.C.M.G., C.B. Noted for his
industry and ability for trenchant analysis, he achieved the height of his influence
as Deputy Under-Secretary of State for Foreign Affairs 1925–36. He wrote three
books: *Conversations with Napoleon III* (London, 1934), *Diplomacy in Fetters* (London,
1944), and *Recollections of a Soldier-Diplomat* (London, 1947). In addition to mastering
the art of forceful prose, Wellesley was a keen amateur artist. Not least, he was
a shrewd observer of King Leopold's Congo.

[3] John Thomas Pratt, K.B.E., C.M.G. After serving in the Consular Service in
China, Pratt became Adviser on Far Eastern Affairs in the Foreign Office for
thirteen years, retiring in 1938. His book, *War and Politics in China* (London, 1943),
is probably the most important work on Far Eastern policy written by a British
official. Pratt highly distrusted Japan and occasionally referred to her 'Franken-
stein movements' in China—an analogy of interest because his brother was the
actor, Boris Karloff.

people are hampered by the immigration laws of a number of countries such as Australia, Canada and the United States of America.[4]

Wellesley's interpretation of modern Japanese history in relation to China can also be stated succinctly in his own words. He wrote during the Manchurian crisis in 1932 that Japan was:

(1) Defensive (1890–95): The Sino-Japanese War was fought to keep off the Chinese menace from the shores of Japan.

(2) Intrusive (1895–1914): To obtain in China a position *equal* to that of the Treaty Powers. This involved the war with Russia, who had challenged this intrusion where she herself wished to intrude, and the acquisition of territorial rights in South Manchuria.

(3) Aggressive (1914–21): The attempt during the war to obtain *special* rights, superior to those of other Powers, *e.g.*, hegemony in China. This attempt was unsuccessful and recoiled upon Japan. It ended in the abrogation of the Anglo-Japanese Alliance, and what was virtually a trial of Japan before a court of the nations at Washington.

(4) Conciliatory (1922–27): Commercial interests in Japan, with increasing extension of business and fear of boycotts, were co-operating with the Foreign Office (after its Washington experience) in developing a policy of friendly relations— . . . as opposed to the military policies of force and bullying. In 1923 came the great earthquake, which for some years shattered the self-confidence of Japan.

(5) Resentful (1927–32): A change for the worse, due to the failure of a friendly policy and the increasing Nationalist sentiment in China . . . the real struggle was developing in Manchuria over the Chinese policy of encirclement of the South Manchurian line. This led to the outbreak of the present struggle in September 1931, after the Japanese had been trying for at least five years to

---

[4] Memorandum by Wellesley, 6 February 1932 [F 1033/1/10], F.O. 371/16146; cf. *Documents on British Foreign Policy* [hereafter abbreviated throughout the entire book as *D.B.F.P.*], Second Series, IX, No. 356. The *D.B.F.P.* are models of scholarly editing, but they suffer two serious handicaps: they rarely reproduce minutes, thus disguising who actually shaped British policy and the dialectical and frank nature of the process; and, with few exceptions, they deal only with Foreign Office documents. Sometimes the Cabinet and the Prime Ministers of the Empire made the important decisions about foreign policy, as will be especially evident in chapter II. Reading the *D.B.F.P.* one might scarcely guess that the Imperial Conference ever took place, or at least that it had any particular significance.

solve the railway and other problems in Manchuria by peaceful negotiation.[5]

As he observed many times, Britain's policy in China differed fundamentally from Japan's. Britain worked for a strong and united China where British trade would flourish; he believed that Japan, on the other hand, wished to keep China weak and disunited. 'If we want to understand the Japanese attitude,' he had written earlier, 'we cannot do better than ask ourselves how we would welcome a Japanese invitation to co-operate in a policy aiming at the unification of a strong and unfriendly Europe.'[6]

To use Sir John Pratt's ideas as illustrative of British official thought about China, they can be summed up in a single sentence: 'Her vast territory, occupied by one-quarter of the human race endowed with almost every gift except a sense of political realities and a capacity for centralised government, is still an undeveloped market of almost fabulous potentialities.'[7] The real importance of the China market to Britain was slight, consisting of only 2·5 per cent of British exports. China ranked about fifteenth as a British customer and British investments there represented less than 5 per cent of total British investments abroad. Yet China held a place in British aspirations out of all proportion to those figures. Since the days of Marco Polo, men dreamed of the magnificent potential for trade. British policy aimed to prevent this great potential market from being sealed off. Pratt summarized that theme of China's history since the beginning of the twentieth century in the following way:

China has always . . . been the occasion of political activities by Japan and the Great Powers of Europe and America out of all proportion to the volume of trade actually passing over her borders. At the beginning of the 20th century two related developments were the cause of considerable anxiety: the increasing weakness of China, which laid her open to aggression and spoliation; and the ambitions and growing rivalry of Russia and Japan. The general object of British policy was to prevent this great potential market being closed

[5] Memorandum by Wellesley, 1 February 1932 [F 654/1/10], F.O. 371/16143; cf. *D.B.F.P.*, Second Series, IX, No. 239.

[6] Minute by Wellesley, 10 March 1928 [F 1123/7/10], F.O. 371/13165.

[7] Memorandum by Pratt, 1 December 1933 [F 7818/5189/61].

against us either by obstructive action on the part of China herself or by the predatory activities of other Powers.[8]

He went on to emphasize that Britain had been the first of the western powers to open China to the outside world, and that Britain had taken the lead in the development of China's system of communications:

We had been the first to force China to open the treaty ports to the trade of all the world, and, our constant endeavour had been to induce China to open the door still wider and extend the field for foreign trade and enterprise. By our pioneer work in railway construction and by securing the opening of the inland waterways to steam navigation, we had accomplished something towards the opening up of the interior of China, but, in the absence of a Government capable of efficient administration or of understanding the problems involved in modern commercial and international relations, progress had been disappointingly slow.[9]

Summarizing the reason for concluding the Anglo-Japanese Alliance, Pratt continued:

At the end of the 19th century we occupied the foremost position in the Far East, but, in proportion as the march of events gradually drew China nearer to the main currents of world affairs, this position was more and more threatened by the approaching conflict between Russia and Japan and by the aggressive activities of European Powers. China now began to be cut up into spheres of influence, from which British enterprise was excluded, and railway and other concessions were extorted from her as instruments of imperialistic penetration. We did not wish to see China fall under the political or economic domination of any Power or group of Powers; nor did we wish to see Japan destroyed by Russia. . . . We therefore entered into an Alliance with Japan, which enabled her to roll back the Russian menace both from her own shores and from China.[10]

Another comment by Pratt reveals a typical British interpretation of the Boxer rebellion.

The Boxer rebellion was the last convulsive effort of Old China to get rid of its difficulties and its problems by driving the foreign virus out of China altogether. This having failed, room was made for the new forces that were from now on to shape the destiny of China, and that consciously aimed at learning the secrets of the West and at fitting China to take her place alongside of the other great States composing the civilised world. The reform movement affected every

[8] Ibid.   [9] Ibid.   [10] Ibid.

phase of the national life and directed it into the channels in which it is still flowing. We were anxious that the movement should be encouraged and afforded every opportunity of succeeding. We adopted, accordingly, a sympathetic attitude towards the reasonable and legitimate aspirations of the Chinese people.[11]

Pratt may have exaggerated the British virtues of progress, free trade, and sympathy for China, but, as will be seen in chapter V, Great Britain did take the initiative in trying to reform the Unequal Treaties.

The Foreign Office resented charges of British 'imperialism' or 'capitalism' in China. In 1928 Pratt wrote:

China having barely begun to emerge from the stage of domestic industry, the total amount of all capital invested in factories is insignificant. Nearly the whole of this capital is Chinese, only a small percentage being British. The interests of the British in China are therefore overwhelmingly those of the trader and only to a very insignificant extent those of the capitalist or employer of labour.

The development of a factory system in China is, and must continue to be, the work not of foreign capitalists, but of the Chinese themselves. The influence of foreign capitalists, both British and Japanese, inasmuch as it has set up higher standards and introduced humanitarian ideas, has been entirely beneficial.[12]

Leaving aside the question of beneficence, the statistics of the China trade are notoriously unreliable. In 1933 Pratt welcomed the publication of C. F. Remer's *Foreign Investments in China* (New York, 1933), which to the Foreign Office satisfactorily clarified many obscure issues. Pratt quoted the following table indicating investments in China.

	Million £	Per cent of Total
Great Britain	197·9	56·2
Japan	74·0	21·0
Russia	1·3	0·4
United States of America	31·9	9·0
France	19·5	5·5
Germany	15·4	4·4
Belgium	8·5	2·5
Netherlands	2·0	0·6
Italy	0·9	0·3
Scandinavia	0·4	0·1
	352·3	100·0

[11] Ibid.
[12] Memorandum by Pratt, 25 February 1927 [F 1932/144/10], F.O. 371/12446.

He then observed:

We thus get the very striking result that the British business investment in China is no less than 56 per cent of the total foreign investment, and is nearly three times as large as that of her nearest rival, Japan. Of the British business investment in China, 76·5 per cent is invested in Shanghai, and 23·5 per cent in the whole of the rest of China. The British investment in Shanghai is $3\frac{1}{2}$ times as large as the Japanese.[13]

British investments in China therefore were relatively substantial. And, as will be seen in chapter VII, the vision of a great—but changing—China market persisted to the eve of the war.

With the possible exception of Pratt, Sir Victor Wellesley probably devoted more sustained attention to economic problems of the Far East than any other member of the Foreign Office. To his own surprise, he learned when he compiled figures in 1932 that Britain's trade with Japan almost equalled that with China (though, like Pratt, he believed that potential trade with China remained infinitely greater).

	In thousand £:	
	1929	1930
British exports to Japan	13,435	8,229
British re-exports to Japan	207	168
British imports from Japan	9,132	8,064
British exports to China	14,029	8,572
British re-exports to China	117	86
British imports from China	12,157	9,914

'(These figures do not include British Dominions trade, which is of considerable importance, both with China and Japan. Next to the United States and China, British India is Japan's best customer).'

Another set of statistics, Wellesley wrote, spoke for itself:

	Millions of yen:	
	1928	1929
Total exports from Japan	2,196	2,216
Total imports to Japan	1,971	2,148
Japanese exports to United States	826	914
Japanese imports from United States	625	654
Japanese exports to China	373	346
Japanese imports from China	234	209

[13] Memorandum by Pratt, 23 January 1934 [F 414/68/10], F.O. 371/18078.

	Millions of Yen:	
	1928	1929
Japanese exports to British India	146	198
Japanese imports from British India	285	288
Japanese exports to Great Britain	58	63
Japanese imports from Great Britain	164	153

The United States of America, controlling about 40 per cent of Japan's foreign trade, holds a weapon mightier than the army and navy of Japan. But would she ever consent to use it? and would the Government of India (Japan's third most formidable customer) support her policy? Would the embargo produce an *immediate* collapse of Japan's offensive power? Would the collapse, unless immediate and complete, avert the danger of the situation?[14]

Those questions remained unanswered. As will be seen from the first three chapters, and especially chapter VI on the Manchurian crisis, Anglo-American friction persisted. The Foreign Office distrusted the State Department. To repeat an opinion of Wellesley quoted below, 'the policy of the United States of America in China (as elsewhere) has been erratic and inconsiderate in the past. . . . The United States Government is quite capable of backing out after we had agreed to give our support, leaving us to clear up the resultant mess.'

I also repeat two quotations from Wellesley's writings in order to emphasize changing variables:

If we probe this problem to its depths it cannot be disguised that in the last analysis it is primarily and fundamentally racial in character, and that the political and economic aspects, important as they are, are in reality only secondary compared with the underlying racial problem.

The root trouble in the Far Eastern problem will be found to lie (as is the case with most international problems) in economic causes.

The two statements are obviously contradictory, but understandably so. The first was written before the depression, the second during the depression. 'Racism' thus emerges as a major theme during the opening chapters of this book, wanes during those dealing with the 1930s, but re-emerges when I attempt from time to time to consider some of the broader causes of the Pacific war.

[14] Memorandum by Wellesley, 1 February 1932 [F 654/1/10], F.O. 371/16143; *D.B.F.P.*, Second Series, IX, No. 239.

Perhaps men of affairs do learn lessons from history. During the Chinese revolution, Foreign Office officials occasionally pointed out the futility and danger of intervention in a revolution, as had been proved in Russia. As will be seen in chapter IV, the British, perhaps making a virtue out of their waning power, followed a policy of restraint during the Chinese revolution and congratulated themselves when the Russians got their fingers burned. To give another example of the lessons of history,[15] after the Munich crisis, British officials resolved not to make the same mistakes in the Far East, and, as will be seen in the last chapter, Britain did not pursue a line of appeasement, in the pejorative sense, towards Japan. This is ironic, because a more forward policy of conciliation in the positive sense of removal of genuine misunderstandings might have made more sense in the Far East than in Europe. The case has been strongly stated recently by a person of long experience in Japan, Captain Malcolm D. Kennedy, O.B.E., who concludes: 'It is one of the tragic ironies of history that Japan, our valued friend and ally for twenty years, became our mortal enemy in the Pacific War twenty years later.'[16]

My narrative begins after the peace settlement of 1919. There are two developments that occurred at the Paris Peace Conference, however, that need to be emphasized in order to understand many of the events I discuss below: first, the denial of racial equality to the Japanese; second, the handling of the Shantung issue. Both issues were misunderstood at the time and had profound repercussions. Statesmen underestimated the significance the Japanese attached to racial equality, at least nominal racial equality, and failed to comprehend the impact in

[15] And here is another, which I include now because I did not find an appropriate place for it in the text. Wellesley wrote during the Shanghai crisis of 1932: 'There is a parallel between the present situation in the Far East and that in the Near East after the war. . . . Greece, like Japan, had invaded the territory of a neighbouring State (Turkey) in order to extend her economic and territorial empire. The result was to stimulate Nationalist opposition among the Turks until eventually the Greeks could stand it no longer and were driven out—their retreat involving the destruction of Smyrna with the international trading interests in that great city, which have not yet recovered. The warning of this analogy is that Shanghai may prove to be another Smyrna.' Memorandum by Wellesley, 6 February 1932 [F 1033/1/10], F.O. 371/16146; *D.B.F.P.*, Second Series, IX, No. 356.

[16] Malcolm D. Kennedy, *The Estrangement of Great Britain and Japan, 1917–35* (Manchester University Press, 1969), p. 1.

China of the principle of self-determination. As a Japanese official explained to an Australian military officer in 1920:

Mr. Hanihara begs leave to remind Major Piesse that the utterances of Japanese delegates and steps taken by them at the Conference, demonstrated that Japan's object was not 'the removal of restrictions on immigration', but the elimination of racial discrimination— a discrimination which, for no reason but of the colour of skin, deprives men of equal opportunity in life, and often subjects them to an unbearable humiliation.[17]

On the subject of self-determination, in 1925 the British Minister in Peking submitted a confidential memorandum to the Foreign Office written by a prominent Englishman of long experience in China. He reminded his compatriots that Britain had adopted the principle of self-determination during the war, yet China continued to be subjected to foreign control. 'During the Great War the Anglo-Saxons declared that they were fighting for democracy, for the right of weak peoples to self-determination. The wind was sown then and the whirlwind is being reaped now.'[18]

I conclude with a guess: if such China hands as Wellesley and Pratt were alive today, they would judge that Japan's presence on the Asian mainland acted as the catalyst of twentieth-century Asia. It helped to unite the Chinese, and gave strength to the Chinese Communist movement. Manchukuo proved to be Japan's downfall, or at least point of no return. Pratt wrote in 1937: 'Japan on the mainland of Asia is an irritating bacillus producing an ailment in the body politic only to be cured by the expulsion or destruction of the bacillus.'[19] Both Pratt and Wellesley believed that Japan's intrusion into China would foster Communism, though both were wary of giving a precise definition of that movement or its meaning in a Chinese context.[20] Their sentiments about Communism in China were

---

[17] As recorded in Alston to Curzon, No. 33, 23 January 1920 [F 67/67/23], *D.B.F.P.*, First Series, VI, No. 695.

[18] Confidential memorandum enclosed in Macleay to Chamberlain, No. 23 Conference, 16 December 1925 [F 1092/8/10], F.O. 371/10925.

[19] Minute by Pratt, 28 July 1937 [F 3975/14/10], F.O. 371/20965.

[20] There was a general tendency among British officials (not particularly shared by Pratt or Wellesley) to view the issue of Communism in China as a Russian plot and to regard the Far Eastern problem as merely one element in the worldwide struggle between Great Britain and Bolshevist Russia. The clearest statement of

widely shared at the time, not least by intellectuals who visited there. Auden and Isherwood apparently took at face value Madame Chiang Kai-shek's statement to them in 1938: 'It is not a question . . . of our co-operating with the Communists. The question is: Will the Communists co-operate with *us*? . . . As long as the Communists want to fight for China we are all friends.'[21]

Finally, for the benefit of those who know little or nothing about the Far East (as I did when I began this book), let me turn to three definitions by Sir Eric Teichman, an official who spent his lifetime in China:

A *treaty port* in China is a place opened to foreign residence and trade by agreement between the Chinese and a foreign government. There are also a number of other open ports, some opened by mutual arrangement and others by China of her own volition. In all there are two to three dozen open ports in China, the status of some of which is vague and controversial. Amongst the more important and

---

this idea that I have found was written in 1926 by Sir William (Lord) Tyrrell of the Foreign Office:

'[E]ver since the Bolshevist régime was established in Russia its activities have been mainly directed against this country and . . . in every part of the world we have been met by its persistent and consistent hostility. The reason for this is to be found in the unbridgeable character of the policies of the two countries, our respective aims being diametrically opposed to each other. British policy aims at securing the safety of the Empire and the promotion of its trade, upon which its life and prosperity are based. For this purpose we are working everywhere for peace and settlement, with a view to achieve a return to normal economic conditions. Russian policy on the other hand, aims at the establishment of communism, which it can only achieve by the destruction of the present order of things. To promote this revolution it aims at fomenting disturbance and disorder everywhere. Its chief weapon is a ruthless propaganda all over the world, which everywhere assumes an anti-British character, not only because we are a world-wide Empire, but because our overthrow is the chief aim and object of Moscow.

In the Far East we have a Bolshevist Russia, pursuing the same aims as the Czarist Russia, the main difference being that the Bolshevists are far more efficient and unscrupulous in the pursuit of that policy than their predecessors ever were. (Memorandum, 26 July 1926, C.P. 303, Secret, CAB. 24/181).'

Tyrrell's statement is an excellent example of how British officials conceived of the nature and purpose of the British Empire as well as their preconceptions about Bolshevism.

[21] W. H. Auden and Christopher Isherwood, *Journey to a War* (London, 1939), p. 68. It could be, though, that Madame Chiang's statement conformed with a prefatory remark by the authors: 'Some of our informants may have been unreliable, some merely polite, some deliberately pulling our leg.'

old-established treaty ports, reading along the coast from south to
north, are Canton, Swatow, Amoy, Foochow, Ningpo, Shanghai,
Tsingtao, Chefoo, Tientsin and Newchwang; and, going up the
Yangtze Valley, Chinkiang, Nanking, Wuhu, Kiukiang, Hankow,
Changsha, Ichang and Chungking. . . .

A *Concession* is an area at a treaty port which has been leased in
perpetuity to a foreign Government for occupation of its nationals.

A *Settlement* is an area at a treaty port set aside by the Chinese
Government in which foreigners may reside and acquire land. In the
case of both settlement and concession areas administrative authority
is exercised by the foreign Power or Powers; either by specific or
prescriptive right.[22]

Note Teichman's description of British life in a treaty port:

Life for the foreign treaty-port communities is intellectually cramped
and narrow, but materially easy and agreeable. The Chinese are the
best servants in the world. Native food supplies are abundant, cheap
and very good. The shooting, for those who have the opportunity to
wander far enough afield, is still the best to be had in any un-
preserved region in the world. The pheasant is extraordinarily
abundant in the mountains of the north-western provinces and
reed-beds and coppices of Central China; the spring and autumn
snipe come in their thousands; and clouds of duck darken the sky at
flighting time along the Yangtze river. And shooting rights are free to
all. The 'China pony', and polo at a fraction of the cost of the same
sports in India, England and America; and games of all kinds
catered for by well-run clubs.[23]

The treaty ports, concessions, and settlements were nineteenth-
century relics. They rested on a position of force that had
created the treaty port system in the mid-nineteenth century.
During the crisis of 1926–7, 13,000 British troops landed at
Shanghai to protect the lives and property of their compatriots.
It was virtually the only significant display of force during this
era to prove that Britain remained a Lion and was not a paper
tiger. In the inter-war years Great Britain had neither the
might nor the will to maintain indefinitely the status of a
nineteenth-century imperial power. On the whole, British
statesmen optimistically believed that 'fair play towards

[22] Sir Eric Teichman, *Affairs of China: A Survey of the Recent History and Present
Circumstances of the Republic of China* (London, 1938), pp. 137–9.
[23] Ibid., p. 282.

China', in the sense of a gradual readjustment of the treaty system and the abolition of extraterritoriality, might eventually win lasting Chinese friendship. Had the Manchurian crisis and other decisive events leading to war not developed, they might have been right, even though friction over Shanghai was bound to persist.

A word about the title. I use the word 'strategy' in its broadest sense (not in its narrow military meaning) merely to distinguish the book from others in the same field, and to suggest that I have attempted something rather more than a study of British 'policy' as it is sometimes stringently defined. Even so, legitimate criticism could be made of the book for its neglect of such topics as the role of the Dominions after the Imperial Conference, the fighting services, Parliament, public opinion, and governmental agencies such as the Treasury. Similar criticism might be levelled that I have not dealt at all extensively with such important topics as the Brussels Conference and have not even attempted to discuss the Ottawa agreements and their meaning for the Empire at large and the Far East. These omissions for the most part are deliberate. This book, based mainly on Cabinet and Foreign Office documents, is a thematic survey and by necessity contains many gaps that will have to be filled by other scholars.

Unless otherwise specified, the unpublished documents referred to in the footnotes are deposited at the Public Record Office, which holds the copyright. The principal abbreviations are CAB. (Cabinet), F.O. (Foreign Office) and C.O. (Colonial Office).

I am grateful to Professors Dorothy Borg, Charles Boxer, Akira Iriye, Ernest R. May and Richard H. Ullman, and to my colleagues at Yale who read the manuscript either in whole or in part, and who gave me guidance on points of detail. I also wish to give my most hearty thanks to Dr. Ian Nish and A. J. P. Taylor. I am also grateful to Miss Casey Miller, Miss Jennifer Horne, and Mrs. Sonia Argyle for help in preparing the manuscript. After reading the draft Mr. Geoffrey Hudson gave me some written comments on Prime Ministers Hughes and Meighen, the Washington Treaties and the Singapore Base, and 'appeasement' in the Far East, which I have included as end notes in quotations with his initials after them in order properly to acknowledge his ideas.

I must also thank the Search Officers of the Public Record Office who helped me to master cumbersome systems of classification and who introduced me to various sets of private papers (none of which proved to be very helpful for my purpose).

For over a decade I have greatly benefited from my association with St. Antony's College, and I take this opportunity to dedicate this book to three of my closest friends there, Mr. Geoffrey Hudson, Professor Kenneth Kirkwood, and Miss Elizabeth Monroe.

This book represents my contribution to the Far Eastern International History Seminar at Yale University. It deliberately focuses almost exclusively on the British and does not attempt to compare their attitudes with those of American or Asian statesmen. When the other work of the seminar is complete, we shall attempt a comparative synthesis.

There is at least one advantage to writing in committee: far from having to say that I accept total responsibility for errors of fact and interpretation, I shall be glad to share them with my friends James B. Crowley and Gaddis Smith.

Easter 1970 W. R. L.

I

TRADE RIVALRY IN CHINA AND
THE ANGLO-JAPANESE ALLIANCE

AT THE end of the First World War, British statesmen
viewed Japan's position in China as the key issue that
would determine the future of the Far East. They held as
an unquestioned premise that during the war Japan had pursued a policy aiming at political and commercial supremacy on
the Asian mainland, as proved by the attempt to reduce China
to the status of a 'vassal State' of Japan through the Twenty-
one Demands of 1915. Their views reflected the same concern
for a 'balance of power' in Asia as in Europe: if Japan were
allowed to harness the manpower and exploit the resources of
China, Britain's commerce and strategic position in the Far
East would suffer catastrophically.

In a word, British officials in 1919 attributed to Japan the
worst characteristics of their European neighbours: the militarism of Germany and the commercial monopolism of France.
And the power of stereotyped thought demonstrated itself in
another important way. To solve the China problem, British
officials seized upon the traditional nineteenth-century panacea
of Free Trade. If China's door were kept open to the trade of all
nations equally, British commerce would prosper, Japan's expansion would find a 'legitimate' outlet, and China would
develop to the benefit of Chinese, Japanese, Americans, and
Englishmen alike. That doctrine was known in British circles as
the 'courageous policy of reconstruction in China'. Less idea-
listically phrased, it was a policy designed to restrain Japanese
commercial monopoly and control of railways by regulating
Chinese finances through an International Consortium. Japan's
attitude towards the Consortium served as the weathervane by
which British statesmen attempted to predict the future of
China and Japan's relations with the western powers. Their
evaluations of Japanese intent contributed to the non-renewal
of the Anglo-Japanese Alliance; but, as they viewed the China

problem in the broader spectrum of the Far East and Pacific, they questioned their strategic and commercial assumptions and became more sympathetic to Japan's expansion on the Asian mainland.

The British image of China was at once complex and simplistic: complex, in that British statesmen fully grasped the magnitude of the problem of foreign encroachments in China, simplistic in its bold interpretation of Chinese history. No one could begin to re-examine the basic western policy of the Open Door in China (defined by the British as the 'creation of Equal Opportunity') without opening a Pandora's box containing the problems of the leased territories and spheres of influence, foreign settlements, economic rights and privileges, extra-territoriality, control of railways, harbours, and customs—in short, all of the foreign impingements that threatened 'the territorial integrity and administrative independence of China'.

None of those issues in turn could be raised without investigating the internal situation in China, where British officials above all saw, in the words of Lord Curzon (Secretary of State for Foreign Affairs), 'administrative chaos and governing ineptitude'. They spoke of a China more properly conceived as a continent than as a country, as an 'agglomeration' of peoples rather than a nation. The peace-loving, 'teeming' population of China, in the British view, worked industriously, but 'political immaturity' made China a 'torpid polity' rather than a modern state. The British described China's government as a democracy of sorts, whose central administration was reduced to impotence because of provincial autonomy and lack of a modern system of communications. They traced the basis of China's troubles to the traditional struggle between the south and the north. In Curzon's straightforward words: 'The old historic fight between North and South is going on. It is unresolved.' According to another typical British view:

The present state of affairs in China can only be described as chaotic in the extreme. It would be difficult to name a time when the Central Government at Peking stood at a lower ebb than it stands today. The revolution of 1911 and the disappearance of the Manchu Dynasty has left China a legacy of political turmoil and internecine strife, from the throes of which she has not yet emerged. The Central Government is almost impotent, utterly discredited, verging on bankruptcy, and entirely at the mercy of the Provincial Military Governors of the provinces who are the product of the revolution and the real rulers of China.[1]

The situation could be summed up by stating that China, with a vast population, resources and trading potential that could rival the world's best markets, had survived the European war intact but wracked with civil disorder and on the verge of financial bankruptcy. This condition made her, in the recurrent phrase, 'a very easy prey'. As a Foreign Office committee defined the nub of the problem: 'Potentially strong but politically weak, China must, in our opinion, unless she receives foreign support, continue to remain a standing temptation to the Japanese policy of absorption.'[2]

British efforts to understand the reasons for Japanese 'Imperialism' led to lengthy discussions about the economic problems of Japan and the 'national character' of the Japanese people. Curzon, for example, gave this explanation:

Japan [is a power with] a people possessing great and intellectual gifts, a people orderly and disciplined in temperament, with a fierce patriotism, resolute in determination, but rather unscrupulous in the means they employ. These people inhabit a group of small islands, where they have only a limited area to sustain a population already too large for it—islands which are poor in resources, and which barely support the 50 or 60 millions who live upon them. They are a people who must expand. They have done so, in so far as this was open to them, during the last twenty years, and have done it, if not with an excess of scruple, with fairly successful consequences. . . . Thus you have this restless and aggressive Power, full of energy, somewhat like the Germans in mentality, seeking in every direction to push out and find an outlet for their perfectly legitimate ambitions.

Within sight of their shores you have the great helpless, hopeless, and inert mass of China, one of the most densely populated countries in the world, utterly deficient in cohesion or strength, engaged in perpetual conflict between the North and South, destitute of military capacity or ardour, an easy prey to a nation of the character that I have described.[3]

[1] Memorandum by Victor Wellesley (at this time Superintendent of the Far Eastern Department), 20 October 1921 [F 3823/2635/10], F.O. 371/6660.

[2] Report of the Anglo-Japanese Alliance Committee, Secret, 21 January 1921 [F 1169/63/23], F.O. 371/6672.

[3] Stenographic Notes of a Meeting of Representatives of the United Kingdom, The Dominions and India (hereafter cited as Imperial Conference Minutes, I.C.M.), 8th Meeting, Secret, 28 June 1921, p. 5, CAB. 32/2.

How could Britain check Japanese 'Imperialism'? With a severely inferior number of British businessmen in China to compete commercially with the Japanese and with no intention ever of committing British troops against Japanese forces there, British statesmen had to rely in large part on their famous ability 'to exhort morally'. Again, Curzon responded most eloquently. His main line of argument was that the 'break-up period' of China's history had passed, that 'economic imperialism' was an anachronism. Recalling the era of the Scramble for colonies, Curzon once said: 'the old days, 20 or 30 years old, in which the tendencies of the Powers of the world were, so to speak, to map out different areas in China as their spheres of influence, the British in the Yangtse, and other Powers elsewhere, have disappeared.'[4] The reason lay in the belief that China was not—as had been conceived in the late nineteenth century—a dying or decadent state, but a nation awakening to national consciousness. In the words of the British Minister at Peking from 1906 to 1920, Sir John Jordan, China was 'a great nation . . . rousing herself from sleep and bidding fair to renew her mighty youth.'[5] China, in short, was emerging from a long period of stagnation. Curzon repeatedly pleaded with the Japanese Ambassador to urge his government to take into thorough account the significance of this fundamental change in the affairs of China and to grasp the changing spirit of the times. The period of economic concessions and spheres of influence, he argued, had passed, and Japan's 'economic imperialism', her 'selfish', 'inconsiderate', 'opportunistic', policy, if pursued, would only lead to a crisis of the utmost magnitude.

As they used such highly moral arguments, the British

[4] Ibid., p. 7.

[5] Sir John Jordan to Balfour, No. 564, 23 December 1918 [30547/10499/10], *D.B.F.P.*, First Series (all further references to *D.B.F.P.* in this chapter are to the First Series), VI, pp. 566ff. Sir John Jordan was one of the most distinguished China hands of this century, renowned for his knowledge and forthright manner. 'Jordan's character had both the sternness and fine characteristic of the North Irish stock from which he owed his patient industry. He was often a fierce critic of the Chinese officials, though he won their respect more than any other foreigner of his time. Deception roused him to outspoken anger. On one occasion a Chinese statesman, camouflaging the truth, was sharply interrupted by the accusing words, 'Y're a liar! Y're a liar!' He was certainly no diplomatist in the sense in which the word is usually employed.' *The Times*, 15 September 1925.

occasionally and uneasily reminded themselves of their own record in China. They spoke in the idealistic language of the First World War, but they recognized their own 'moral' dilemma. The Japanese, wrote the British Minister and Chargé d'Affaires in Tokyo, Beilby Alston, 'in the secret of their souls . . . think that no wickedness or aggression they have been guilty of in respect of China comes anywhere near our early aggression and conclusion of treaties with that country.'[6]

When the Japanese drew attention to the international rivalries of the nineteenth century, the British claimed absolution from guilt by present action. Britain pledged herself to uphold a free and independent China; Japan, according to a Foreign Office memorandum, 'apparently desires to retain a disunited and feeble China where she can fish in troubled waters'.[7] 'We wish to have done with "spheres of influence" in China.' Alston wrote; 'Japan's desire seems rather to perpetuate them.'[8] Curzon emphasized to the Japanese Ambassador as he did to his colleagues that China now could not be 'cut up'. 'That day had passed, and the future of China did not lie in this sort of subdivision. Neither did it lie in the assumption by Japan of the overlordship of the Far East.'[9] Curzon's frank remark referred specifically to Japan's 'economic imperialism' in the Shantung peninsula, where Japanese activities seemed to indicate aggressive intentions in Asia as a whole.

The Japanese had seized the leased German territory of Tsingtao in the Shantung peninsula in 1914. At the Peace Conference Japan pledged herself to return the territory to China in full sovereignty, retaining only certain economic privileges. Despite that assurance, the British feared that Japan was attempting to convert Shantung into a Japanese colony. According to Jordan:

In spite of protestations in Europe of mere economic interest, the local evidence of Japanese political and military intentions is too patent to be overlooked by the people whilst the ostentation of their methods adds sting to the sense of injury. They retain complete

[6] Alston to Curzon, No. 314 Confidential, 18 July 1919 [118979/6579/23], F.O. 371/3817.
[7] Memorandum by C. H. Bentinck, 28 February 1920 [F 199/199/23], F.O. 371/5358.
[8] Alston to Tilley, 7 October 1919 [150925/951/23], F.O. 371/3816.
[9] Curzon to Alston, No. 125, 18 July 1919 [106210/16000/10], F.O. 371/3695.

control of the railway running through the province, their powerful
wireless stations stand in the provincial capital, and the province is
flooded with hordes of disreputable Japanese citizens who associate
with bandit chiefs and act as providers of drugs and other lures
tending to disturb the public order and to debauch the manhood of
the people. . . . At present the whole place is virtually a Japanese
colony, liberally subsidized by the mother-country, and ruled by
some 1,500 Japanese officials whose personal interests are involved in
the perpetuation of the present system of government.[10]

Since the territory was vital in every respect to China's territorial integrity, the British could not look with indifference on
Japan's 'encroachment'. 'Shantung is in the heart of China, the
birthplace of Confucius, densely populated, and developed by a
highly civilised people.'[11] Furthermore, Tsingtao possessed the
finest natural harbour in all China. If the Japanese were
allowed to entrench themselves there, they would control the
strategic railway stretching inland, which in turn would allow
them to tap the trade of the interior all the way to Tibet. In the
months following the war the British looked with alarm on the
prospect of the greater part of China being sealed off and lost
forever to British trade because of the consequences of Japan's
occupation of Shantung. This alarmist view gave rise to a
theory of geo-politics in the Far East that reflected growing
suspicion of Japan and a ringing affirmation of the belief in the
China trade.

That theory held that economic concessions carried with them
political control, and, more specifically, that the key to commercial development was the construction of railways, which

[10] Jordan to Curzon, No. 525, 22 November 1919 [170011/16000/10], F.O.
371/3696; cf. *D.B.F.P.*, VI, No. 597. For background of the Shantung controversy,
see Kurt Bloch, *German Interests and Policies in the Far East* (New York, 1939); the
issue at the Paris Peace Conference can be conveniently followed in Russell H.
Fifield, *Woodrow Wilson and the Far East* (Hamden, Conn., 1969 edn.), and Seth P.
Tillman, *Anglo-American Relations at the Paris Peace Conference of 1919* (Princeton,
1961). See also Wunsz King, *China at the Paris Peace Conference in 1919* (St. John's
University Press, 1961). For the situation in China, Chow Tse-tsung, *The May
Fourth Movement: Intellectual Revolution in Modern China* (Harvard University Press,
1960). The Anglo-Japanese aspects of this and all other issues of the Alliance are
receiving definite treatment by Ian Nish, *Alliance in Decline* (forthcoming); for the
earlier history of the Alliance, see his previous work, *The Anglo-Japanese Alliance*
(London, 1966).

[11] Memorandum by Ashton-Gwatkin, 7 July 1920 [F 2142/2142/10], F.O.
371/5345.

had strategic and political as well as commercial value. A statement made by Curzon to the Japanese Ambassador in July 1919 illustrates the first point, as perceived from British experience in the Middle and Far East for over half a century. When asked by the Ambassador whether Britain would be content with Japanese military withdrawal from Shantung, while retaining economic concessions, Curzon replied:

I felt some difficulty in giving a reply to this question without going seriatim into the various concessions of a commercial, financial, industrial or administrative character, of which Japan claimed to be the heir [of Germany in Shantung]. But, broadly speaking, I did hold the view that it was undesirable that Japan or any other Power should acquire such a preference in China. In my own experience, the possession of such concessions was found, as a rule, to carry with it, at any rate in Eastern countries, a command of the country's policy and resources quite as effective in its way as that which resulted from the presence of troops.[12]

Specifically, the British objected to Japan's control of the harbour of Tsingtao, not only because of overtones of political authority but also because of maladministration. In retrospect even German sway compared favourably with the oppressive and corrupt Japanese rule by martial law.

' [T]he Japanese are guided by principles which far surpass anything in the way of exclusiveness and commercial monopoly, and which are in conflict with every British conception of fair trade and equal opportunity.' . . . In its administration of the Harbour and Customs at Tsingtao, in its general discrimination against other foreigners in such matters as wharf charges, shipping accommodation, etc., in its operation of the railway . . . and, above all, in its treatment of the natives, the Japanese régime is tenfold more objectionable to foreigners and Chinese alike than the German one ever was.[13]

---

[12] Curzon to Alston, No. 129, 22 July 1919 [106793/16000/10], F.O. 371/3694, cf. *D.B.F.P.*, VI, No. 436. For the problem of economic concessions and railways (a subject badly in need of re-investigation), see, for example, Westel W. Willoughby, *Foreign Rights and Interests in China* (2 vols., Baltimore, 1927); Carl W. Young, *The International Relations of Manchuria* (Chicago, 1929); Grover Clark, *Economic Rivalries in China* (New Haven, 1932); Kia-ngau Chang, *China's Struggle for Railway Development* (New York, 1943); Paul Hibbert Clyde, *International Rivalries in Manchuria* (New York, 1946 edn.) for specific British background, E-tu Zen Sun's *Chinese Railways and British Interests* (New York, 1954).

[13] Jordan to Curzon, No. 411 Confidential, 5 September 1919 [150764/16000/10], F.O. 371/3695. Jordan quotes from a report by Archibald Rose, Commercial Secretary of the British Legation at Peking.

Thus when the British spoke of 'economic imperialism' in China, they meant primarily the methods used by the Japanese in such matters as customs and the preferential treatment given to Japanese nationals. In Shantung the Open Door to Englishmen had become a 'standing jest'—meaning, open to Japanese only. Having witnessed similar Japanese penetration in Korea and Manchuria, British officials in China now feared that the closing of the Open Door in Shantung would lead eventually to annexation. Sir John Jordan succinctly conveyed the implications of Japan's economic grip over the peninsula when he wrote: 'Rights and privileges which Japan wishes to retain in Shantung are those of economic Imperialism, which she has utilised so effectually as means of territorial absorption in Corea and Manchuria.'[14]

The instrument of territorial expansion was the railway. Occupying Shantung, the Japanese controlled the railway running from Tsingtao to the capital of the province. In British eyes this line of communication would provide the base from which Japanese construction would proceed to Peking and on into northern and western China. 'The future status of the Tsintao-Tsinau railway,' Jordan reported, '. . . remains the crux of the situation.'

I have been a close observer of railway construction in Corea and Manchuria during the past twenty years, and I have no hesitation in affirming that a railway running from the principal port in China to the capital of a province containing 35,000,000 people, owned, policed and controlled by Japanese, is not an economic concession, but a political one. . . .[15]

As they projected the construction of a Japanese railway into the interior, British officials envisaged it controlling the approaches to Peking and connecting with the 'future railways' of southern Manchuria and eastern Mongolia. With railway schemes running from Korea through northern Manchuria and Mongolia (and possibly even from Foochow, in southern China, going into the heart of the Yangtze valley), the Japanese

[14] Jordan to Curzon, No. 416 Tel., 4 August 1919 [112287/16000/10], F.O. 371/3695.
[15] Jordan to Curzon, No. 411 Confidential, 5 September 1919 [150764/16000/10], F.O. 371/3695.

seemed to be systematically planning to choke off British and other western trade in all of China.

This speculation had interesting ramifications. Just as British statesmen in the late nineteenth century held the geo-political view that the power controlling the sources of the Nile controlled Egypt and the routes to the East, so they now attached great importance to Mongolia. If by railway expansion from Shantung and Korea the Japanese could exploit Mongolia, the consequences would be disastrous for Britain's strategic position in the Far East. According to a report by the British Military Attaché in Peking:

Mongolia is of great natural wealth in every way, but as it is undeveloped it is often looked upon as of minor importance. If however the schemes of the Japanese General Staff should ever be realised, and railways open up the country, an enormous transformation will occur. A glance at the . . . map shows the central position of Mongolia and the importance it might have both in a political and in a military sense. The Power which controls this region should be in a position to control the Far Eastern Continent.[16]

The British Minister repeated the argument: 'Though at present undeveloped, and sparsely populated, this portion of the continent [Mongolia] is capable of vast expansion and strategically dominates the rest of China'.[17] Such an increase of Japanese political and economic influence would create a 'stranglehold' on British trade in the Yangtze valley. To prevent this, Shantung should not be allowed to go the way of Korea, and Mongolia held open at all costs. Geo-political theories are usually exact in attempting to find the ultimate locus of power, and this one was no exception. If pressed to its logical extreme, or perhaps *reductio ad absurdum*, it held that the power controlling eastern inner Mongolia would control the Asian continent.

As opposed to Japan's use of railways for purposes of territorial aggrandizement, railway construction might cure the political and economic ills of China. Jordan argued:

The railways in China have been used to dismember the country.

[16] D. S. Robertson, Report on Mongolia and Chinese Frontier Questions, 29 September 1919, enclosed in Jordan to Curzon, No. 446, 1 October 1919 [151590/104499/10], F.O. 371/3696. The map referred to is enclosed in his report.

[17] Ibid.

3—B.S.F.E.

They could be made the most potent factor in its reunion. A solution of the problem of communications would go far to solve the questions of political unity, efficient administration, and security for life, property, and trade. Questions of taxation, currency, mining, trademarks, and practically every subject of current official discussion, are dependent upon such a solution.[18]

As Lord Curzon explained to the Japanese Ambassador, 'I could not but think that an international policy as regards the railways of China as a whole would be one of the most fruitful instruments of her regeneration'.[19] Sir John Jordan optimistically believed that between the Japanese, British, American, French, and Belgians, 50,000 miles of railway would be built in 25 years. If this construction could be united by 'international' effort and developed in the spirit as well as in the letter of free trade agreements, he had no doubt that the commerce of China would develop at a dizzying pace. Even within ten years, concerted railway building would revolutionize China's economy and make her truly politically independent.

Building of these railways would occupy our united resources for at least 10 years but it would be a work which would enormously strengthen and rehabilitate China and make this country one of the greatest markets in the world. Trade of China continues to increase by leaps and bounds in spite of all obstacles and with adequate railway facilities, more especially in the Yangtze Valley, it will attain proportions undreamed of at present.[20]

Thus the dream of a vast China market revived after the First World War. The dimensions of the China trade and the necessity for Britain not to allow other nations to monopolize it was emphasized in a most striking nineteenth-century fashion by none other than the Prime Minister, David Lloyd George: 'This country was just awaking, and that whereas the amount of trade in China was only £1 per head of the population, in Japan it was something like £10 per head, and there were possibilities that trade in China might eventually total £4,000,000,000'.[21]

[18] Jordan to Balfour, No. 564, 23 December 1918 [30547/10499/10], *D.B.F.P.*, VI, p. 568.
[19] Curzon to Alston, No. 125, 18 July 1919 [106210/16000/10], F.O. 371/3695.
[20] Jordan to Curzon, No. 473 Tel., 26 August 1919 [122086/8369/10], F.O. 371/3691.
[21] Cabinet Minutes, Secret, 30 June 1921, CAB. 23/26.

Lamentably, in the Foreign Office's opinion, British traders were not aggressive enough in developing this great market. They were not competitive enough with their Japanese and American rivals. 'I cannot overlook the fact', Jordan wrote, 'that the really interested parties, the British mercantile community, have trusted too much to the efficacy of a political formula and too little to their own initiative.'[22] British apathy might result in the China market being 'stolen' by the Japanese and the Americans. At times the latter in British eyes appeared to be as great a danger as the Japanese. 'We should not leave China to be walked over by America and for the latter to get the whole of China's trade,' Lloyd George once said.[23] Trade rivalry accounts for part of that exaggerated statement, but the British also resented American accusations of 'John Bull's Imperialism' and in turn deplored the United States' 'unreliable', 'unpredictable', and 'flabby' policy toward China. Nevertheless the British regarded the United States as the saviour of the Far East. Ultimately they saw the United States and Japan as the two major Far Eastern powers; the fate of Britain's commercial position would probably depend on the outcome of the struggle between them. In the view of Victor Wellesley, who of all Foreign Office officials probably devoted closest attention to the China problem at this time:

It is hardly an exaggeration to say that 'young China', in its most promising aspect, is an Americanized China. But America has found an eager and persistent competitor in Japan, who has launched into a rival policy of ostensibly peaceful, but actually brutal penetration, which was pursued with redoubled vigour and with methods closely resembling those of Prussian imperialism at the very moment when President Wilson and the Allies were engaged in overthrowing Prussianism in the West.

The mutual irritation and distrust that have consequently arisen between America and Japan are no longer concealed, and the Far Eastern question is visibly resolving itself into a duel between those two countries to decide the fate of China. America's best means to dispel her fear of Japan is to realise her great hope, the reconstruction of China on lines that will ensure equality of opportunity, free

---

[22] Jordan to Curzon, No. 525, 22 November 1919 [170011/16000/10], F.O. 371/3696; cf *D.B.F.P.*, VI, No. 597.

[23] Same as note [21].

play to international co-operation, and the exclusion of Japanese imperialism.[24]

Clearly Britain's sympathy lay with the United States. 'The closer our co-operation with America, the wider the open door.'

To co-ordinate Anglo-American policies in the Far East, the Foreign Office responded enthusiastically to the State Department's proposal to establish an International Consortium. The purpose of the Consortium, in the words of one of the British China experts, was 'to eliminate special claims in particular spheres of interest and to throw open the whole of China without reserve to the combined activities of an international group.'[25] There was no disagreement between the British and the Americans about the desirability of this international group governing the financial affairs of all of China and securing the Open Door; but the Japanese objected to placing Manchuria and Mongolia within the sphere of the Consortium's activities. The Foreign Office regarded the Japanese claim to special interests in those territories as 'totally inadmissible'. Curzon adopted the attitude that he 'would not yield for one moment.'[26] From July 1919 until a year and a half later, when the Consortium actually started to function, Curzon urged the Japanese to pursue a policy of 'large-minded statesmanship' and 'judicious and conciliatory action'. Phrased in noble language, his words conveyed the political message that Japan must prove her 'good faith' in China in return for Britain's favourably considering the renewal of the Anglo-Japanese Alliance.

On 18 July 1919, the Foreign Secretary initiated a series of candid interviews with the Japanese Ambassador, Baron Chinda. They reviewed all major aspects of the China problem, and the tone of their remarks reveals the tenor of Anglo-Japanese relations in the year following the Peace Conference. In the first conversation, which lasted nearly an hour and a half, Curzon eloquently and perhaps a little pompously denounced Japan's tactics, 'pursued in the most systematic and unblushing manner', in China. He criticized the agreements concluded by

[24] Memorandum by Wellesley, 1 June 1929 [F 2159/199/23], F.O. 371/5360.
[25] Wright to Müller, 14 July 1919 [102801/8369/10], F.O. 371/3691. For the State Department's initiative, see Frederick V. Field, *American Participation in the Chinese Consortiums* (Chicago, 1931).
[26] Ibid, minute by Curzon.

Japan with China and said that Japan's insistence on her 'technical rights' in Shantung had created world-wide suspicion of Japanese designs.

[T]he whole policy of Japan was wrapt in a mist of doubt and suspicion which was creating very general alarm. If Japan was actuated by the friendly sentiments which she professed; if she meant to adhere to her earlier pledges to give up Tsingtau and Shantung; if she was prepared to withdraw the whole of her troops, civil administrators, and police; if, in fact, she was prepared to make a 'bona fide' restitution of whatever she had acquired from Germany to China, why should she not come out into the open and say so? Why allow the atmosphere to be further poisoned by long concealment and delay?

Curzon's comments evoked a heated response from Chinda, who defended Japanese policy by emphasizing that his country's national honour was at stake in China, that the British had no reason to believe that the Japanese would not fulfil their pledges, and that Japan would indeed evacuate Shantung 'at her own time'. But Japan did want to retain the economic rights inherited from Germany. With 'extreme diffidence' Curzon then explained why Britain objected to those rights.

As to the economic rights or privileges claimed by Japan, they seemed to me to be another way of perpetuating the era of spheres of influence, which the Ambassador concurred with me in deprecating. . . . To me it seemed that a preferential position was out of harmony with the spirit of the times. More particularly did these arguments apply to the railway system of China. Proposals had recently been made, and were even now under examination, for the unification under international control of the Chinese railways, but I had seen that Japan had endeavoured to exclude from any such arrangement the railways of Manchuria and Mongolia, and it might also be of Shantung, on the grounds that they were in spheres of Japanese influence. This again, I said, was the perpetuation of a bad system.[27]

As for the question of national honour, Curzon assured the Ambassador that public opinion would applaud Japan's prudence in giving up the economic concessions rather than taunt her with surrender. Curzon was surprised at the extent to which Chinda appeared to agree with him.

[27] Curzon to Alston, No. 125, 18 July 1919 [106210/16000/10], F.O. 371/3695.

Also surprised, Chinda apparently found it hard to believe that Curzon had so scathingly indicted Japanese policy. Four days later the Ambassador returned to the Foreign Office, stating that Curzon's remarks seemed to be of such moment that he wanted further clarification before he communicated them to his Government. He gathered that Curzon had given an 'adverse verdict' on Japanese policy in China. Had the British therefore changed their views? He asked because Japan had kept the Foreign Office informed at every stage in the negotiations with China, and the British had raised no objections. Curzon in reply again emphasized 'the ferment of new ideas created by the war' that made economic imperialism out of date. He explained that he was acting as Japan's best friend by offering advice about how to correct the unfavourable impression created by Japan's actions on the Asian mainland. He proceeded to advise the Ambassador that Britain would brook no interference in her negotiations with the Chinese Government about the Tibetan boundary. He also stated at length that Japan's administration of Korea was scandalous, comparable with Germany's record in Belgium. Without wishing 'to dictate' to the Japanese, he urged them to introduce a more liberal system of government in Korea. He drew a parallel between Korea and Ireland.

We ourselves had our own difficulties, such as those in Ireland; but they arose from the fact that there were in Ireland two nations instead of one, and that, instead of having conceded too little, we had given too much. The problem in Korea was a very much simpler one, and could easily be solved by the exercise of humanity, moderation, and common sense.[28]

In further interviews Curzon continued freely to express his opinion about the shortcomings of Japanese policy and to criticize their efforts 'to fix the clutch of Japan upon China'. Japan's schemes in this regard appeared to have many ramifications, but in British eyes the major point at issue, apart from Shantung, was railway construction in Manchuria and Mongolia.

On 1 September 1919, Chinda informed the Foreign Office that the Japanese Government accepted the proposals to estab-

[28] Curzon to Alston, No. 129, 22 July 1919 [106793/16000/10], F.O. 371/3694.

lish the International Consortium; but he explicitly stated that the Consortium must not operate to the prejudice of Japan's special rights and interests in southern Manchuria and eastern inner Mongolia. He justified this exclusion partly because of the need to establish a barrier against possible aggression in the Far East by a recovered Russia or Germany, partly because of Japanese sacrifices during the war, but above all because of 'geographical propinquity'. He argued that eastern Mongolia and southern Manchuria were the hinterlands of the natural Japanese sphere and exclusive control was necessary to guarantee Japan's security.[29] Curzon failed to be persuaded, and the discussion continued on into the year. In November the Foreign Secretary attempted to refute the argument that the Consortium's work in Manchuria and Mongolia would endanger the 'strategical security' of Japan. He gave the Japanese Ambassador the benefit of the doubt by granting two quite 'unlikely' hypotheses—that the Consortium might allow a railway under Chinese control to be constructed to the frontiers of Korea, and that China might be permitted to build a naval harbour on the coast facing Korea. These fears, Curzon said, had to be evaluated both in the light of probability and, one of his favourite phrases, common sense. He asked the Ambassador:

If Japan herself was a member of the Consortium, was it in the least likely that any proposal would be contemplated or sanctioned that would involve so direct a challenge to her legitimate interests? Was it not on the contrary quite certain that, in areas contiguous to those of a great Power like Japan, preference and priority would naturally be given to the interests and point of view of that Power? Was it really necessary, in constructing an international agreement of this sort, to provide against fanciful contingencies which were not in the least likely to occur? If, however, such apprehensions as these filled the Ambassador's mind, why, I said, should he not suggest to me some formula which should guard against at least that particular peril?[30]

Curzon regarded this request for specific information as most important. He would not alter his general attitude, he told

[29] Curzon to Alston, No. 156, 1 September 1919 [123925/8369/10], F.O. 371/3691.
[30] Curzon to Alston, No. 212, 20 November 1919 [154117/8369/10], F.O. 371/3691.

Chinda; but he would respectfully consider any proposal that would safeguard Japan's 'strategical security'. Over a month later, he asked Chinda whether the Japanese Government had now formed an opinion on this point and was surprised to learn that 'the Ambassador seemed to have forgotten what had passed upon the subject, and said that he had omitted to consult his Government upon the matter.'[31] Curzon frequently complained of this breakdown of communication, but suspected it might be intentional on the Ambassador's part. In any case it helps to explain why the initiative in resolving the Consortium issue came from the Americans and not the British. In March 1920 the American banker Thomas W. Lamont, 'in the bluntest and frankest terms', bludgeoned the Japanese into accepting the Anglo-American Consortium proposals by threatening to withdraw American 'financial assistance' to Japan.[32] Japan backed down and southern Manchuria and eastern inner Mongolia were included in the Consortium's sphere.

One might have gathered from the gist of the British documents that Japan's acquiescence in the creation of the Consortium would have been regarded as the triumph of Free Trade over Japanese monopoly and as a safeguard against possible Japanese ambitions for a continental empire. But the tone of the British response to this development continued to be critical rather than commendatory. So far from congratulating the Japanese for co-operating in the Open Door policy, the British chided them for having taken so long to come around to an enlightened point of view. Part of the reason for this disposition lay in the deep-seated suspicion of Japanese motives and the general preconceptions of the problems of the Far East. The Foreign Office consistently held that Japan's imperial ambitions menaced the stability of eastern Asia, and that Japan, as a developing industrial nation, would increasingly threaten

[31] Curzon to Alston, No. 248, 30 December 1919 [166554/16000/10], F.O. 371/3696. 'Although the Ambassador has a very tenacious memory, and displays a scrupulous attention to detail, he sometimes omits to inform his Government of some of the most important features in our interviews.' Ibid.

[32] Memorandum by Ashton-Gwatkin, 23 March 1920 [F 304/199/23], F.O. 371/5358. For Lamont, see Thomas W. Lamont, *Across World Frontiers* (New York, 1950). For the Consortium agreement, see Cmd. 124 of 1921, *Correspondence respecting the new Financial Consortium in China*, pp. 53–5.

Britain's China trade. At the same time, the British more optimistically thought that Japan's expansionist impulses might be controlled, and they occasionally reflected that Japan's reputation as a super-efficient and highly industrial nation—the Germany of the Far East—might be more myth than reality.

In one of the few disagreements about the policy to be pursued towards Japan, the British Minister in Tokyo, Beilby Alston, clashed with the Minister in Peking, Jordan, and with the Foreign Office on the issue of how best to sublimate Japanese imperialism. As one of the officials most familiar with the Far East, Alston had witnessed the Twenty-one Demands with dismay. Following the war he continued to be critical of Japanese policy and pessimistic about Japan's wish for a 'rehabilitated' China. Nevertheless he urged a far more concilatory course than the hard-line policy of the Foreign Office. His discussions with the Japanese Minister of War and other prominent officials led him to believe that it might be more dangerous to adopt an unyielding position than to make certain concessions that would induce the Japanese Government to be more co-operative. During the Consortium negotiations, Alston reported that the Ministers of War and Finance objected strongly to the scope of the Consortium's sphere of operations because, among other reasons, 'Manchuria and Mongolia are outposts of Corea and Corea is the outpost of Japan[;] no step should therefore be taken to endanger the one since it would mean endangering the other.' If Britain insisted, the consequence might be war:

If she [Japan] is isolated difficulty of rehabilitating China will be materially increased as will dangers of complications leading to war. Possibility of great social changes taking place in Japan and of military party losing in power are not entirely (? stable) facts on which to rely. Military party might, thinking their own position being endangered, very conceivably precipitate war and with mercurial high-spirited and aggressive nation like this we could not be certain that social changes would result in a mood of sober-mindedness.

Rather than isolate Japan, Alston proposed to exclude Manchuria and Mongolia from the Consortium, and in return demand that Japan surrender unconditionally all rights in Shantung and co-operate wholeheartedly in 'rehabilitating'

China. 'Her refusal would be tantamount to (?hoist)ing of her true colours.'[33]

In Peking Jordan dissented vigorously. 'There can to my mind be no compromise between policy of international co-operation for unification of entire railway system of China and that which would allow certain regions to be alienated for exclusive benefit of any one Power.'[34] In London Curzon noted that he agreed with Jordan. 'Mr. Alston's proposed bargain is one which I think we should on no account encourage.'[35] Thus the British Government, after considering the choices, decided to adopt an uncompromising attitude.

In fact there was no real divergence of views. Alston merely thought it better to get Japan into the Consortium at the expense of Manchuria and Mongolia rather than to have her excluded; with Japan in, some measure of control could be exerted over her.[36] He was relieved that at last Lord Curzon had spoken frankly to the Japanese. Plain speaking plus tact, Alston held, was the heart of the diplomatic business of getting the Japanese to behave as the British wanted. With too heavy-handed an approach, 'they may shut up altogether and become mulish. If they are treated with tact I find they are very amenable. . . . The Japanese are easily led if handled with care, and are as appreciative of tact as they are resentful of brusqueness.'[37] When Japan accepted the Consortium proposals, Alston and his colleagues attributed the success to their avuncular talks with the Japanese as well as to their co-operation with the Americans.

The British also identified domestic and economic reasons why Japan could not withstand joint Anglo-American insistence to join fully in the Consortium. When the American banker, Lamont, visited Japan in March 1920 he informed Alston that he was disappointed with the 'unbusinesslike' methods of the Japanese and amazed that Japan was 'treated as

[33] Alston to Curzon, No. 352 Tel., 22 August 1919 [120554/8369/10], F.O. 371/3691; cf. *D.B.F.P.*, VI, No. 476.

[34] Jordan to Curzon, No. 473 Tel., 26 August 1919 [122086/8369/10], F.O. 371/3691; *D.B.F.P.*, VI, No. 477.

[35] Ibid., minute by Curzon, 30 August 1919.

[36] Alston to Curzon, No. 359 Tel., 30 August 1919 [123938/8369/10], F.O. 371/3691.

[37] Alston to Tilley, 30 December 1919 [178071/951/23], *D.B.F.P.*, VI, No. 649.

a first class Power instead of being regarded as a third rate Power, which would in his opinion be nearer the mark.' Alston agreed: 'the gravest defect in modern Japan is inadequate attention to efficiency. . . . Super-efficiency is perhaps the prize myth of Japan, but it is foreign writers, not Japanese, and visitors and self-styled investigators, not residents, who have created the myth.'[38] The same idea was expressed by Sir John Tilley of Kivu-Mfumbiro fame, who as early as September 1919 surmised that the Japanese would join the Consortium essentially for domestic reasons: 'We may get our way. My impression is that Japan is not in a position to carry through a strong policy: her army & her exchequer are weak & her internal position uncertain.'[39] By analysing the problem in another way he might have concluded that a free trade policy in China should be pursued to the hilt. With the backing of a strong economy, Britain's products could compete favourably with relatively inferior Japanese goods.

A study of the internal politics of Japan led some Foreign Office officials to believe that the Japanese were becoming more democratic. A democratic Japan, so the logic ran, would be less militaristic and aggressive. This argument found fullest expression in a memorandum written in March 1920 by a junior official, F. Ashton-Gwatkin. Surveying Japan's history and recent constitutional developments, he concluded that the Japanese people were 'sick of "sabre politics"'. Commercial prosperity, he wrote, had sapped the strength of the militarist tradition.

Up to the present, Japan has been ruled by a bureaucratic and militarist oligarchy, whose foreign policy has aimed at establishing Japan's position among the great Powers of the world by maintaining a strong army and navy and by obtaining a paramount position in Eastern Asia. But there seems no doubt that this period of Japan's history has almost run its course. . . .

There is reason to believe that such a 'democratisation' of Japanese institutions would modify the aggressive character of the

[38] Alston to Tilley, No. 159, Very Confidential, 29 March 1920 [F 784/2/10], F.O. 371/5299.
[39] Minute by Tilley on Alston to Curzon, No. 365 Tel., 8 September 1919 [126874/8369/10], F.O. 371/3691. Tilley later became Ambassador in Tokyo, see his autobiography, *London to Tokyo* (London, 1942). His other book (with Stephen Gasellee), *The Foreign Office* (London, 1933) is one of the best works on the subject.

country's foreign policy. . . . under the more democratic régime which may reasonably be expected to establish itself in Japan within the next few years—

1. The menace to the British Empire in the Far East will decrease;
2. A rapprochement between Japan and a Russo-German combination will become still more improbable;
3. Japan's attitude towards China will of itself improve.

Ashton-Gwatkin optimistically concluded that even the tension between Japan and the United States would relax.[40]

Some of Ashton-Gwatkin's colleagues thought he was guilty of wishful thinking. 'I fear I am not so sanguine,' noted C. H. Bentinck, 'as to the bureaucratic and militaristic rule having almost run its course and as to the aggressive character of Japan's foreign policy being likely to undergo much modification in the near future.' He was not optimistic about any improvement in the China problem, and, even if Japan did become more democratic, there still were dangers involved:

I cannot myself see much hope of Japan's attitude towards China improving unless checked by British or American influence, nor does it appear probable that the tension between Japan and America will relax. Were Japan to become too democratic, I should consider the danger of her joining a possible future Russo-German combination greater than at present.[41]

Bentinck invited the observations of H. G. Parlett and E. M. Hobart Hampden, who between them had held the position of Secretary of the British Embassy in Tokyo for over a decade. Parlett wrote:

Unless we have a very definite promise of American co-operation & support we cannot afford to leave Japan isolated & thus a potential enemy. I agree with Mr. Bentinck in his opinion that it is mainly to British (or American) influence that we must look for any improvement in Japan's attitude to China, and the existence of an understanding with Japan would enable us to continue to exercise that friendly pressure on her in the future which we have found on

---

[40] Memorandum by Ashton-Gwatkin, 23 March 1920 [F 304/199/23], F.O. 371/5358; cf. *D.B.F.P.*, VI, No. 789. Ashton-Gwatkin after his retirement wrote *The British Foreign Service* (Syracuse, N.Y. 1950). He sporadically influenced British Far Eastern policy to the end of the appeasement era. See below, chapter VIII, note 59.
[41] Ibid.

occasion distinctly beneficial in the past. The Japanese *are* amenable to representations made in a really honest & friendly spirit.[42]

Hobart Hampden concluded in the same vein:

[T]he war has impressed the country with the imperative necessity to secure new sources for the self supply of materials, such as iron, which are deficient at home. Therefore the policy of expansion and penetration in Asia and the Pacific will surely survive political changes, if not from a continued national ambition to dominate the East, then at least from considerations of urgent commercial and industrial development and a growing population.[43]

Two major points of general agreement emerged from these estimates of the internal condition of Japan: it was entirely uncertain that Japanese domestic developments, whatever form they took, would play in Britain's favour; and the Anglo-Japanese Alliance should probably be renewed.

In Lord Curzon's view, the renewal of the Alliance in some form would, above all, give Britain a control over Japan that otherwise would not exist: 'our naval position in the Pacific renders it desirable to have a friendly Japan, while the existence of some form of agreement with that country would also make it easier for His Majesty's Government to keep a watch upon her movements in China, to demand of her in her dealings with us a greater measure of freedom and frankness than it would otherwise be possible to expect, and to exercise a moderating influence on her policy generally.'[44] Thus in early 1920 the advantages of renewing the Alliance seemed to outweigh the disadvantages.

A year later the Foreign Office reversed that judgement and decided that the Alliance should be dropped, to be replaced, if possible, by a tripartite agreement among Britain, Japan, and the United States. Why the transition? As British statesmen evaluated the Alliance, they saw it more and more as a Pacific as well as a Far Eastern question involving Canada, Australia, New Zealand, and the United States as well as Great Britain and

---

[42] Ibid.   [43] Ibid.

[44] Ibid., filed letters from War Office and Admiralty. Both the Admiralty and the War Office generally concurred, though the Admiralty somewhat surprisingly advocated an 'understanding' with Japan rather than a continuation of the Alliance; the War Office agreed about the desirability of an Alliance or understanding with Japan because 'it is clear that our military position in the Far East might be most embarrassing, to say the least of it in the event of hostilities with Japan.'

Japan. The complexity of the situation staggered even the most keenly analytical minds; but, with a thoroughness probably unsurpassed by any group of officials in the world at that time, they resolutely examined every aspect of the Alliance, including not only the major political and economic problems but also an array of subordinate questions. Extensive general memoranda on the Far Eastern side of the problem were drawn up on:

A. British Commitments in the Pacific Ocean.
B. British Neutrality in the Event of a Japanese-American War.
C. Japan's Outlying Possessions and Colonies.
D. Japanese Sphere of Interest.
E. Present Situation in China.
F. Present Situation in Japan.
G. Intervention in China.
H. British Interests in China and our Competitors.
I. Japan and the Open Door.
J. Macao.

More specifically, the Foreign Office systematically examined:

I. Cable and Wireless Development in China.
II. Chinese Eastern Railway.
III. Consortium.
IV. Currency Reform in China.
V. Disbandment of Soldiers in China.
VI. Exterritoriality [*sic*].
VII. Foreign Concessions and Settlements in China.
VIII. Foreign Control in Chinese Government Services.
IX. Foreign Leased Territories and Spheres of Influence in China.
X. Mongolia.
XI. The 'Open Door' in China.
XII. Philippines.
XIII. Racial Discrimination and Immigration.
XIV. Remission of the Boxer Indemnity.
XV. Recognition by His Majesty's Government of Japan's Special Position in China.
XVI. Shantung.
XVII. Siberia and Saghalien.
XVIII. Tariff Revision in China.
XIX. Tibet.
XX. Unification of China's Railways.[45]

[45] Memorandum by Wellesley, 20 October 1921 [F 3823/2635/10], F.O. 371/6660.

All these reports only supplemented exhaustive papers on the Alliance itself and the naval situation in the Far East. Nor, of course, was the Foreign Office the only agency that studied the issue. The Foreign Office worked in conjunction with the Colonial Office, War Office, Admiralty, Board of Trade, and other interested offices, all of whose activities were systematically co-ordinated by the Committee of Imperial Defence.

Of all those involved, the most forceful and opposing voices in the debate about the Alliance were those of the Assistant Secretary superintending the Far Eastern Department, Victor Wellesley, and the Ambassador in Tokyo after April 1920, Sir Charles Eliot. Wellesley was the principal analyst who opposed renewal. Eliot was the champion of the Alliance.

Wellesley held that the Alliance had 'notoriously failed' to preserve the integrity of China.

The policy of Japan has shown itself to be one of peaceful penetration not less thorough and certainly more ruthless, more brutal and more insidious than that employed by Germany all the world over before the war, having for its ultimate aim a complete Japanese hegemony over China, politically, economically and probably militar[il]y. . . .

The Anglo-Japanese Alliance has therefore come to be an unnatural and artificial compact based neither on identity of interest nor on sympathy with common aims and ideals. Its perpetuation will stamp it as a 'Mariage de convenance' dictated on the side of Japan by fear of political isolation and on ours by the conviction that it affords us only the means of exercising a restraining and moderating influence on Japanese ambitions.

Wellesley continued to argue that, regardless of the Alliance, Japan would pursue a set course determined by her economic needs and growing nationalism. She would continue to tighten her grip on China, and this would lead to open conflict with Britain. What would happen if the Chinese rebelled against increasing Japanese penetration?

A prostrate and exhausted China on the verge of disruption appealing to us for protection against an Ally who has succeeded by surreptitious means in strangling her to death in cynical disregard of the spirit if not the letter of the Treaty obligations to maintain her integrity; would that not place His Majesty's Government in a situation of extreme embarrassment? . . . we shall almost of necessity be forced to acquiesce in the 'fait accompli' and fall back on a policy of saving what we can for British interests from the general wreckage.

That would be a most ignominious position for His Majesty's Government and a sad ending to the high-falutin phrases about China's integrity and equal opportunities for all.

He concluded that, if the Alliance were replaced by a tripartite agreement with the United States, Britain would be in a stronger position to restrain Japan.[46]

Eliot defended Japan against charges of 'cynicism', 'untrustworthiness', and 'agressiveness', and put forward powerful reasons why the two nations should not be allowed to drift apart. Explaining why the Japanese favoured renewal of the Alliance, he emphasized their pride and sentiment—'it pleases the Japanese to think that they are on the same footing as the Great Powers because they are the Ally of one of them.' Moreover, he reported, the Japanese feared isolation, and termination of the Alliance might cause Japan to turn towards Russia or Germany. On the other hand, Britain had much to gain by continuing the partnership. Despite their reputation of being 'lukewarm', the Japanese were loyal allies, as the history of the war had proved. The Alliance gave Britain some control over Japanese foreign policy, and Eliot believed that the Japanese would become more amenable if approached cordially and honourably. Practically, if the Alliance were severed, he foresaw that in the event of war Britain's Far Eastern possessions would be in an 'uncomfortable position'. After dealing with other aspects of the Alliance, Eliot ended his defence with an appeal to the English sense of fair play. The most serious charge brought against the Japanese, he wrote, was that they 'persistently resort to unfair and insidious methods in order to favour unduly Japanese merchants and injure or expel foreign competitors.' Was it not peculiar, Eliot implied, that these complaints, however justified, came 'from countries which refuse to admit Japanese'? Eliot's dispassionate argument won the approval of Sir Eyre Crowe (Assistant Under-Secretary), who wrote that it was 'good reading and carries conviction'. Curzon agreed that it was 'a good general statement of the case', but also remarked that it said 'little or nothing' about one of the main British concerns—China.[47]

---

[46] Memorandum by Wellesley, 1 June 1920 [F 2159/199/23], F.O. 371/5360.
[47] Eliot to Curzon, No. 296, 17 June 1920 [F 1559/199/23], F.O. 371/5360, with minutes by Crowe and Curzon. Eliot, a man of acknowledged brilliance and the

The problem of Shantung remained uppermost in the minds of British officials as they analysed the alternative proposals for the renewal of the Alliance. In carefully weighed language, Wellesley wrote in September 1920 that Japan had still not agreed to include the Shantung railways in the unification scheme: 'It cannot be too strongly emphasized that so long as this railway remains in the hands of the Japanese it presents a real danger to the Peace of the Far East and Shantung can hardly fail to become a second Manchuria with infinitely more disastrous consequences for it means Japanese penetration into the very vitals of China.' If Japan refused to yield on the railway question, the British would have evidence of her true intention —to dominate China.[48]

Britain feared the possibility of a militant Japan ruthlessly exploiting the resources of China and gaining strength to confront even an Anglo-American combination; conversely, according to Wellesley's analysis, Japan dreaded the prospect of Anglo-American co-operation and therefore attached supreme importance to the Anglo-Japanese Alliance.

She is acutely conscious of her political isolation as the result of the defeat of Germany and the collapse of Russia, and the one thing she fears above all is closer co-operation between us and the United States. She realises that she cannot stand up against an Anglo-American combination in the Pacific. A Russo-German-Japanese alliance might be of advantage to Japan on the Asiatic side of the Pacific, but Japan is an island empire, and therefore sea power is to her of great importance and such a combination would not give her the supremacy of the sea as against an Anglo-American combination and would therefore not benefit her to the same extent.

The only way in which Japan can hope ultimately to be able to withstand an Anglo-American combination would be by obtaining complete control of the resources of China. As the Alliance opposes no obstacles to her policy of exploiting China it has in Japanese eyes the double attraction that it prevents an Anglo-American

---

author of a distinguished book on Japanese Buddhism, frequently irritated the Foreign Office by his intellectual gymnastics. Typical minutes ran that Eliot would begin by posing a false hypothesis, continue to refute it, and then confute all issues at stake by proving the impossibility of definite proof. For anecdotes about Eliot, see the introduction by Sir Harold Parlett to Eliot's book, *Japanese Buddhism* (New York, 1959 edn.).

[48] Memorandum by Wellesley, Secret, 1 September 1920 [F 2200/199/23], F.O. 371/5361.

combination for the present and does not prevent her strengthening her hold upon China which will guard her against the eventualities of the future. Therefore the Anglo-Japanese Alliance is the cornerstone of her foreign policy.

Thus Britain had the advantage. 'Whatever be decided upon' about the Alliance, Wellesley stressed, 'it is well to remember that we hold the trump cards in our hands. It is not Great Britain but Japan who is so desperately anxious to secure a renewal of the Treaty.'[49]

In Tokyo, Eliot thought that the Foreign Office exaggerated the strength of Japan's industrial plant and too alarmingly attributed imperialist motives to the Japanese leaders. When asked to submit a comprehensive report on the economic conditions in Japan with reference to foreign policy, Eliot reported that only the cotton industry could be described as well organized. He warned against envisaging Japanese business groups through inappropriate western lenses that erroneously perceived German cartels or American trusts. He concluded that the Japanese Government had no intention of using commerce for political or seditious purposes in British possessions such as India. He minimized the importance of the Labour movement and stated that the circumstances of revolution in Russia and China did not exist in Japan. Summarizing the greatest danger, he wrote: 'a belief in Japan's mission in China is universal, and a more popular Government might express it in a more aggressive form. At present Japan's main object is economic expansion.' In December 1920, in a secret telegram giving his major opinion about the Alliance, Eliot recapitulated the central issue in this way:

I regard Japan as a moderately strong Power at present, less threatened by internal troubles than most countries. In a few years, if her naval and military programme is executed and no internal trouble occurs, she will be very strong, and if we do not make her our Ally she will be decidedly hostile. I anticipate grave difficulties in India and our other Asiatic possession in near future, and we cannot count on American sympathy there. I do not think that we can afford to risk enmity of Japan.

Eliot therefore favoured renewal.[50]

[49] Ibid.
[50] Eliot to Curzon, No. 462 Tel., Secret, 12 December 1920 [F3205/199/23], F.O. 371/5361.

From October 1920 to January of the next year, a Foreign Office Committee thoroughly reviewed the question of the renewal of the Alliance and the future policy of the British Government in the Far East. The Committee consisted of four of the most knowledgeable British experts on the Far East in London, Sir John Jordan, Sir Conyngham Greene (British Ambassador in Tokyo, 1912–19), Victor Wellesley, and Sir William Tyrrell (at that time an Assistant Under-Secretary). They defined the goal of British policy in the Far East as 'the maintenance of peace, the security of British possessions and interests in that part of the globe, the preservation of the independence of China and equal opportunity for all in matters of trade and commerce.' The principal obstacle in achieving this policy was Britain's ally, Japan. After analysing the main factors governing the relations between China and Japan, the Committee recognized that economic expansion for Japan was a 'vital necessity'. Their report continued:

We cannot, however, conceal from ourselves that, whatever justification she may have, her aims have revealed an increasing variance from the principles for which British policy has always stood, and upon which the Alliance is founded.

We wish to reply at once to the criticism that the absence of any Alliance will remove all restraint on Japanese expansion by saying that in the opinion of all competent observers the Alliance has never acted as an effective brake on Japanese activities; but we admit the force of the criticism to the extent of suggesting an alternative in the form of an *Entente* between Great Britain, Japan and the United States of America.

An *Entente* between those three powers would discourage naval competition between its members. It would also foster the 'cardinal feature' of British foreign policy in the post-war world: 'to cultivate the closest relations with the United States and to secure their whole-hearted co-operation in maintenance of peace in every part of the world.' Renewal of the Alliance would thwart that aim and would not check Japan's policy in China.

In the last analysis the independence and integrity of China, which is among our foremost aims, depends upon the reality or otherwise of the open door policy. That is the crux of the whole situation. . . . In our opinion, the best safeguard against a danger which lies as much in the weakness of China as in the aggressive tendencies of Japan, is to be found in a constructive policy for the rehabilitation of China. . . .

We would, however, repeat that in our opinion it would be hopeless to embark upon such a policy singlehanded, or without adequate naval support. Japan could thwart us at every turn. The war has left us too exhausted to cope with so great a problem. To succeed in such an effort we believe the co-operation of the United States to be indispensable. American ideals in China are identical with our own. Neither Power seeks territorial aggrandisement or privileged position. Both are actuated by a feeling of goodwill towards China and a genuine desire for peace in the Far East as elsewhere.

If the Americans refused to join a tripartite *Entente*, 'we would suggest as an alternative the conclusion of an agreement with Japan, brought up to date and in harmony with the spirit of the League of Nations, and so framed as not to exclude the eventual participation of the United States.'[51]

The opinion of the Cabinet inclined towards renewal. Meeting in late May 1921 to discuss the Alliance, the Cabinet listened to the Foreign Secretary's analysis. Having been ill, Curzon apologized for his hasty preparation and for the circulation of certain documents, 'some of which are rather out of date.'[52] He did not refer to the deliberative judgement of the Foreign Office Committee report, and the Cabinet apparently did not benefit from its considered and systematic conclusions. Curzon fluently reviewed the arguments for and against renewal, and plumped solidly for renewal. Lloyd George found the Foreign Secretary's reasoning 'irresistible', and the subtle mind of A. J. Balfour (now Lord President of the Council) evaluated Curzon's argumentation as 'very convincing'.[53]

The threefold case against renewal had sharp points: the Alliance's rationale no longer existed because of the disintegration of Russia and the disappearance of Germany as a Far

[51] Report of the Anglo-Japanese Committee, Secret, 21 January 1921 [F 1169/63/23], F.O. 371/6672; cf. *D.B.F.P.*, XIV, No. 212. The Committee made their judgements without the benefit of an up-to-date survey of economic conditions in Japan. A report by the Commercial Counsellor in Tokyo arrived in London less than a week after the Committee finished its work. (See Eliot to Curzon, No. 556, 26 November 1920 [F 3350/199/23], F.O. 371/5361). 'Briefly put,' Wellesley noted, 'Japan is politically & economically rather less mature than might have been expected.' Wellesley regretted that the information contained in this report was not available to the Alliance Committee, but did not think it affected the conclusions.

[52] Cabinet Minutes, Secret, 30 May 1921, CAB. 23/25.

[53] Ibid.

Eastern power; the Anglo-Japanese combination caused suspicion in the United States; and, the Alliance alienated China's sympathy. But the case for renewal, Curzon argued, was stronger. The Alliance was a success. 'People at home, indeed, hardly realised what the Alliance had meant to Great Britain in the Pacific, to say nothing of what the Japanese had done in the Indian Ocean and the Mediterranean.' And who would be so bold not to presage a regenerated Russia and a revived Germany? 'It might well be that in ten years' time we might be faced with a combination of these Powers in the Far East, and to meet such a situation an Alliance with Japan would be the natural guarantee.' With an alliance, Britain could exert pressure on Japan and China. From the military and naval point of view, Britain if allied with Japan, would not need to maintain a large Far Eastern fleet. Warming to his subject, Curzon maintained that Britain's Allies favoured the combination:

He [Lord Curzon] ventured to think that France, on account of her Possessions in the Far East, would regard with dismay any proposal on our part not to renew the Alliance. Holland would unquestionably take the same view, on account of her Possessions in the East Indies, since it would be a great temptation to an unfriendly Japan to pounce on and seize these Possessions.[54]

Finally, Curzon argued that Britain should be considerate of Japanese sensibilities:

[T]he feeling in Japan itself had to be considered, and there was no question that the Japanese as a whole were in favour of the renewal of the Alliance. Our general experience had been that the Japanese were scrupulous and faithful in carrying out their obligations. . . . No doubt, as was often said, the Japanese were not above intrigue, but he would like to ask if they were the only people who did this? He personally could not think of a single instance when the Japanese had not carried out their word.[55]

Balfour added that he had always found the Japanese an honourable people. Later in the discussion Lloyd George summarized the tone of the Cabinet's charitable disposition when he said, 'Frankly he (Mr. Lloyd George) liked the Japanese. The reasons they gave very often for doing things were quite

[54] Ibid.   [55] Ibid.

unintelligible, and they might have no conscience, but they did stand by those who stood by them, and they had given unfailing support to their Allies at the International Conferences.'[56] Compared with the fickle Americans, the steadfast, gallant little Japs appeared to be Britain's true friends.

Despite the bizarre theme of Japanese virtue that ran through the discussion, the Cabinet members also evaluated the dangerous side of Japan's national character. Commenting on the 'unwieldy and helpless country China', Curzon pointed out that Japan thwarted Britain's policy of building up stable, free trade on the Asian mainland.

Almost at the door of this great, helpless body there existed Japan, whose national temperament was fiercely imperialistic and where the German spirit of disciplined aggression had been imbibed to a great extent. Japan herself was incapable of maintaining more than her present population, and it was natural that she should look to China. This was the great factor in the Far Eastern world, and he [Curzon] would like to remind his colleagues of the degree to which, by her action in Korea, Formosa, the Pescadores, Manchuria, and Shantung, Japan was already forming a ring around China.[57]

Winston Churchill (Colonial Secretary) later emphasized that China's weakness 'was at the root of all the trouble.' It tempted Japanese expansion. But, to be fair, where could the Japanese find a population outlet? Balfour reminded the Cabinet of Sir Edward Grey's policy, and of the dilemma facing Britain:

At different times he had talked a good deal to Earl Grey about the question, and the latter had always taken the view that His Majesty's Government must be very careful as to how far they tried to keep Japan out of China. It had to be remembered that the Japanese were not allowed to go to Australia or to New Zealand, or to California, or to the Philippines, or, in fact, to any place where there was a white population. It was, therefore, somewhat unreasonable to say she was not to expand in a country where there was a yellow race.[58]

The issue of race in that way rested at the heart of power politics in the Far East.

How would the United States react to a renewal of Britain's Alliance with an Asian power? According to Lord Lee (First Lord of the Admiralty), the Americans intensely disliked the

[56] Ibid.　　　　[57] Ibid.　　　　[58] Ibid.

combination. 'If anyone talked of the Alliance in America everyone was at once on their hind legs.' He emphasized the danger that the continuation of the Alliance might accelerate the shipbuilding race. In order to bring up-to-date views before the Cabinet, he had talked to an American Admiral, W. S. Sims.

> The American Admiral had told him [Lee] that the American people were vehemently opposed to the Alliance, and that so long as it existed it would be very difficult to get reasonable people in the United States to curb the cry for additional arms. . . . The extent to which America could build ships was unlimited. She could not only build against Japan, but also against Great Britain and Japan combined.[59]

Winston Churchill also took the view that the Alliance would exacerbate the shipbuilding problem.

> His Majesty's Government had decided to maintain a one-Power naval standard, and an adherence to this policy was going to be very expensive if America and Japan continued a competition in naval armaments. United States Naval Officers would naturally go to their Ministers and say that England was Japan's ally, and that the position was very dangerous unless the United States built against both countries. In that case a very dangerous situation would be created, and there would be a constant feeling of antagonism by which foreign politics could not help being affected. It would be a ghastly state of affairs if we were to drift into direct naval rivalry with the United States. . . .[60]

If the Americans responded to the Alliance's renewal by building against both powers, Britain's combination with Japan would jeopardize, not stabilize, the world's peace.

On the other hand, those who wished to take a hard line towards the United States believed that the renewal of the Alliance would sober American chauvinists. Lloyd George characteristically did not want to leave the impression that Britain refused to stand up to the Americans. If the Alliance were terminated, 'the people would say that His Majesty's Government had been frightened of America and it would certainly have an unfavourable effect on our prestige in the Far East, if not throughout the whole world.'[61] Curzon quoted passages from despatches to the effect that a strong Anglo-Japanese combination would intimidate reckless American

[59] Ibid.   [60] Ibid.   [61] Ibid.

politicians who cried for additional naval armaments. He explained why a tripartite agreement between Britain, Japan, and
the United States would not work:

The difficulty about making any arrangement of that kind would be
that the anti-British party in America would probably not tolerate
any such Agreement, and, even though it were to be agreed to by the
House of Representatives, it would fail in the Senate. Further, there
could be no guarantee of American stability.

Curzon therefore recommended that the terms of the Alliance
be brought into line with the League's Covenant and renewed
for a period of four or five years. 'Though it might be possible to
provide for the participation of the United States at a later date
should they so desire, he would not propose their inclusion now,
since the policy of the American Government was so apt to
change abruptly with the changes in the Administration.'[62]
American policy in the Far East appeared to be hopelessly
unpredictable.

The Cabinet decided in favour of convening an international
conference to discuss the affairs of the Pacific. But, in view of the
mercurial tendency of the State Department, the British did not
place much hope in its success. At best the Americans might be
brought to see that their true interests would be served by co-
operating wholeheartedly with their racial cousins, the peoples
of Britain and the Dominions. At worst the United States might
attempt to split the Anglo-Japanese Alliance and shift the
centre of the English-speaking world from London to Washington. The Cabinet therefore proceeded cautiously. Britain would
go along with the American idea of reaching agreement on
security in the Pacific; but Japan would be told that Britain had
no intention of dropping the Alliance, and Canada cautioned
against an American kiss of death to the British Empire. This
ambivalence reflected British indecisiveness in trying to make
long-range security plans with the Americans, who appeared to
be incapable of systematic planning, or short-term agreements
with their traditional but dangerous ally, the Japanese. Militarily (as pointed out in analytical study prepared by the
Committee of Imperial Defence in consequence of the Cabinet's

---

[62] Ibid. Curzon's remark about the House of Representatives and the Senate
shows, of course, ignorance of American constitutional procedures.

discussion), Britain had everything to lose and nothing to gain by the Alliance's termination. Even with an arrangement with the United States, Britain would have to strengthen her eastern fleet—at great expense—and face the possibility of an eventually hostile Japan perhaps aligned with Russia and Germany. On the other hand (as argued by the Foreign Office Committee), Britain's long range security lay in Anglo-American co-operation—and in maintaining the British Empire. Great Britain had to decide on a fundamental policy towards Japan and the United States, at the same time that the nature of the Empire was in a state of transition. In 1921 the British Empire stood at the parting of the ways in the Far East.

II

THE FAR EAST AND THE
IMPERIAL CONFERENCE OF 1921

THE year 1921 was a critical juncture of events and decisions for the British Empire. The sun never set on a multitude of worldwide troubles, from Ireland to the Middle and Far East, from blistering domestic difficulties to opaque constitutional problems. From 20 June to 2 August the Prime Ministers of Great Britain, Canada, South Africa, Australia, New Zealand, and the Representatives of India, met to discuss how best to answer these vexing questions that perplexed even the best minds of a brilliant Imperial Conference. What was the future of the League? How to prepare against a resuscitated Germany and a revived Russia, and against the possible combination of those two powers? How to deal with that vacillating giant in the west, the United States? Above all, how to preserve the unity of the Empire at a time when the Dominions were becoming increasingly autonomous and independent in their foreign policies? None of those questions could be raised without in turn asking how the Empire should maintain worldwide security—in particular, how Britain should approach the issues of shipbuilding and naval disarmament. At the heart of that question lay Britain's most acute dilemma, whether or not to renew the Anglo-Japanese Alliance, commonly believed to expire on 13 July 1921. The Imperial Conference now reconsidered the whole question with a sense of urgency and incisiveness reminiscent of the most exuberant Imperial Cabinet meetings of the First World War.[1]

[1] The classic work on the Conference remains the essay by J. Bartlet Brebner, 'Canada, The Anglo-Japanese Alliance and the Washington Conference', *Political Science Quarterly*, **50**, 1 (March, 1935), 45–58. Despite its contentious theme of the influence of the Canadian Prime Minister, the article is remarkable for its fairness, perception and felicity of style. The other principal essay is by M. G. Fry, who makes important modifications of the Brebner article in the light of more extensive evidence: 'The North Atlantic Triangle and the Abrogation of the Anglo-Japanese Alliance', *Journal of Modern History*, **39**, 1 (March 1967), 46–64. See also

To the historian one of the striking features of the Imperial Conference is the continuity between the principal spokesmen and those who made the peace two years earlier. They were the same. The Prime Minister, David Lloyd George, still presided with all his political genius intact. Lord Curzon, now Foreign Secretary, still gave his grandiloquent and often trenchant interpretations of foreign affairs viewed in a historical perspective that any professional historian could well envy. Winston Churchill, now Colonial Secretary, vigorously dealt with the problems of the dependent colonial empire. A. J. Balfour, now in a less demanding role as Lord President of the Council, still delicately questioned every side of every issue, speaking one moment on behalf of the League of Nations, the next as spokesman for the Committee of Imperial Defence. His philosophical cousin, General J. C. Smuts, now Prime Minister of South Africa, continued to abstract the arguments and to come up with answers so sweeping that often as not they solved everything and nothing, or, to use Curzon's complaint, with answers that were half helpful and half embarrassing. William M. Hughes, Prime Minister of Australia, denounced the United States as shrilly as ever, and continued to receive the stolid support of his New Zealand colleague, Prime Minister William F. Massey. Arthur Meighen of Canada, the only newcomer to the circle of Prime Ministers, tenaciously upheld the view that Anglo-American friendship should be the basis of the Empire's world policy. The Indian Representatives for the most part sat in silence, proffering occasional thanks for admission to the highest council of the Empire. One misses Lord Milner and Sir Robert Borden of Canada, both now in retirement. But on the whole the decisions were being made by the same men, weary from the domestic aftermath of the war as well as the war itself, but nevertheless responding robustly to the great problem of the world's security in the post-war era: shipbuilding and armament in the Far East and Pacific.[2]

Charles N. Spinks, 'The Termination of the Anglo-Japanese Alliance', *Pacific Historical Review*, 6 (1937), 321–40; John Galbraith, 'The Imperial Conference of 1921 and the Washington Conference', *Canadian Historical Review*, **29**, 2 (June, 1948), 143–52; M. Tate and F. Foy, 'More Light on the Abrogation of the Anglo-Japanese Alliance', *Political Science Quarterly*, **74**, 4 (1959), 523–54.

[2] There is no single satisfactory account of the personalities of the statesmen at the Conference, though many insights into Lloyd George and his colleagues can be

Partly in order to prepare their strategy at the Imperial
Conference, partly because of the pressing need for decision,
the Committee of Imperial Defence began to give sustained
attention to the problem of naval policy in the Pacific in
December 1920. At one session, in which the Secretariat
emphasized the *VERY SECRET nature* of the proceedings,
Lloyd George stated that the British Government had never
before been confronted with such a complex situation. Stated
as simply as possible, 'the problem which faced the Committee
that morning was the kind of Navy upon which they would have
to depend in the future for the defence of the Empire and for
the protection of the Imperial lines of communication.' Should
Great Britain embark on a shipbuilding programme? The
first step in making that decision, Lloyd George said, was to
determine the 'probable enemy'. He ruled out Germany,
Russia, Italy, and even France as potential antagonists in the
immediate future, and emphasized that the post-war situation
differed entirely from the pre-1914 balance of naval power:
'There were ... two formidable new Powers in the world—
formidable to-day and possibly overwhelmingly so in a few
years' time. Both at present were friendly nations, and they
were Japan and the United States.'[3]

If those two powers built against each other, one of the fleets
eventually might be used against Britain. They probably would
not act in concert. And Britain could not consider the United
States to be a possible enemy. Lloyd George continued:

[W]e could not fight the United States for economical as well as for
military reasons. For instance, the long Canadian frontier was not
really defensible. If the Committee were to decide now that Great
Britain must enter into competition with the United States in naval
shipbuilding, it would be the biggest decision they had taken since

gained from A. J. P. Taylor's *English History, 1914–1945* (Oxford, 1965). His
bibliography discusses the standard biographies, which are singularly unhelpful
for an understanding of the Imperial Conference. For the Dominion statesmen, the
point of departure is W. K. Hancock, *Smuts: the Fields of Force, 1919–1950* (Cambridge, 1968), also thin on the Conference's substantive issues.

[3] Committee of Imperial Defence, Minutes of the 134th Meeting, Secret, 14
December 1920, CAB. 2/3. British and American naval policies are thoroughly
discussed by Stephen Roskill, *Naval Policy between the Wars: the Period of Anglo-
American Antagonism, 1919–1929* (London, 1968). For American policy, see also
George T. Davis, *A Navy Second to None* (New York, 1940).

1914, and conceivably greater than that taken in 1914, for various reasons. . . . There would follow precisely the same tension as had resulted from our naval competition with Germany. The two countries would begin to scowl and to snarl at each other; newspapers on both sides would stir up public feeling; inflammatory speeches would be made, and generally there would be an attitude of rivalry, hostility and antagonism aroused. The first result of this would be that America would insist upon her debt being paid in full. . . .

We should be up against the greatest resources of the world. We should be up against a growing and intensely virile population. This was the competition that we should have to face, and it could be faced by no one without the most serious misgivings. . . . No British statesman, therefore, could commit his country to what might be a disastrous rivalry, except for the most imperative and convincing reasons.[4]

None of the members of the Committee of Imperial Defence disputed Lloyd George's conclusion about the necessity to avoid shipbuilding rivalry with the United States. But Winston Churchill lamented Britain's relative loss of supremacy at sea and the decline from the traditional principle of the two power standard, by which Britain should be prepared to engage the fleets of any two combined powers. With the deterioration of Britain's relative strength, from the two- to the one-power standard, he 'did not see why we should not be able to defend our position in this respect by comparisons with the second naval power without arousing irritation on the other side of the Atlantic.' Some officials hoped that an American Republican Government would curtail the shipbuilding programme there. On the other hand:

Lord Beatty [First Sea Lord and Chief of Naval Staff] pointed out that as far as the United States were concerned the competition had already started, and that the new Administration, even if possessed of the best motives in the world, could scarcely be expected to refrain from completing the ships already laid down. This would leave us in a greatly inferior position unless we took the necessary steps now.[5]

Willy-nilly, Britain had to build or to accept American superiority—or to continue the Alliance with Japan.

[4] C.I.D., 134th Meeting, Secret, 14 December 1920, CAB. 2/3.
[5] Ibid.

Continuation of the Alliance might counterbalance American strength, but might it not also accelerate the armament race? The Committee of Imperial Defence had difficulty in answering that important question. Those who spoke mainly from a broadly political point of view, such as Curzon and Lloyd George, tended to favour the Alliance as a means of restraining American naval construction and bridling Japanese imperialism; those with more pro-American views and with naval experience, such as Beatty and Churchill, urged caution. Curzon emphasized the Alliance's value in curbing Japanese imperialism: 'The Japanese were insidious and unscrupulous in their methods, and if they were not controlled and kept in order by their Alliance with this country they would be at liberty to pursue their aggressive policy in China and elsewhere unchecked, even to the length of waging war with the United States of America.'[6] Lloyd George believed that the Alliance would curtail the free use of the American navy by forcing the United States to concentrate her fleet in the Pacific. Furthermore, American bluster was a good reason for the extension of the Alliance: 'it was possible that the bellicose attitude of the United States might conceivably drive us into a defensive Alliance with Japan.' As he developed his ideas, he became more irritated at the Americans. He asked the First Sea Lord what would happen in the event of Britain's waging war with the United States, with Japan remaining neutral.

Lord Beatty thought that the existence of a strong Japanese Navy would no doubt, in the conditions suggested, make the United States rather nervous, but he thought they would have no option but to exert all their forces against the Power with which they were at war, retaining of course some coast-defence vessels for home defence. He thought nothing would please the Japanese more than to see the only other two Naval Powers of any account engaged in a war which might have the effect of leaving Japan the supreme Naval Power.

Churchill strongly held that it would be disastrous if the Alliance led to Anglo-American naval competition, not to mention war.

Mr. Churchill welcomed the opportunity of recording his opinion that no more fatal policy could be contemplated than that of basing our naval policy on a possible combination with Japan against the United States.

[6] Ibid.

The Prime Minister suggested there was one more fatal policy, namely, one whereby we would be at the mercy of the United States.[7]

Britain could remain independent of the United States and supreme as a world power if the Empire, as distinct from England and her colonies, concerted its policy towards the United States and Japan. The co-ordinator of the Empire, the Colonial Secretary, thought that the key to harmonious action lay with the Pacific Dominions, and that they would all agree that the Alliance should be dropped: 'Canada, Australia and New Zealand had very strong racial objections to the Japanese, and would be disposed to throw in their lot with the United States against Japan. . . .'[8] In fact Churchill was wrong. The Pacific Dominions held radically different views about Japan and the United States, and about the entire question of security in the Pacific.

The rift became quite apparent in the spring of 1921.[9] Curzon reported to the Cabinet in May that Australia and New Zealand championed the Alliance while Canada emphatically urged its termination.

Somewhat to his [Curzon's] surprise, Mr Hughes was strongly in favour of its renewal, and Mr. Massey also took the same view, although he (Lord Curzon) had not expected him to do so. In fact, the Prime Minister of New Zealand had said that we had a good deal to gain and nothing to lose, by renewing the Treaty. . . .
On the other hand, Canada was frankly hostile. This was only natural, as they were thinking of their own interests, living, as they did, side by side with the United States of America: and every day one saw how everything in Canada was influenced by their close touch with their southern neighbour. People in Canada were also profoundly affected by the question of Japanese immigration on the West Coast, and were painfully impressed with Japan's attitude in Korea.[10]

Like a signalman seeing two locomotives on a collision course,

[7] Ibid. [8] Ibid.
[9] During this time the issue of the Alliance was discussed by the Parliaments of each of the Dominions. The debates are most conveniently followed in the *Journal of the Parliaments of the Empire*; there is a good discussion of the various points of view by Gwendolen M. Carter, *The British Commonwealth and International Security: the Role of the Dominions, 1919–1939* (Toronto, 1947), chapter II.
[10] Cabinet Minutes 43(21), Secret, 30 May 1921, CAB. 23/25.

the Imperial Government now faced the most difficult exercise of shunting the Canadians or the Australasians onto a parallel track.

Canada had initiated the debate about the Dominions and Japan. In an exchange of telegrams with Lloyd George, Prime Minister Meighen made it clear that the Alliance blocked accord in the English-speaking world. Canada therefore recommended the termination of the Alliance and the convening of a Pacific Conference to reach agreement on the affairs of the Far East. The Alliance could thus be terminated gracefully, the Empire's policy reconciled with American interests in China, and the principles of the League given concrete application by repudiating the old pre-war system of Alliances. Lloyd George replied by pointing out the complexity of the question: the issue involved the problem of shipbuilding as well as the future of the League, and New Zealand and Australia in any event would have to be consulted about the Alliance's renewal. Lloyd George held that the Imperial Conference should have complete liberty to decide the issue in June; Meighen retorted that failure to act before then would prejudice the outcome of the Conference. This exchange demonstrated, above all, the weakness of the Imperial Government.[11] When all was said, London was powerless to prevent Canada from taking independent action with the United States—an alarming thought, since Canadian-American unity might signal a shift in the centre of gravity of the English-speaking world from London to Washington. According to Sir William Tyrrell of the Foreign Office:

If Canada insists on moving at Washington . . . without having come to an agreement with us, she will be playing into the hands of Senator Lodge and his party who hope to utilize the question of the Japanese Alliance for the purpose of detaching her and possibly Australia with a view to shift the centre of the English-speaking communities from London to Washington. Every effort should be made to prevent this.[12]

Lloyd George assured the Canadian Government that the Empire's freedom of action would not be restricted by waiting

[11] Copies of this correspondence with minutes in F.O. 371/6672 and 6673; summary in *D.B.F.P.*, First Series (all subsequent references to *D.B.F.P.* in this chapter are to the First Series), XIV, No. 261.

[12] Minute by Tyrrell, 8 April 1921, F.O. 371/6672; *D.B.F.P.*, XIV, No. 261.

for the discussion of the Imperial Conference, and that Japan would be asked to extend the Treaty three months in order to give the Conference time to decide whether the Alliance should be renewed or terminated. Canada did not reply. The Imperial Government interpreted Canadian silence as acquiescence. The Canadians did not. According to Meighen, as he later recalled the exchange, 'We did not communicate agreeing to a renewal in any form, whether for three months or any time.'

The date of 13 July 1921 was crucial to the misunderstanding between the Canadian and Imperial Governments, and to the entire issue of renewal. Did the Alliance automatically expire on that date, or did it continue until denunciation? Until the summer of 1921, both Britain and Japan had assumed that the Alliance would remain in force unless steps were taken to terminate the Treaty. A complication arose when the two governments submitted a declaration to the League of Nations in the previous year, on 8 July 1920, stating that the Alliance if continued would not conflict with the League's Covenant.[13] Both governments interpreted this communication merely as a notification that the letter as well as the spirit of the Treaty would be brought into harmony with the Covenant if the Alliance continued. However, on 10 July 1921, less than two weeks before the Imperial Conference, Sir Cecil Hurst, the Legal Adviser to the Foreign Office, notified Lord Curzon that the notification to the League amounted to *denunciation*. In a manner characteristic of many of his other judgements, Hurst viewed the issue in a narrow, legalistic fashion without taking fully into account the political intent of the two parties. Curzon noted: 'I am not a lawyer. But I am greatly astonished to learn that the joint communication to the L. of N. constituted a denunciation.' If Britain decided to open negotiations for a Pacific Conference, could the Alliance be temporarily continued? 'Am I to be told this is impossible?' he asked. 'Surely not. . . . In other words I agree with the Japs.'[14] Nevertheless Curzon bowed to Hurst's legal exactitude. When the Imperial Conference met in late June, the participants faced the immediacy of the Alliance's expiry in only a fortnight's time.

---

[13] See *D.B.F.P.*, XIV, Nos. 45, 51, 55, and 65; *League of Nations Official Journal*, No. 5, 1920, 252–3.

[14] Minute by Curzon, 14 June 1921, *D.B.F.P.*, XIV, No. 288.

'One of the most urgent and important of foreign questions,' Lloyd George stated to the Conference when it opened at noon on Monday 20 June was Britain's relations with Japan and the United States. There was no quarter of the world, he said, where Britain desired peace and avoidance of an armaments race more than in the Far East and Pacific. After recapitulating Japan's loyal service to Britain during the war, he immediately came to the heart of the issue: race.

No greater calamity could overtake the world than any further accentuation of the world's divisions upon the lines of race. The British Empire has done signal service to humanity in bridging those divisions in the past; the loyalty of the King Emperor's Asiatic peoples is the proof. To depart from that policy, to fail in that duty, would not only greatly increase the dangers of international war; it would divide the British Empire against itself. Our foreign policy can never range itself in any sense upon the difference of race and civilisation between East and West. It would be fatal to the Empire.

He put the case just as positively in relation to the United States:

Friendly co-operation with the United States is for us a cardinal principle, dictated by what seems to us the proper nature of things, dictated by instinct quite as much as by reason and common sense. We desire to work with the great Republic in all parts of the world. Like it, we want stability and peace, on the basis of liberty and justice. Like it, we desire to avoid the growth of armaments, whether in the Pacific or elsewhere, and we rejoice that American opinion should be showing so much earnestness in that direction at the present time.[15]

His colleagues regarded Lloyd George's speech, which contained many similar persuasive and idealistic passages, as one of the most powerful statements of the Empire's purpose ever articulated. Its general gist may be summarized by two of his sentences: 'The British Empire is a saving fact in a very distracted world. It is the most hopeful experiment in human organization which the world has seen.' Lloyd George achieved his rhetorical best. But in his remarks concerning Japan and the United States a sceptical observer might have drawn two negative implications: race did constitute a residual problem within

---

[15] Stenographic Notes of a Meeting of Representatives of the United Kingdom, the Dominions, and India (hereafter cited as Imperial Conference Minutes, I.C.M.), Secret, 20 June 1921, 1st Meeting, CAB. 32/2.

the Empire and in its relations with Japan; and the United States could not be trusted to pursue a naval policy conducive to the Empire's security.

On the sensitive issues of race and naval defence, the Conference agreed that there should be some but not total publicity given to the discussions about policy. Lloyd George attached great importance in publishing the opening speeches by the Prime Ministers 'because so much depends on the atmosphere that is created.' But all thought that the sessions should be secret in order to discuss all matters freely. 'My own opinion is that open diplomacy is impossible,' said Prime Minister Massey. The rest agreed, though the Canadian Prime Minister urged that 'it is better to err on the side of publicity than on the side of secrecy.' Only by the fullest and frankest discussions—which if reported to the public would rankle opinion abroad—could the Empire decide on a sound foreign policy. Three assumptions about that policy underlay all of the discussions about the Far East. First, its supreme importance. Negatively, in the words of Prime Minister Hughes, 'Wars are hatched by foreign policy.' Positively, according to Prime Minister Smuts, armaments depended upon policy and British policy therefore should aim at making an armaments race impossible. Second, the most important regional focus of British policy has shifted since the war. In Hughes's words: 'The war and the Panama Canal has shifted the world's stage from the Mediterranean and the Atlantic to the Pacific. The stage upon which the great world drama is to be played in the future is in the Pacific.' Third, British policy had the power to relax racial tensions or to inflame them, and there could be no doubt that Britain should attempt to sooth racial friction. According to Meighen, there was 'the paramount necessity of seeing to it that no step is taken that leaves out of the mind the importance of mitigating racial divisions.' In similar vein the Indian Representative emphasized the British Empire 'as a Confederation of Races into which willing and free peoples had been admitted—willing and free peoples; consent is incongruous with inequality of races, and freedom, necessarily implies admission of all people to the rights of citizenship without reservation.'[16] In short, to those sitting

[16] I.C.M., 2nd Meeting, Secret, 21 June 1921, CAB. 32/2.

in Conference in London in June 1921, the British Empire clearly represented a force for peace and racial harmony.

During the opening days of the Conference, the delegates listened to salutatory orations, a spirited report by Churchill on the colonies and other dependencies, and a brilliant analysis by Curzon of foreign affairs, which, to use Hughes's words, left a profound impression of 'the vastness and splendour of the pageantry of the Empire'. On 28 June Curzon reviewed the history of the Anglo-Japanese Alliance. He pointed out that the Treaty when renewed in 1911 contained the new and 'well-known article 4', which was inserted in order to exclude the possibility of war between Britain and the United States by explicitly stating that neither contracting party would be required to go to war with a power with which a Treaty of Arbitration was in force. In 1914 Britain concluded such an arrangement with the United States, a Peace Commission Treaty.[17] The Foreign Office informed the Japanese that this agreement should be regarded as the equivalent of an Arbitration Treaty and that the stipulations of Article 4 therefore applied. Nevertheless a substantial part of the American public appeared to think that the Anglo-Japanese Treaty could bring Britain into conflict with the United States. Curzon thus raised a major point: American suspicion of the Anglo-Japanese combination.

In analysing the familiar arguments for and against the Alliance, the Foreign Secretary developed a delicate theme: the dilemma of security and race. Summarizing all aspects of this complex issue, he subtly emphasized the contingencies if the Americans faced renewal and the Japanese cancellation. If Britain continued the Alliance, the American public would regard it as 'disastrous'—the word reported by the British Ambassador in Washington—and consequent American shipbuilding in the Pacific would certainly be disastrous in turn for Britain's security and economy if an armaments race ensued. On the other hand, if the Alliance were dropped the progress made in race relations would be destroyed.

Supposing you cut off your Agreement with Japan now, you again

---

[17] See Bradford Perkins, *The Great Rapprochement: England and the United States* (New York, 1968), pp. 234–5.

revive the old position in the Far East—the white men against the dark men or the yellow men. Now our policy during the last twenty years has been to try to remove and obliterate these colour prejudices, and undoubtedly our agreement with Japan has led to an increase in the prestige of the dark races as against the view that Europeans will not have anything to do with the dark races and look upon them from a point of superiority and despise them.

When we took Japan on the footing of equality of races we immeasurably increased the sense of self-respect entertained by those races ... if we were to throw away this Alliance I really think you would be throwing away an asset of very considerable value on an international scale and from the widest point of view.[18]

Was Anglo-American friendship worth the sacrificing of the Alliance with the 'yellow men', who, as Allies, would be disinclined to join a Russo-German axis? Curzon's summary of the problem led him to conclude that the Alliance should not be cancelled. There were then three other choices: (1) renewal, but with modifications to bring the Treaty into line with the League's Covenant; (2) expansion of the Alliance into a tripartite agreement including the United States, though Curzon warned that 'it seems to be doubtful whether the Senate would pass it, or if American public opinion is prepared for it.'; and (3) renewal after consultation with the United States and China, perhaps after a Conference of the Pacific powers. All in all, in Curzon's judgement, Britain's security would be endangered most by a rupture with Japan, but he did not exclude the possibility of somehow reconciling Japan and the United States.

Balfour continued the argument. He spoke, improbably, as the Chairman of the Standing Committee of Imperial Defence and as British Representative of the League of Nations. With characteristic verve, breadth of vision, and sweeping dialectic, he managed to reconcile Britain's defence with the spirit of the Covenant. Supporting Curzon, he said that under no circumstances could he envisage a war with the United States. But, if one looked at the strategic situation in the Pacific, the American naval programme could not be viewed with equanimity.

America is steadily putting ships in the Pacific, I understand, and although I am not in the least way conceiving a war with America as a possibility, yet if you look at the thing from a purely strategic point

[18] I.C.M., 8th Meeting, Secret, 29 June 1921, CAB. 32/2.

of view, and omit politics and sentiment and look at it with an open
mind, undoubtedly it is a fact that if we had not Japan on our side we
should be second or third Power in the Pacific after a considerable
number of years. . . . Therefore, in our view, so long as our relatively
unprepared condition lasts, it is, from a strategic point of view, of
very great importance that the Japanese Alliance should be
maintained.

He emphasized how technological advances had enhanced
Britain's difficulties in the Pacific. Modern battle fleets in the
future would be increasingly fuelled by oil, not coal. Until
Britain could build adequate fuelling facilities at Singapore, the
gate of the Pacific, a British fleet concentrated in that ocean
would be immobile and relatively useless. For that reason
Britain would of necessity have to remain on friendly terms with
Japan. Termination of the Alliance, he said, would have most
adverse military results.

[T]wo evil consequences at least will follow from bringing the
Japanese Alliance to an end. The first is, that we can no longer
count on any assistance from Japan. We can no longer pretend to
control her actions or modify her policy in the Far East, but worse
than that, we may turn a faithful friend into a very formidable
enemy, and to turn a faithful friend into a formidable enemy at a
moment when you find yourselves relatively unprepared to meet any
attack from the former friend and the present enemy is the worst
policy you could possibly pursue from a strictly military point of
view.[19]

In short, Britain could not defend herself against a hostile
Japan—a compelling military reason for continuing the
Alliance.

Balfour next demonstrated that the Alliance could easily be
brought into line with the League's principles. Article 21 of the
Covenant stated that regional agreements such as the Monroe
Doctrine would remain valid; he proposed that the Alliance
should be transformed into a Monroe Doctrine for the Pacific,
perhaps with American participation. Because Britain's
Alliance with Japan was essentially defensive, 'in essence
pacific', he did not think it would require much ingenuity or
skill to draft a treaty fully in harmony with the spirit and the
letter of the Covenant. Then not even the Americans could
protest.

[19] Ibid.

[I]t is quite clear that the pacific character, the defensive character, of the whole transaction would be patent to the eyes of the world if it were done under the auspices and with the complete accord of the League of Nations. It would then be framed with its defensive and unaggressive character patent in every line, with the League of Nations as its godfather, and it would be a very embittered controversialist who could find in such a transaction a menace or threat, or anything else, to any third Power, or indeed anything otherwise than as a controlling influence over any imperialistic tendencies which the Japanese Government or any Party in the Japanese State might be supposed to entertain.[20]

Balfour's reasoning in dual channels of national security and international accord gave additional support to Curzon's weighty opinion that the Alliance in some form should be renewed. Following Curzon's lead, however, Balfour's case for the Alliance also did not preclude American participation or resolution of the problem by international conference. The principal spokesmen for the Imperial Government held moderate ground between the more extreme positions of the antipodean Dominions and Canada, and were still flexible enough to move in either direction.

During the first week and a half of the Conference, the thrust of the discussions seemed to be leading directly to renewal. On 21 June, in the ninth meeting, the Prime Minister of Canada challenged that concensus and began to try to reverse the logic developed by the Conference. Speaking with deference to Curzon's perspicacity, and as the Prime Minister least experienced in foreign affairs, Meighen forthrightly said at the outset that he would oppose continuation of the Alliance in any form. To align the Empire with Japan because of two 'impotential foes', one half smitten and the other prostrate, seemed to him to be a policy based on 'speculative possibility' and wildly out of line with reality. Canadians and Americans would not tolerate a return to the old diplomacy of pre-war days.

Speaking generally as to Alliances, I am quite sure I am speaking the opinion of the Dominion of Canada when I say it naturally is averse to any Alliances at the present time. . . . if, for example, Japan and Great Britain are, under the shadow of the League, to form an Alliance for the purpose of preventing possible designs of

[20] Ibid. Cf. Blance E. C. Dugdale, *Arthur James Balfour* (New York, 1937), p. 317.

Russia and Germany in the Far East, then, other Alliances would be formed for counter purposes. Alliances will grow, and there becomes really no difference between the situation that results and that from which we have escaped.[21]

With words ringing of Wilsonian idealism (or rather, its Canadian equivalent inspired by Sir Robert Borden), Meighen's speech displayed the same sympathy towards China and suspicion of Japan that characterized the President's initial attitude at the Paris Peace Conference. If one of the objects of the Alliance was the preservation of China's integrity, then it had failed egregiously.

[H]aving made the Treaty for definite objects, Japan has far exceeded her rights, and progressively violated her covenant. It cannot well be imagined how in the short space of less than twenty years she could expect under any conditions to achieve more in the way of aggrandisement, and it is only reasonable to say that if we do enter into another Treaty, we have every ground to expect them, hold the check rein as we will, to succeed in duplicating the performance of the last twenty years in the further invasion of this very independence and integrity of China. . . .

We may restrain, we may do all we can. We say now that we have done so to the best of our ability, but there is Korea, there is Formosa, there is Manchuria, there is Shantung. There are the twenty-one demands. They have done all these things during the twenty years, and strive as we will to have the United States people believe that this is perpetrated with our hand on their collar, we cannot get them so to believe. They will believe it has been done with the connivance of Great Britain, in order to subvert the purposes of the United States, and to give us a great hold on and enchancement of our eastern interests.[22]

In short, the Alliance made Britain *particeps criminis* and thus affected the Empire's standing with other nations—notably the United States.

Meighen held as axiomatic that Anglo-American friendship constituted the basis of Britain's world policy. It was equally self-evident that nothing could antagonize the United States more than the reincarnation of the Anglo-Japanese Alliance. Nor would renewal stabilize the situation in the Far East. With

[21] I.C.M., 9th Meeting, Secret, 29 June 1921, CAB. 32/2.
[22] Ibid.

Britain as Japan's ally, and apparently unable to curb the rapacity of that ally, China and the United States would drift together. Britain in effect would be giving both the Japanese and the Americans a free hand in China, which, ethical considerations aside, would be unwise economically. 'Our interests there [China] are equal to those of the United States; the importance of the Chinese trade and the goodwill of China are very great.' To prevent the gravitation of China to the United States, the Alliance would have to be dropped. Otherwise the Americans, blood-brothers of the peoples of the Empire, would be the odd men out and no Anglo-Japanese treaty, no matter how skilfully worded, would persuade the American public that an Anglo-Japanese combination did not menace American security.

[W]hat is to be expected of the United States who are asked to stand out altogether while we renew a special exclusive relationship with Japan? There would be some show of reason behind a sense of estrangement on the part of that country, even though the possibility of antagonism with them is provided against in the arrangement; they are nevertheless out, and they are the same blood as ourselves.[23]

Renewal of the Alliance from the Canadian point of view would be to start the Empire down the path of disaster, and Meighen made vividly clear that Canada would be the victim.

If from any cause, or from the initiation of any disastrous policy, we should become involved in worse relationships than we are now, Canada will suffer most of all. And if, in the last awful event—God forbid it should ever come!—we reach the penalty of war, Canada will be the Belgium.[24]

He rejected out of hand the notion that the Alliance would safeguard the Empire against American aggression, or against any hostile combination of European powers. In sombre tone he stated unequivocally that Canada would part company if the Empire pursued the renewal of the Alliance.

If this renewal is intended to create a combination against an American menace which is to succeed the German menace, which in turn succeeded the Russian menace of 1902, then there can be no hope of ever carrying Canada into the plan.

23 Ibid.   24 Ibid.

The claim is sometimes made, sometimes left to be implied, that this Alliance with Japan is to be the pivot of a new world alignment. That only needs to be stated to excite despair in the minds of the people of our country. The future is dark if we have to start now on that path. I can only add that there is no possibility of convincing Canada or making any appeal at all to her with those words in our mouth—none at all.[25]

The Prime Minister of Canada had, in effect, given an ultimatum to the Conference.

Hughes savagely attacked Meighen's argument. Living up to his reputation of an Australian nationalist whose powerful mind gave no quarter and asked none, he abrasively denounced the Canadian Prime Minister for extolling the United States and condemning Britain. The position taken by Canada, he bluntly charged, was more American than British. 'I must regard Mr. Meighen's presentation of the case as not the case for the Empire, but as the case for the United States of America.' The Canadian logic ran that the Alliance should not be renewed because the Americans did not want renewal. But how, Hughes asked, could the Conference be certain of the American attitude?

Mr. Hughes: ... Mr. Meighen tells us that the renewal of the Treaty will be objectionable to America. ... He says it does not matter in what form we renew, it will still be objectionable. He does not ... say 'There is nothing inimical to our interests in the Treaty.' But even so, he says that his nebulous intangible thing which he calls 'the voice of America' will regard something which will militate against America's interests. It is very difficult to deal with such an argument because in the very nature of things who is able to say what is the voice of the people of America? It is said that the voice of the people is the voice of God.

Mr. Massey: Not always.

Mr. Hughes: Precisely, you cannot tell whether the God speaks or merely rumbles in uneasy slumbers, or peradventure, speaks with a forked tongue saying many and quite inconsistent things.[26]

Hughes made it quite clear that the diabolical inconsistency of the United States, in his opinion, lay at the root of the world's troubles, especially in the Pacific. He reminded Meighen of the American fiasco of creating the League, then abandoning it.

[25] Ibid.
[26] I.C.M., 9th and 10th Meetings, Secret, 29 June 1921, CAB. 32/2.

He spoke with irony of Canada's putting national defence above the security of the Empire.

Mr. Meighen has not suggested for a moment—not directly, at any rate—that one of the consequences to Canada of refusing to renew the Treaty might be to endanger its national safety. He does not suggest that for a moment, for its borders march for nearly 4,000 miles with those of a nation of 110,000,000 of people. He did not say so, but it is a fact, and one of the most striking proofs of the inconsistencies of mankind, that the nation primarily responsible for that League of Nations which was to banish war forever, is now committed to the most ambitious naval programme the world has yet seen. . . .

Here is a nation responsible—more than any other nation—for the Covenant, that imposing and sacrosanct instrument, which was to ensure the peace of the world and banish war for ever from the earth; yet from which, amongst all the civilised nations, excepting only Bolshevik Russia, she alone has remained aloof, and which she has now condemned with bell, book and candle, thus drowning her contemptuous rejection of the only existing means of preserving the world's peace.[27]

Speaking as if he might be addressing President Wilson instead of the Prime Minister of Canada, Hughes continued:

The League of Nations stands, if anything does, for all those principles upon which Mr. Meighen has been so inconsistent this morning. The peace of the world, disarmament, the end of the suicidal struggle for naval supremacy which preceded the great war and which is now being renewed—a policy which has reduced the world to a state of chaos and which, if persisted in, will destroy civilisation—for all these things the League of Nations stands. We are members of the League. The United States is not. The declared policy of the United States is to build the biggest navy in the world.[28]

By their actions, the Americans demonstrated that they feared attack, and Hughes argued that they were preparing above all against Japan. Dread of Japan together with an anti-British sentiment constituted the basis of the American protest against the Alliance. 'Mr. Meighen has not touched upon two facts which stand out; one, that America's real objection to this Treaty in any form is the fear of Japan; and the other, the hatred of Britain by certain sections in America.' The preoccupation with possible Anglo-Japanese aggression had

[27] Ibid.   [28] Ibid.

brought about a case of American schizophrenia. Even in regard to Britain one personality fought against the other. 'America speaks with two voices. One voice assures us . . . that the great heart of America beats in sympathy with us; the other voice denounces us and all our works.' By contrast with Meighen, Hughes thought that strong, independent action would cure the demented anti-British mind in America.

Mr. Meighen says 'You will get the friendship of the great American people.' Frankly I do not believe it. Now, Sir, I venture to say that if we do this thing, if we repulse an Ally who stood by us during the critical days of the war, if we bow the knee to faction, if we attempt to interpret the raucous voice of the faction as the voice of the great American people, we shall not only fail to win their friendship, but shall most assuredly bring ourselves into contempt amongst them. How does a strong nation act? It does that which it thinks to be right.[29]

The right policy, according to Hughes, was to renew the Alliance and not to allow the United States to dictate to the British Empire.

As he berated the United States, Hughes praised Japan. The Empire could not have won the war without Japan's assistance. 'Without her help it is most improbable that the Allies would have triumphed over the Central Powers. Had she elected to fight on the side of Germany, we should almost certainly have been defeated.' As an ally whose loyalty to Britain stood beyond question, Japan had every reason to expect British gratitude by the continuance of the Alliance. From Britain's point of view, to cold-shoulder Japan after twenty years of friendship would violate the ultimate canon of the British way of life by being ungentlemanly. Furthermore, it would be dangerous. Hughes pursued this point in regard to Australia. He admitted that his views might be coloured. To use one of his favourite metaphors, his ideas reflected his environment, just as the dyer's hands showed his work. But he did not want the Conference to think that he was narrow minded. He held that what was true for Australia was true for the Empire as a whole, with the possible exception of Canada. The pre-eminent truth was that sea power secured the safety and commerce of the Empire.

[29] Ibid.

This Empire rests on sea power, and while sea power exists as the most potent factor in determining the destiny of mankind, we must see to it that the navy is adequate to our circumstances. That, shortly, is the position. I want the Conference to consider it in its application to Australia. If we do not renew this Treaty with Japan, where will Australia stand? If you will look, Sir, at the map you will see the position that Australia occupies. . . .

Will anybody who looks at that map say that, living as we do, remote from Europe, from the Western World, occupying a rich and almost empty Continent, dependent absolutely on sea power, not only for our prosperity, which comes from the sale of goods in overseas markets, but dependent for our very existence on sea power, say that it would be wise for us to alienate by a rude and abrupt refusal to renew this Treaty, our nearest neighbour, a great and powerful nation, whose circumstances compel her to seek new territory for her overcrowded population, and who has behind her effective means of making us feel the full force of her resentment.[30]

At this particular stage of the discussion, Meighen, who perhaps thought that Hughes's remarks were irrelevant to Canada, went off to lunch with the Prince of Wales. Few statesmen could not have been perturbed by Hughes's invective and the power of his argument. Lloyd George, obviously relishing Hughes's discourse, interrupted and suggested that Mr. Meighen would certainly like to hear more.

That afternoon Hughes waxed even more vituperatively eloquent. He again reminded his colleagues of basic geographical and military facts of the war that pertained not only to Australia but to the entire Empire.

Look at the map and ask yourselves what would have happened to that great splash of red right down from India through Australia down to New Zealand, but for the Anglo-Japanese Treaty. How much of these great rich territories and portions of our Empire would have escaped had Japan been neutral? How much if she had been our enemy? It is certain the naval power of the Empire could not have saved India and Australia and still been strong enough to hold Germany bottled up in the narrow seas.[31]

In the event of a future war, the southern British Empire could not, like Canada, nestle under the United States' wing for

[30] Ibid.
[31] Ibid. For the clash between Hughes and Meighen seen in broad geo-political context, see end note.

safety. Australia and New Zealand in particular would be at the mercy of Japan unless she remained a friend. To Hughes's mind it was therefore imperative to maintain Anglo-Japanese friendship and the surest way to do that would be to continue the Alliance. It was no use beating in the air about American friendship, Hughes said—look at the facts. Two facts impressed him most of all: the United States was unpredictable and undependable, and the Treaty, if not renewed, would turn a friend into an enemy.

We have to face the facts as they are. If we do not renew this Treaty with Japan, what will the position be? Look at the map, and note the geographical position of Australia. A great continent with $5\frac{1}{2}$ millions of population, and Japan a small group of islands, densely populated and occupying a dominating strategic position, as its nearest neighbour. The population of Japan is increasing with great rapidity; the economic pressure upon the means of subsistence is daily becoming more intense. The position is unstable, it cannot continue for any length of time. Japan cannot continue to spend half her total revenue on military and naval armaments. She must expand. She is the strongest naval Power in the Pacific. In the face of these facts is it to be wondered at, that Australia views with apprehension the possibility of the Japanese Treaty being denounced?[32]

Britain could not dare to brush aside contemptuously an ally of twenty years who also happened to be a great naval power. If the Treaty were cancelled, Hughes said, 'We shall turn on the hymn of hate which this other voice now chants into loud shouts of eternal friendship.' In peroration he said he would yield to no man, not even Meighen, in an effort to bring about a Union of the English-speaking Peoples. But he did not believe that the Conference would enhance American esteem for the Empire if they treacherously overthrew a loyal ally. The Empire's policy had to be founded on justice, 'compatible alike with the welfare of mankind and the greatness of this Empire'. To Hughes that meant the unequivocal renewal of the Alliance. 'I am for the renewal of this Treaty, and I am against delay.' The Prime Minister of Australia thus presented an ultimatum equally emphatic to Meighen's.

Smuts was shocked. With considerable understatement he said that the discussion had become somewhat controversial.

[32] Ibid.

'The language used by these two Prime Ministers is such as to frighten a man who stands outside of this great issue.' Both Meighen and Hughes had spoken primarily of the Alliance; but the real issue at stake was much larger: without being precise, Smuts said that the Alliance 'raises in a very fundamental form many of the great issues on which the future of the world depends, many of which are fundamental questions of our future foreign relations . . . which affect the Empire.' Like Lloyd George, he emphasized the importance of bridging the differences between Europe and Asia; ultimately he attached greatest importance to friendship with the United States. Smuts concluded that if the Alliance were renewed it would create a cleavage among the peoples of English-speaking stock, and that such a split in turn would break up the Empire. He proposed that the problem should be settled by a system of Pacific conferences held under the auspices of the League. Britain's real enemy, Japan, might thus be controlled and her true friend, the United States, contribute to a stable peace in the Pacific.[33] This balanced attitude said both much and little: it expressed the major issues without giving a definite formula for their solution. It gave little comfort to the spokesmen of the Imperial Government who hoped to persuade the Conference to renew the Alliance. As Curzon summarized Smuts's speech to the Cabinet later that day, 'the general points made by General Smuts had been that we must do nothing to antagonise Japan, the Prussia of the East, while maintaining good relations with the United States of America.'[34]

Lloyd George and Curzon responded more warmly to the oration of the Prime Minister of New Zealand. Massey said nothing original, but his rebuttal of Meighen's ideas signified that almost the entire Conference opposed the Canadian view. Like his colleagues, Massey chose the issue of race as one of the main themes of his descant. As an observer of both the United States and Japan for many years, he pessimistically predicted that the next war would be a war between yellow and white, or between white and brown. 'That is exactly where our Empire comes in. We have both white men and brown men in the Empire. We should have had much more serious difficulty in

---

[33] I.C.M., 10th Meeting, Secret, 29 June 1921, CAB. 32/2.
[34] Cabinet Minutes 56(21), Secret, 30 June 1921, CAB. 23/26.

winning the war had they not been thoroughly loyal to us, and I
think that deserves to be remembered when we are discussing
such a matter as this.' Like the brown subjects of Great Britain,
the Japanese were loyal. Racial differences in the Empire and
between Allies need not lead to wars, Massey implied, because
Britain knew how to deal with coloured peoples. The racial
situation in the United States, however, filled him with despair.

As for America's future, I consider that the future of America itself
is the biggest problem of the world to-day. No one can look at all
those mixed races in the United States; 13 million negroes and
millions of people from Southern Europe, Northern Europe, all
sorts and conditions of men and women, without wondering what
the population will be like in another forty or fifty years from now or
even a much shorter period, and I say it is quite impossible for
anybody to predict the result.[35]

Massey admired the 'genuine' Americans of old stock. But with
pro-Germans, pro-Bolsheviks and pro-Sein Feiners, and with
the increasing mongrelization of America's population, New
Zealand and the other Dominions would have to continue to
look to the Empire and not to the United States for protection.
As he expanded his argument, Massey emphasized that the
Empire succeeded in governing coloured subjects and maintaining the Alliance with Japan because of the English spirit of
fair play. He pointed with pride to New Zealand's immigration
act as the strictest in the world. Japan did not protest. From
New Zealand's point of view, the Alliance above all rested on a
gentleman's agreement.[36]

   A sense of fair play towards Japan and smouldering resentment of the United States formed the dominant attitude of the
Cabinet members when they faced up to the dilemma presented
by the Conference. Lloyd George summarized the nub of the
problem by pointing out that Great Britain could not afford to
quarrel with the United States, but that it was essential not to
offend Japan. He again emphasized American inconstancy and
Japanese fidelity. 'To cast off, in the manner suggested, a

---

[35] I.C.M., 10th Meeting, Secret, 29 June 1921, CAB. 32/2. These racial attitudes
are well analysed in regard to New Zealand by P. S. O'Connor, 'Keeping New
Zealand White, 1908–1920', *New Zealand Journal of History*, **2**, 1 (April, 1968),
41–65.

[36] I.C.M., 10th and 11th Meetings, Secret, 29 and 30 June, CAB. 32/2.

Power which had stood by us like Japan was to his mind an inconceivable action, and he [Lloyd George] regarded it as fundamental that Japan should not be insulted.' The Prime Minister of Canada, Lloyd George implied, appeared to have the Conference over a legal barrel. By blocking the renewal of the Alliance, Canada would make the Treaty expire automatically, thus creating the impression that the Empire had cut Japan dead. Knowing that diplomatic instruments can often mean whatever one wants them to mean, Lloyd George demanded that the legal question be reconsidered. This is the crucial passage from the secret minutes of the Cabinet:

Regarding the question of the renewal of the Alliance, he [Lloyd George] wondered whether it would be possible now to get out of the difficulty by saying to Japan either that we would withdraw that notification or treat it as not being a denunciation of the Alliance. If this were done it would modify the situation considerably, and Mr. Meighen, instead of pleading for the non-renewal of the Alliance, would have to plead for the issue of a notice denouncing it.[37]

In other words, Meighen would be faced with automatic continuation rather than expiry, and would have to carry the Conference to denounce rather than veto a proposal for renewal. The Lord Chancellor accordingly received instructions to study the matter.

When the Conference re-convened on 30 June, Lloyd George took a hard line almost identical with Hughes's:

Mr. Lloyd George: ... We must not insult Japan. She stood by her compact to the very letter. She has never been at a Peace Conference where she has not stood by us right through and through. In the war she stood by us and she stood by us in peace, and now to drop her is something, I think, which, so far from winning the friendship of America, would win the contempt of America.

Mr. Hughes: Hear, hear.

Mr. Lloyd George: That is my view. The American is not that type of man. If we were beginning from the start, I do not know what we should do, but two years after the war, when this gallant little people in the East backed us through thick and thin, now to drop them—we cannot do it. I think the British Empire must behave like a gentleman.[38]

[37] Cabinet Minutes 56(21), Secret, 30 June 1921, CAB. 32/2.
[38] I.C.M., 11th Meeting, Secret, 30 June 1921, CAB. 32/2.

Lloyd George also held that British honour and interests should be maintained in China. As an ally, Japan could be controlled and the Chinese people made to see that the Alliance promoted their interests. He again reiterated the importance of the China trade and the necessity of preventing American domination.

[T]he trade of China is only one pound sterling per head of the population, whereas the trade of Japan is ten pounds sterling per head. If you had the same thing in China you would have a trade of about 4,000 millions. . . . We should not allow China to be left entirely in charge of the United States of America. Let us not allow the United States of America to create the impression in China that she is China's only friend.[39]

After further attempts, in his words, to reconcile the unreconcilable, the Prime Minister dropped his legal bombshell by calling on the Lord Chancellor to report.

The remarks of Lord Birkenhead, the Lord Chancellor, were unambiguous. He pointed out that the Law Officers had been unaware of political and diplomatic intent on the part of both the Foreign Office and Japan when they gave their decision that the communication to the League constituted denunciation. He held flatly that denunciation had not taken place, that the Treaty would continue automatically.

Lord Birkenhead: . . . I have no hesitation whatsoever in saying that we should adhere to the view that no denunciation has taken place. There is no technical reason whatever why we should not adopt that course, and indeed, it is one I should feel no difficulty in supporting and in vindicating in any legal company. . . .

Mr. Lloyd George: That seems to me completely to change the whole situation. You see it is a different proposition now.

Mr. Meighen: The situation is this, as I understand it, between Japan and ourselves things are not exactly in the same position in regard to the Treaty as if no communication had been made to the League of Nations. That is to say, it does not expire on the 13th or until a year's notice of denunciation has been given, but as between Japan and Great Britain on the one side and the League on the other. Japan and Great Britain are under an obligation to remodel the words of the agreement. Lord Chancellor, is it your opinion that it should end on the 13th July?

Lord Chancellor: No.

Mr. Meighen: I agree.

[39] Ibid.

Lord Chancellor: I am very glad to have your agreement.

Mr. Meighen: Then we are in this position that we are discussing something quite different.

General Smuts: The policy still remains.

Mr. Lloyd George: Yes, the policy still remains. The Conference certainly is of value.

Mr. Meighen: I should certainly have reconsidered my remarks had I known it.[40]

The meeting eventually ended in consternation.

With the legal ball now rebounding into the Canadian court, Meighen had to re-evaluate his position. On Friday 1 July he reconstructed the Canadian case before the Conference. He said that he regretted Hughes's attack and Lloyd George's support of the Australian onslaught. Meighen defended himself simply and effectively by refusing to accept their interpretation of Canadian foreign policy. Without mincing words, he stated that they had presented a caricature. He resented above all the accusation that Canada had urged an 'ungentlemanly' policy of contemptuously casting aside a loyal ally, and that he had been charged 'with espousing the cause of the United States of America, and with having argued the whole matter from their standpoint, instead of the standpoint of the British Empire.' He assumed, however, that the necessity of friendship with the American Republic did form part of the Empire's world policy. 'If America and British concert and concord and friendship is a loadstar at all of our foreign policy, then in deciding our course, selfishly from our standpoint alone, we must give foremost consideration to the effect of that step upon American relations.' Redefining the legal position, he acquiesced in the proposition that the Alliance would run on for at least a year. He faced the disagreeable fact that Great Britain and Japan would appear at the Pacific conference as Allies.

I would therefore urge this, that the Foreign Secretary. . . . should make known the position of this country, its friendship for Japan, its friendship for America, its friendship for China, and he should endeavour to get the assent of them all to what he described as the Pacific Conference. He should endeavour . . . to ensure its success so that before this year expires, and as early as all the parties can agree, an understanding among these four Powers arrived at through

[40] Ibid.

a Pacific Conference shall be substituted for an exclusive confidential relations with Japan.[41]

No one disagreed. Lloyd George said that the alternative of the Treaty with Japan and friendship with the United States could be reconciled. Even Hughes said he took no exception to the Canadian Prime Minister's statement.

Nevertheless the issues remained real and not semantic. Hughes and Meighen, to use the latter's words, were still 'worlds apart'. Their opposing views reflected two entirely different temperaments, two approaches to world politics. Hughes was essentially pessimistic, conservative in the sense of being profoundly distrustful of the 'new diplomacy' and international institutions designed to preserve the peace. His solution to the problem of the Alliance amounted to making the best of a bad situation. In the abstract, he said he preferred the Americans to the Japanese. But he despaired of the United States. Failing American support, he chose to uphold the Alliance for the simple reason that it was imperative to have a friendly Japan and to do everything possible to prevent her from becoming an enemy. Meighen, on the other hand, was more optimistic about the United States, more idealistic about the future of the League. Like Wilson and Borden, he rejected the idea that security in the Pacific could be attained by the old system of alliances that had contributed to the causes of the war, especially when the ally appeared to represent militant imperialism. He believed that the United States was Britain's natural ally, that the Americans would co-operate with the Empire, and that Anglo-American friendship could provide the only real basis of world order. By articulating those tenets of international idealism, he won the qualified support of General Smuts and perhaps Balfour, but it was Meighen's own unyielding voice that blocked an outright re-affirmation of the Alliance by the Conference. In the end, as everyone knows, the Canadian view won out: the Washington Conference's Four Power Treaty concluded by Great Britain, the United States, Japan, and France replaced the Alliance. It remains one of the great historical 'ifs' whether Hughes's answer of renewing the Alliance would have provided a better solution.

After the confrontation between Meighen and Hughes, the

[41] I.C.M., 12th Meeting, Secret, 1 July 1921, CAB. 32/2.

Lord Chancellor's announcement that the Treaty had not been denounced, and Meighen's careful reconciliation, the rest of the Conference became anticlimactic. When President Harding proclaimed American interest in a Pacific conference on 11 July everyone, including Hughes, agreed that an attempt should be made to bring the United States into a tripartite arrangement. They discussed at length how to make preparations for the Washington Conference without prejudicing its outcome. Those exchanges belong more appropriately to an introduction of the history of the Washington Conference rather than to an analysis of the significance of the Imperial Conference, but one important point should be made in conclusion to modify much of the historical writing about the road to Washington. It is the ingenuity of the Imperial Government. The main point is not that Meighen reversed the policy of the Conference and certainly not that Hughes became increasingly 'angry and bewildered at the way in which the ground had shifted under his feet.'[42] Everyone, including Hughes, wanted American co-operation. Fundamentally they saw the reason as racial. Lloyd George summarized:

They are getting suspicious of us in Japan, and they think we are doing something. They say, 'Well, they are white races, they are the cousins of the Americans. They quarrel amongst themselves, but when trouble comes they act together.' That is true, the last war showed it. When there is trouble they begin to feel that we are nearer to the Americans than we are to them. The people who govern in America are our people. They are our kith and kin. The other breeds are not on top. It is the men of our race who govern in America. I do not know whether they are in the minority or not, but in the main they are on top.[43]

[42] Brebner, 'Canada and the Anglo-Japanese Alliance', p. 56. Brebner later developed his theme of Canadian triumph even more strongly: 'In 1921 Arthur Meighen, Conservative Prime Minister of Canada, single handedly persuaded an Imperial Conference to reverse itself and suspend the renewal of the Anglo-Japanese Alliance. . . . The London incident must be regarded as an exceptional, indeed practically unique, instance of Canadian capacity to bring her two great colleagues together by making one of them change her mind.' John Bartlet Brebner, *North Atlantic Triangle: the Interplay of Canada, the United States and Great Britain* (New Haven, 1945), pp. 281–2.

[43] Half embarrassed when he recalled the audience he was addressing, Lloyd George continued: 'The only exception is General Smuts's race. He is very much the same. We all came from Holland.' I.C.M., 30th Meeting, Secret, 26 July 1921, CAB. 32/2.

If the Americans could be brought into the Alliance or a similar arrangement, so much the better. So it transpired at Washington. But what would have happened if the Washington Conference had ended inconclusively? Meighen would have been proved wrong, at least temporarily. Hughes would have been vindicated. And the Alliance? Hughes argued that it would continue *ipso facto*. With the disposition of the Imperial Government, it probably would have, since Canada would again have been in the position of having to argue for denunciation rather than being able to veto its continuation. Therein lay the Imperial Government's skilfulness of design. Either way the issue went, Great Britain, with London at the centre of the Empire, would still appear to play, in Curzon's words, 'the role for which her history and her character fitted her, namely, that of the impartial arbiter of the East.'

END NOTE

HUGHES AND MEIGHEN. 'Although these two Dominion Prime Ministers were certainly different in temperament and outlook, often too much stress is laid on their personalities as distinct from the disparity in situation of their respective countries. Canada as the immediate neighbour of the U.S.A. would be virtually defenceless against American power in the event of a British-American war; on the other hand, it could have a reasonable confidence in American help, however isolationist the U.S. might be, in the event of a Japanese attack on a coast between Seattle and Alaska. For Australia the situation was the opposite; Australia would be in no particular danger in a British-American war, unless Britain herself were to be overthrown, whereas in a British-Japanese war Australia would be in peril from Japanese sea-power in the Pacific, while American intervention could not be expected as it could against a Japanese invasion of North America. Hence it was quite natural in terms of national interest for Hughes and Meighen to take the lines they did in the controversy over the renewal of the Japanese Alliance.'— G. F. H.

III

THE WASHINGTON CONFERENCE

THE principal, unanswered question about Great Britain and the Washington Conference on Naval Disarmament and Far Eastern Affairs is this: who made the decisions and why? Like most important questions, the answer, or at least part of it, is basically simple. Britain's contribution to the Conference was, above all, the work of two men, the Marquess Curzon and Arthur James Balfour. Guided by traditional concepts of Britain's national security and her worldwide position as an imperial power, Curzon as Foreign Secretary presided over the policy-making process until the time the Conference opened on 12 November 1921. As Britain's representative to the Conference, Balfour then executed that policy. Many historians, of course, have analysed the work of Curzon and Balfour before, some even concluding that Great Britain had no policy at Washington.[1] Leaving aside for the moment the philosophical question of what constitutes 'policy', it is clear that no historian has thoroughly examined the suppositions on which Curzon and Balfour worked with Far Eastern issues, or has attempted fully to answer these questions: How did they envisage the future of international affairs in the Far East? How did they attempt to reconcile the contradictory advice given to them by Canada and the antipodean Dominions? What was their assessment of the policy of the United States in the Far East? To what extent did the China problem enter into their calculations? How realistic were they in their appraisal of the Far East? This chapter will attempt to answer

[1] A. J. P. Taylor, *English History, 1914–1945* (Oxford, 1965), p. 151. The most readable account of the Conference is by Harold and Margaret Sprout, *Toward a New Order of Sea Power* (Princeton, 1940). There are many works on the subject, but see especially R. L. Buell, The *Washington Conference* (New York, 1922) for an acute contemporary analysis. For Britain's role in the Conference, the pertinent works are fully listed in the bibliography of Stephen Roskill, *Naval Policy between the Wars*, whose own work is indispensable in comprehending the naval issues of the Conference.

these questions from the perspective of those two statesmen, not only because of their central position, but also because, as the Belgian saying goes, it is tedious to follow in the footsteps of other historians![2]

Curzon and Balfour differed so radically in temperament and style that at first sight it might appear surprising that they agreed fundamentally on Britain's Far Eastern policy. Yet if one dips beneath the clichés of Curzon's 'Roman manner', his 'pompous rigidity', and 'arrogance', and Balfour's 'non-chalance', his 'philosophic indifference', and 'slipperiness', one finds two remarkably complex possibilities holding profoundly erudite and sensitive views about the nature of world politics. Their outlook on basic issues was similar, deriving from an aristocratic tradition of foreign policy perfected by Balfour's uncle, Lord Salisbury, the Prime Minister whom Curzon served as Parliamentary Under-Secretary in 1895–8. In a sense they were relics of an earlier age who had survived the upheavals of the Great War and proved capable of accommodating, in different ways, the trends of the 'new diplomacy'. They stand in English history as the last of the old guard of the Foreign Office. They brought to their task of solving the problems of the Far East and Pacific an unrivalled experience and knowledge together with certain unquestioned assumptions about the British Empire and Britain's destiny in guiding 'the dark peoples of the earth'.

Curzon made clear his fundamental, life-long tenet of imperialism in the dedication to his book, the *Problems of the Far East*, published in 1894: 'To those who believe that the British Empire is, under Providence, the greatest instrument for good that the world has ever seen.' In Curzon's mind there were three British Empires: the newly acquired tropical African domain, occupied by black barbarians who welcomed British tutelage but who constituted the least culturally significant part of the Empire; the white Dominions of Canada, South Africa, Australia, and New Zealand, whose peoples historically established Great Britain as the greatest colonizing power; and the

---

[2] I also take this approach to avoid collision with other historians working on related topics, notably Ian Nish on the Anglo-Japanese Alliance; J. Kenneth McDonald on British naval policy in the Far East; and Ernest R. May on the Washington Conference.

Eastern Empire extending from Egypt to Hong Kong—from 'Suez to Singapore'—with India as its magnificent centre. The Eastern Empire formed Curzon's major interest and dominated his career as an imperialist. 'No Englishman,' he once wrote, 'can land at Hong Kong without feeling a thrill of pride for his nationality. Here is the furthermost link in the chain of fortresses which, from Spain to China, girdles half the globe.'[3] Beyond the confines of this splendid Eastern realm lay Britain's insular ally since 1902, Japan. The Japanese Curzon respected as intelligent and industrious—and dangerous. They no less than the Indian subjects fitted into a world order based on a *Pax Britannica*. Though the Japanese stood on a different footing from other Asian peoples, they also were coloured, and in a sense represented another British ward. Curzon stated many times in this regard that Great Britain by Providence had a divine mission in the East. His key words in this doctrine were to *control* or *direct*. As the British controlled India, they attempted to direct Japan. Curzon explained to the Imperial Conference of 1921:'There can be no doubt that while the Anglo-Japanese Alliance has lasted . . . it has enabled us to exercise a very powerful controlling influence on the sometimes dangerous ambitions of Japan.'[4] He therefore favoured the renewal of the Anglo-Japanese Alliance as a means of fulfilling Britain's Eastern mission. And beneath that idealism lay a perceptive awareness of military reality in the Far East. Though he philosophized about the Empire as an instrument of divine purpose, Curzon also saw himself responsible 'to maintain British interests, British honour, British territory, British independence.' Termination of the Alliance with Japan—one of the key issues in British policy in 1921—would risk turning a faithful servant into a powerful enemy who might eventually destroy the Eastern Empire.

While he attached paramount importance to Britain's remaining a friend of Japan, Curzon also hoped to cultivate better relations with the United States. He deplored the American 'defection' in international affairs following the war, and

[3] Quoted by Harold Nicolson, *Curzon: the Last Phase, 1919–1925. A Study in Post-War Diplomacy* (New York, 1934), p. 13.
[4] Imperial Conference Minutes (I.C.M.), 4th Meeting, Secret, 22 June 1921, CAB. 23/3.

regretted 'that this great country, which had shared in our sacrifices and helped to win our victory, became, by the foolish policy of her own President [Wilson], nervous, useless and impotent at the critical period after the war was stopped.'[5] He viewed with great alarm the American shipbuilding programme, which, if carried out, would provide the United States 'with the most powerful fleet that the world has ever known.' He welcomed with relief indications that the Americans might be coming to their senses by taking such measures as the Senate's authorization of the President to discuss naval disarmament with Britain and Japan.[6] He hoped that President Harding's administration would bring the United States back into a more responsible pattern of behaviour. 'America is coming back voluntarily,' Curzon said optimistically in June 1921.

> Let us meet her with open arms; her participation will not only be valuable, it will also be a help in the reconstruction of the world, and nothing will be wanting on the part of the Foreign Office to promote and encourage it in every way. . . .
> My own belief is that in the troubles and turmoils of the east, if we can look to the west and re-establish excellent relations with America, we shall see a dawning of light in the sky which is so overcast in almost every other quarter of the globe.[7]

If the Americans could be brought around to a more enlightened view of the Anglo-Japanese Alliance, it could be expanded to include them, thereby stabilizing the Far East and the Pacific.

At heart Curzon did not believe the tripartite solution would work. He thought the Americans were far too erratic, far too suspicious of both Japan and Great Britain, and far too incompetent to resolve by diplomacy the issue of naval disarmament. Despite his American wife, Curzon had slight regard for the United States. He believed that the Irish problem would continue to obstruct Anglo-American understanding. Unlike

---

[5] I.C.M., 5th Meeting, Secret, 22 June 1921, CAB. 32/3.

[6] For the United States and the Conference, see John Chalmers Vinson, *The Parchment Peace: the United States Senate and the Washington Conference, 1921–1922* (Athens, Georgia, 1955); also, by the same author, 'The Drafting of the Four Power Treaty of the Washington Conference', *Journal of Modern History* (March 1953).

[7] I.C.M., 5th Meeting, Secret, 22 June 1921, CAB. 32/3.

Balfour, he had little faith in international institutions such as the League, America's forsaken creation. He disliked diplomacy by conference, which he once described as 'long, complicated and often vexatious discussions'.[8] In short, Curzon believed that a Conference on naval disarmament and Far Eastern affairs would fail. In preparing for that contingency he attached supreme importance to the continuation, rather than the abrogation, of the Anglo-Japanese Alliance as the keystone of British policy in the Far East.

In the meetings of the Prime Ministers of the United Kingdom and the Dominions in the summer of 1921, Curzon guided the discussions about the Alliance. One of the major points at issue was this question: if the proposed conference on naval disarmament ended inconclusively or in failure, would the Alliance continue automatically? Curzon and the British Cabinet together with the Australasian Prime Ministers held that it would; the representatives of Canada and South Africa were reluctant to admit the perpetuity of the Alliance. Following a controversial exchange on this point, Curzon, at his colleagues' invitation, drew up his own instructions. He would meet with the American, Japanese, and Chinese Ambassadors to explain that Britain wished to remain friends with all three nations and to work together in the spirit of the Covenant. He would find out whether those two powers would be willing to confer on the affairs of the Far East and Pacific. He added a most important, parenthetical comment: '(Should the Conference fail, the existing agreement [i.e. the Anglo-Japanese Treaty] as adapted to meet the requirements of the Covenant of the League goes on).' That statement sparked one of the most heated debates of the Imperial Conference. Prime Ministers Meighen of Canada and Smuts of South Africa held that, if the Japanese were informed that the Alliance would continue if the negotiations failed, the outcome of the Conference would be prejudiced from the start. Meighen said:

To suggest that we should first say to Japan, 'If the Conference fails, this Treaty is satisfactory to us and this Treaty is our policy,' and, having said that to Japan, that we should then approach the United States and say: 'Come with us'—the thing is madness in my

[8] Nicolson, *Curzon*, p. 42.

mind. Japan would have the key to the situation, they would be the arbiters of the whole Conference.[9]

Smuts sustained the argument:

We must make every effort not to load the dice in favour of Japan, and, it seems to me, if, in advance, we are going to declare that the Japanese Alliance, failing everything else, is to be our policy, I am afraid Japan is going to make use of that position; she is then going to force the pace and she will try to prevent an agreement with America being reached, and I think that it is of vital interest, while conserving our friendship with Japan, also to get America into that circle of friendship.[10]

Curzon offered to strike the controversial sentence because it was a truism: since the Treaty would not be denounced it would continue. Smuts and Meighen were unwilling to admit this crucial point.

General Smuts: It is not really a truism, Lord Curzon: the last sentence means this, in the case of the failure of these negotiations the Japanese Treaty is our policy, and we go on with it. If the last sentence is left out, it means this, that the road is open for us to reassemble, discuss the matter again and see whether we are to give notice or not. The last sentence prevents our giving notice, and that I think would be going too far. This is the whole point in issue between the two of us here.[11]

At this juncture the Prime Minister, David Lloyd George, intervened and threw his weight behind the Alliance as *policy*:

Mr. Lloyd George: I think it ought to be our policy if this [Washington] Conference fails.

General Smuts: We should leave the decision of that open at this stage. . . . All we ask is that this last sentence whether the Japanese Alliance will be the declared future policy of the Empire should remain open for discussion.[12]

Admitting Smuts's contention, Curzon still had the stronger position. Unless the Treaty were denounced or replaced, it would continue. As Lloyd George correctly pointed out, 'Those who are in favour of the Treaty surely have no right to complain.'

If the word 'policy' means a reasoned course of action, then

[9] I.C.M., 13th Meeting, Secret, 1 July 1921, CAB. 32/3.
[10] Ibid.   [11] Ibid.   [12] Ibid.

Great Britain in every sense of the word had a Far Eastern policy on the eve of the Washington Conference. The same cannot be said of a naval disarmament policy. The Far Eastern policy evolved out of the meetings of the Empire's Prime Ministers in the summer of 1921. Their most rigorous and often angry discussions centred on the problem of what to do with Japan and the United States. They arrived at a policy that amounted to bringing the Americans into a tripartite arrangement to replace the Alliance. Failing that, they would stand by Japan, at least until the matter could be reconsidered by another Imperial Conference. By contrast, a naval disarmament policy did not emerge from their deliberations, except in a general sense that almost destroys the meaning of the concept. They merely agreed that equality with the naval strength of any other power was the minimal guarantee for the safety of the Empire.[13] Since everyone regarded naval disarmament as one of the major issues in international affairs at that time, the reason for the contrast in policies needs explanation. It is not difficult. The two issues of the Far East and disarmament were so closely related that they were inseparable. The latter could not be solved without first resolving the affairs of the Far East. In short, no definite decision could be reached on disarmament until the fate of the Anglo-Japanese Alliance was determined. The Imperial statesmen thus saw two related but distinct problems. That distinction is crucial in understanding the Anglo-American rift in the months preceding the Washington Conference.

When President Harding, on 11 July 1921, issued invitations for a Conference, the British response was ecstatic. At the Imperial Conference, the Colonial Secretary, Winston Churchill, exclaimed 'We have made history sitting round this table—there is no doubt about it.' Lloyd George exuberantly proclaimed a British triumph:

There has been a very dramatic change in the whole situation, and although it has been nominally brought about by the President's invitation, it is really the result of our action here. You will recollect that it was decided here to approach the American, the Japanese

[13] On this point see Roskill, *Naval Policy between the Wars*. Chapters 5–8 discuss in detail the policy debates within the Government and are invaluable in understanding the Admiralty's position.

and the Chinese Ambassadors with a view to suggesting a Conference on the Pacific question. That has produced one of the most remarkable documents of modern times in the form of a direct invitation from the President of the United States of America to a Conference on the question of disarmament, to be preceded by a Conference on the question of the Pacific.[14]

The key word in that passage is *preceded*. The Conference on disarmament would be preceded by a Conference on the Far East and Pacific, because the former issue could not be broached until the latter problem was solved. In Curzon's words, 'A successful Disarmament Conference may mark an epoch in the history of mankind. But a successful Disarmament Conference is impossible without a successful Pacific Conference preceding it. If the latter is a failure the former will fail also; and failure in either case will not leave matters where they were. It will leave them incomparably and it may be fatally worse.'[15] There thus would be two conferences to resolve in logical sequence the two related but distinct problems. The Americans appeared to agree. Harding's own words were, after all, 'The Powers especially interested in these problems should undertake, in connection with this [disarmament] Conference, the consideration of all matters bearing upon their solution with a view to reaching a common understanding with regard to the Far East.' The British read into that ambiguous sentence the intention of convening two separate conferences for the respective issues of the Far East and disarmament. The Foreign Office's memorandum to the American Government in reply to Harding's invitation accordingly emphasized this point. While thanking the President for his 'splendid initiative', Curzon also unambiguously and firmly urged that no solution to the problem of disarmament could be reached unless a preceding conference resolved the Far Eastern question. 'Her Majesty's Government are very strongly of opinion that discussion . . . between the Powers directly concerned—namely the British Empire, the United States, Japan, and China—is an absolutely essential preliminary to the success of the Washington Conference.'[16]

---

[14] I.C.M., 21st Meeting, Secret, 11 July 1921.
[15] Memorandum by Curzon, Confidential, 24 July 1921 [A 5489/18/45], F.O. 371/5617.
[16] Ibid.

If the main Conference were held in Washington, then the preliminary meeting in equity should convene in London—as soon as possible. The matter was urgent. Hughes and Massey would be able to participate before their return to the antipodes. Furthermore, a London Conference would enhance the Empire's prestige. Great Britain would be able to achieve, in Lloyd George's words, a 'real understanding' with the United States and Japan. 'Unless you do that I am afraid it would mean failure at the big Conference,' he said.

There will be resolutions of the Hague type, pious expressions of opinion about the importance of disarming, and all that kind of stuff. It will be purely a hot-air Conference unless there is a previous understanding on these great questions between Japan and America and ourselves.[17]

The more the Prime Minister considered the problem of reaching accord between the three principal parties, the more he doubted whether London would be the best place to conduct the preliminary negotiations.

Personally, I have come round against the London Conference, because I think you are more likely to succeed if you have it on American soil than if you have it here. . . . That is my opinion. You cannot tear this thing away from the conflict which has been raging in the United States for the last year or two, the whole thing turning on President Wilson being bamboozled, having walked into a trap in Europe. It is the bugbear of the Senate. American statesmen coming to Paris and London, and being lured into all sorts of things on European soil without consulting the Senate. I think if you have a Conference in America your chances of success—I do not know America, but I watch American politics, and I am looking at the 'atmosphere'—will be fivefold more than if you have it here.[18]

The Prime Ministers therefore discussed other suitable places, including such picturesque spots as Bar Harbor, Havana, and Honolulu. There were many difficulties not least of which was the uncertainty of the American attitude. The American Ambassador in London seemed enthusiastic about preliminary talks, but the British Ambassador in Washington contradicted him. The British re-studied Harding's invitation. No one

[17] I.C.M., 30th Meeting, Secret, 26 July 1921, CAB. 32/2.
[18] Ibid.

could determine precisely what the President meant. At one stage Hughes said, 'I do not know what Conference I mean, and I do not think anybody else does either.' Apparently the Americans wanted only a single conference. Lloyd George began to think the Empire had been tricked. 'The Americans have manoeuvred us into a very bad position tactically.' He went on:

If there is a Conference in Washington at all, you must invite all the Powers there from the start. What does that mean? It means that Japan and the British Empire would be completely out-manoeuvred at the Conference by the others, and the whole influence and atmosphere of the Conference would be hostile from the start. That is very bad strategy. It is good for the United States and it is good for the rest. It is thoroughly bad for us.[19]

Great Britain, in other words, would stand on the same footing as such powers as Belgium. In a general disarmament conference, the Empire would be outnumbered, outmanoeuvred, and perhaps even outwitted.

The Conference of Prime Ministers grew increasingly suspicious of American motives and more determined to act in concert with Japan. Curzon detected 'a very ominous feature of the situation': China. 'America has an enormous interest in China. She wants to rescue China from what she thinks the dangerous clutches of Japan, not merely for the sake of China, but with some due regard to her own trade and interests in the future.' If Chinese issues such as the Shantung and other complex questions were raised at Washington, the Conference would be doomed to failure and Britain would be placed in the false position of subverting her ally. The Japanese already apparently feared that the British had betrayed them. According to the British Ambassador in Tokyo, 'Undoubtedly, the dominant idea is that America and Great Britain have combined and manoeuvred with a view to placing Japan in a most disadvantageous position.'[20] The whole business appeared to be getting into a hopeless tangle. In Lloyd George's words, the Americans distrusted the British, saying 'Hulloa! What are they up to now.' On the other hand, 'Japan says, "They are selling us in China," and you get all these misunderstandings

[19] I.C.M., 27th Meeting, Secret, 22 July 1921, CAB. 32/2.
[20] Eliot to Curzon, No. 263, Tel., 20 July 1921, copy in I.C.M., 29th Meeting, Secret, 26 July 1921, CAB. 32/2.

amongst us.'[21] Curzon thought that the Japanese were groping in the dark, bemused by the proposal for a conference yet willing to go along with the idea if Britain would help them restrict the agenda so that embarrassing Chinese issues would not be discussed. The Foreign Secretary sympathized. He assured the Japanese Ambassador of British loyalty. He had no complaint about the Japanese Ambassador's response.[22] Curzon's relations with the American Ambassador, on the other hand, were of an entirely different character. By the time the Washington Conference convened, Curzon had greatly reinforced his view about the incompetency of American diplomacy.

Trained in the rigorous traditions of the Foreign Office, Curzon assumed that Ambassadors spoke on the authority of their Governments. In his interviews with the American Ambassador, Colonel George Harvey, a newspaper man by profession, Curzon was occasionally perplexed at the contradictions between the versions of American policy expounded by Harvey, on the one hand, and the British Ambassador in Washington, Sir Auckland Geddes, on the other. The full brunt of discrepancy did not become clear until July 1921, during the discussions about the preliminary conference. In regard to one of the central questions, Harvey once told Curzon that the United States would be indifferent to the renewal of the Alliance; Geddes, however, reported that renewal in any form would create 'a very unfavourable impression' in America.[23] Which report was correct? The Foreign Office found it almost as difficult to evaluate Geddes's despatches as Harvey's verbal representations. Geddes's views, one official wrote, 'vary with bewildering intensity.' Nevertheless Geddes at least faithfully presented Curzon's communications to the Secretary of State. By comparison, Harvey behaved irresponsibly. He led Curzon to believe that the United States favoured

[21] I.C.M., 30th Meeting, Secret, 26 July 1921, CAB. 32/2.

[22] Curzon got on well with Baron Hayashi, the Ambassador. He once warned the British Ambassador in Tokyo: 'Bear in mind extreme importance of not saying anything at Tokio which will compromise position of Japanese Ambassador here or cause difficulty between him and his Government. He sometimes speaks to me with a frankness which his Government might not like.' Minute by Curzon, *D.B.F.P.* First Series (all subsequent references to *D.B.F.P.* in this chapter are to the First Series), XIV, No. 328.

[23] Geddes to Curzon, No. 454 Tel., 2 July 1921 [F 2426/63/23], F.O. 371/6675.

the idea of a preliminary conference. He even put forward the suggestion of Havana 'as having ample hotels and delightful climate in October and latter part of year. Site was central between old and new worlds, and negotiations could take place in a favourable atmosphere.'[24] Harvey agreed that the sooner preliminary talks took place, the better. In mid-July he changed his tune. Curzon, disconcerted, listened to telegrams read by the Ambassador saying that London would be an unsuitable place, that the convenience of the Dominion Prime Ministers must be subordinated to the wider interests of the case, and that only a single conference should be held in Washington. Curzon was uncharacteristically daunted. What good would it do, he asked, to hold a disarmament conference unless the affairs of the Far East could be settled beforehand? He reported to Geddes after one interview with Harvey:'I was appalled.' On 29 July the Foreign Office learned with further dismay that the State Department was 'unalterably opposed' to the preliminary conference.[25]

To Curzon, part of the blame for this caricature of diplomacy rested with the American Secretary of State, Charles Evan Hughes. Curzon agreed with Geddes that Hughes controlled his Ambassadors in a peculiar manner. 'Mr. Hughes appears to dislike him [Harvey] intensely and to have embarked on a policy of keeping him in ignorance.'[26] Hughes appeared to be just as ignorant of his Ambassador's actions in London. When Geddes pointed out that Harvey had encouraged the scheme for a preliminary conference, Hughes reportedly gasped with astonishment. 'We are faced then,' he told Geddes, 'with this position, that [the] British Government believes that American Government has been committed by its Ambassador in London to a course of action which American Government does not approve.' Geddes replied affirmatively. Hughes regretted the misunderstanding but remained 'unalterably opposed to idea

[24] Curzon to Geddes, No. 416 Tel., 9 July 1921 [F 2461/63/23], *D.B.F.P.*, XIV, No. 330.
[25] Geddes to Curzon, No. 519 Tel., 30 July 1921 [A 5551/18/45], *D.B.F.P.*, XIV, No. 345.
[26] Geddes to Curzon, Personal and Confidential [Confidential/General/363/18], 18 July 1921, *D.B.F.P.*, XIV, No. 329. 'In Mr. Harvey's case this traditional mistrust is evidently well founded, as he is a journalist first & an Ambassador second.' Minute by R. Sperling, 1 August 1921, F.O. 371/5617.

of a preliminary Conference.'²⁷ This diplomatic bungling of an issue of such magnitude aroused Curzon's roman wrath. He told the American Ambassador that their work was in shambles, that the 'forensic tone' of the State Department resembled that of a lawyer, not a statesman. He said the British proposals had an almost sentimental ring by comparison. He waxed furiously indignant at the idea of a British attempt to 'hoodwink' the United States and to steal the credit for disarmament. Forced to drop the idea of a preliminary conference because of American mulishness, Curzon wrote angrily to inform the State Department that 'the idea that His Majesty's Government ever wished to rob President Harding of a single leaf of his laurels for originating conference on disarmament or to hoodwink American Government is a fantastic chimera.'²⁸

Anglo-American relations continued to deteriorate not only diplomatically but generally. In August the Foreign Office learned of an anti-British wave sweeping the entire country. A distinguished academician, Professor John Dewey, warned in a series of articles, for example, that British trade interests in southern China would force Britain to wink at Japanese predatory acts in the north.²⁹ The American press generally attacked Lloyd George's Irish policy. Curzon despaired of convincing the Americans of British sincerity in wanting disarmament and a stable Far East. But the situation quickly changed. Like a fickle woman, in the British view, the United States in September began to proclaim steadfast friendship with Great Britain. Geddes wrote that the atmosphere in Washington had been completely transformed, partly because of a turn for the better in the Irish problem. The predominant American mood seemed better than any one dared hope. Geddes was optimistic. He gave his basic reasons by explaining the character of the American people.

That vague generalization, the typical American, is a being compounded of contradictory traits. He can be ruthless, not too scrupulous in business and blatantly Chauvinistic but he is also a great

²⁷ Geddes to Curzon, No. 519 Tel. [A 5551/18/45], July 30 1921, *D.B.F.P.*, XIV, No. 345.
²⁸ Curzon to Geddes, No. 474 Tel., 1 August 1921 [A 5606/18/45], *D.B.F.P.*, XIV, No. 349.
²⁹ A list of Dewey's writings may be found in Chow Tse-tung, *Research Guide to the May Fourth Movement: Intellectual Revolution in Modern China* (Cambridge, Mass. 1963).

idealist with a simple but sincere faith in the ultimate triumph of righteousness. One of his ideals is to be a good neighbour and a good citizen, to play for his town's glory and development.

Within recent months the conception of the English Speaking People as a world unit has begun to lay hold of his imagination. He is already half prepared to transfer some of his allegiance to that ideal unit which to him has a vitality which the League of Nations lacks.[30]

Geddes thought that the better part of the American personality would prevail, especially since Charles Evans Hughes represented its mouthpiece in foreign affairs. The Secretary of State appeared to be persuaded of the ideal of an English-speaking union. 'Mr. Hughes with his intense legalistic mind does not react easily to emotional stimuli but even to him the sense of fundamental Anglo-American unity in ideal, makes its strong appeal.' Geddes sympathized with Hughes personally and deplored the circumstances in which he worked:

In dealing with him [Hughes] it has to be remembered first that he himself easily becomes excited in the face of differences of opinion and that his control over his voice and his muscles of facial expression is not strong. Next, Mr. Hughes is surrounded by the officials of a department which, in the past, has not been efficiently organized and which has tended to place the responsibility for its own failures on the shoulders of some other nation's foreign office. To them it ascribes almost diabolical cunning and sometimes dishonesty. As most of the United States diplomatic failures have occurred in negotiations with Great Britain it follows that to the State Department 'Downing Street' is peculiarly an object of suspicion and distrust.[31]

To disarm American suspicion of British cunning, Geddes recommended candour and compassion. With proper guidance the Americans could be led into making the Washington Conference a success.

Curzon continued to work toward 'a solution of the Chinese acrostic', hoping that the American and Japanese elements might be manipulated to spell peace in the Far East. The

[30] Geddes to Curzon, No. 978, Confidential, 21 September 1921 [A 7148/18/45], *D.B.F.P.*, XIV, No. 381.
[31] Ibid. Geddes, who had medical training, often diagnosed diplomatic problems by analyzing the maladies of his opposite number.

puzzle was difficult, above all, again in the Foreign Secretary's words, because of the Chinese game of 'shilly-shally'. To use a different metaphor Curzon liked, how could the Chinese giant, shackled by 'imperialism', be freed? 'It will not be easy to rebuild China in sections or compartments or to leave her partially free and partially in chains. At any rate all the chains will be violently rattled before they are either left on her atrophied limbs or struck off.'[32] The Americans proposed to solve all of China's problems at one blow by discussing, among other things:

(1) The Open Door or freedom of commercial intercourse in China.

(2) The territorial integrity and administrative independence of China.

(3) Shantung.

(4) Spheres of interest and leased territories. . . .

(5) The question of Siberia, with a view to the discovery of fundamental principles applicable both to Russian Asia and China.[33]

That agenda dismayed the Foreign Secretary. 'And in the meantime while these arduous labours are proceeding,' he asked, 'what is to become of the Disarmament Conference, which is apparently to be waiting while the Pacific Ocean yields up its living and dead?' The list of topics struck him as 'vague, dangerous and obscure [and] filled me with despair. . . .' He wrote to Geddes:

China is the rock on which many barques will founder because while we are all in theory in favour not merely of formulating but of carrying out broad and generous principles, you have a country at this moment one of the least united, and a government one of the feeblest, on the face of the Globe, and to expect that China in her present state of internal dissolution will implement any pledge, or merit any favour, is futile.[34]

Curzon concluded that the Conference would probably 'peter out in talk'.

[32] Memorandum by Curzon, Confidential, 24 July 1921 [A 5489/18/45], F.O. 371/5617.
[33] Ibid.
[34] Curzon to Geddes, Confidential, 25 September 1921, [Confidential/General/363/21], *D.B.F.P.*, XIV, No. 348.

Curzon's principal adviser on the Far East drew up a survey of the political situation in that part of the world for the benefit of the British delegates. In this clear-cut analysis by Victor Wellesley, British apprehension about China and the Washington Conference found its fullest expression. Fundamentally, the question amounted to Japan's expansionist aims and Britain's impotence in restricting them—for economic and racial reasons. Postulating Japan's need to expand because of a growing population of 80,000,000, and poor resources, Wellesley argued that the immigration laws of the white Pacific powers forced the Japanese to look to China.

The policies of exclusion adopted by the British Dominions and the United States, for economic and racial reasons, are to some extent responsible for forcing her to take the line of least resistance and to concentrate her efforts in the direction of the mainland of Asia— principally China. That policy has now developed into something more than mere economic expansion. It has come to aim firstly at the political hegemony of China, and, through China, at the ultimate supremacy of the yellow races under Japanese leadership. This is the mission Japan believes herself destined to fulfil.[35]

Japan at Washington might expediently bow to the wishes of the western powers; ultimately, in a time-span perhaps of centuries, she would continue to pursue her goal. Japan might momentarily change her policy; but she would not change her heart. She would remain a potential danger to British interests in China. She would resist any efforts to modify her China policy at Washington. And the British could not force her to do so.

Japan comes to the Conference in a somewhat suspicious frame of mind; she fears that it is merely a device for interference with her policy of expansion in China which to her is a vital necessity. Sooner than agree to any measures that would effectively check that process she would probably wreck the Conference. It should not be forgotten that she enters the Conference with the trump card in her hand— viz., racial discrimination—which she can use as an effective foil against any attempt to cross her path.[36]

After discussing the complex political and economic facets of the China problem, Wellesley again returned to the racial theme.

[35] Memorandum by Wellesley, 20 October 1921 [F 3823/2635/10], F.O. 371/ 6660.
[36] Ibid.

If we probe this problem to its depths it cannot be disguised that in the last analysis it is primarily and fundamentally racial in character, and that the political and economic aspects, important as they are, are in reality only secondary compared with the underlying racial problem. Although there is no danger of the question of race supremacy being forced to an immediate issue, it would, nevertheless, not be wise to ignore its potential danger in laying the foundation of our future policy. Racial conflict, though it has not yet reached an acute form, already finds expression in the policies of exclusion of Canada, Australia and the United States, though based largely on economic grounds.[37]

The logic of Wellesley's thought, like Curzon's, led him to conclude that the white policy of the Dominions should not be altered, nor could it be. Therefore Japan should be allowed to expand into China on 'reasonable' grounds. In one of the most remarkable statements in the annals of British diplomacy (remarkable not merely because it represents one of the first statements of British 'conciliation' in the Far East, but also because the Marquess Curzon of Keddleston could imagine himself to be a Chinaman!), His Most Honourable Lordship once said to the Chinese Ambassador: 'My own inclination, if I were a Chinaman, would be to allow the Japanese to expand, under reasonable conditions in that direction [Manchuria], rather than to bring them down upon the main body of China.'[38]

While Curzon and the Foreign Office grappled with the problem of the Far East, Balfour and the Committee of Imperial Defence studied the issues of the naval balance of power in the Pacific. The Committee worked on the assumption of a one power standard, though in public they admitted so only reluctantly because such statements reminded Englishmen of the decline of British strength from the days when the fleet could match the combined fleets of any two rivals. The first meeting in preparation for the Washington Conference took place on 14 October 1921. As might be expected with military discussions, many of the remarks were essentially negative and wishful. Japan should not be allowed to build a naval base further south

[37] Ibid. Wellesley also prepared the brief on financial reform in China, concluding that little could be done: 'China must stew in her own juice.' See his memorandum, 'Intervention in China,' 10 October 1921 [F 4192/2635/10], F.O. 371/6660.

[38] Curzon to Alston, No. 1013, 24 October 1921 [F 3924/2635/10], *D.B.F.P.*, XIV, No. 406.

than Formosa because the Japanese could then threaten British communications with Hong Kong; the leased territory of Wei-hai Wei on the Chinese mainland should be retained, not because of its strategic value, but because of its use as a sanatorium; the Singapore base should be developed 'as a defensive measure'. They discussed the danger of submarines to British shipping, of airplanes possibly bombarding England. Balfour at one stage said he 'viewed the situation with profound alarm.' But he had little hope that the Conference could deal effectively with submarines, not to mention aircraft. Britain could negotiate only on the basis of 'capital' ships (i.e. battleships and battle-cruisers); otherwise, on a basis of worldwide tonnage, British capital ships would be restricted *and* deprived of subsidiary support, such as cruisers and destroyers, in an adverse ratio to the other powers. Whatever the formula, it would have to be simple; if cruisers and destroyers were introduced, the types would overlap and any agreement would become unworkable because of complexity. The Admiralty therefore proposed to limit the capital ships of modern, i.e. 'Post Jutland', design. The Committee, accepting the Admiralty's view, agreed: 'That the best basis of limitation for naval armaments was by fixing the number of capital ships and that in addition all other ships being built should be declared.' They discussed vaguely how much bluff should be shown at Washington 'to have something to bargain with', but fortunately left Balfour's hands free. By contrast with the elaborate American naval preparations for the Conference, the British merely rearticulated an already generally accepted principle: 'it was essential that we should maintain a fleet at least equal to any other.'[39]

The brilliance of Secretary Hughes's surprise proposal when the Conference opened on 12 November has been discussed so many times by historians that it needs only to be said that beneath its bold simplicity lay a bewildering complexity of issues which, if thoroughly discussed, would fill a book at least a hundred times the length of this chapter. In barest form, his

[39] See Minutes of the 145th and 146th meetings of the Committee of Imperial Defence, 14 and 21 October 1921, Secret, CAB. 2/3. For a discussion of American and Japanese, as well as British, naval preparation for the Conference, see Roskill, *British Naval Policy*, chapter VIII; his account is also the best analysis of the naval building programme.

proposal consisted of the limitation of capital ships and a naval 'holiday' of ten years.[40] Those two basic propositions will be discussed only in relation to British security and even then restricted to the fundamental issue: the balance of power in Europe and the Far East. Paradoxically, in a conference designed to resolve the problems of the Pacific and Asia, the crucial issues to Britain arose in regard to the Atlantic and Europe. If Britain restricted her navy, there was no guarantee that France would curtail her military force, which might have the eventual capacity to devastate Britain by air attack. If Britain limited her capital ships, France might continue to develop the weapon capable of paralysing the British fleet and merchant marine—the submarine. One need merely glance at the British press during the time of the conference to see that the submarine issue struck fear in the hearts of the British.

It is difficult to imagine any Englishman better suited to head the British Delegation at Washington than Arthur James Balfour. Like Curzon, he takes his place as one of the truly gifted British diplomatists in this century. Unlike Curzon, he

[40] Again, the best account is by Roskill, ibid., who has a full bibliography on the subject. When the Committee of Imperial Defence examined Hughes's proposal they drew up this table comparing the heavy guns carried by the twenty-one British ships and the eighteen American ships that would be retained:

	No. of guns	Calibre inch	Weight of Projectile lb.	lb.
British	88	13·5	1,400	123,200
	100	15	1,920	192,000
Total				315,200
American	64	12	870	55,680
	124	14	1,400	173,600
	8	16	2,100	16,800
Total				246,080

'The British ships are thus stronger in gun power than the American ships, and the advantage in favour of the British ships is more marked than appears at first sight. . . . The general conclusion was that the British ships compared favourably with any other capital ships now in existence.' Churchill, who chaired the meeting, accordingly thought that the American proposals were 'fair and honest'. Committee of Imperial Defence, 149th Meeting, Secret, 14 November 1921, CAB. 2/3.

could move flexibly in almost any direction without altering his fundamental position; if necessary, he could even give way on basic issues simply by admitting he was wrong. He had the ability of intervening decisively on his own initiative (and without reference to his principals in London), and of living up to his reputation of getting nothing done with ease, or, as Curzon would have put it, breaking for tea when the discussions became futile. His intelligence perhaps bordered on genius, but it was not encyclopedic. At a press conference in Washington he was nonplussed when a reporter asked him the number of subject peoples in the British Empire; yet in a matter of seconds in the midst of a speech he could take a list of figures from his secretary and turn it into a harrowing tale of British casualties while aiding France during the war. Reports have it that when he spoke at Washington his voice was firm, his oratory as graceful and persuasive as ever and uncharacteristically enthusiastic. His physical appearance matched his demeanour, that of a tall, rather stooped, white-haired English aristocrat. He appeared what he was, the last Victorian Prime Minister.[41]

Part of Balfour's success at the Conference can be attributed to his ability to separate essential and non-essential issues and to keep clearly in mind the problems that could and could not be resolved at Washington. 'Let me emphasize,' he once stated when his colleagues appeared to be diverted from the major task at hand, 'that it was never possible for this Conference to do more than promote two objects: settlement of the Far East and diminution of naval armaments.' Contrary to the belief of Curzon and the Cabinet, he found he could work towards a solution of those problems simultaneously. As he discussed broad principles designed to stabilize the situation in China, he also analysed the proposal for a naval holiday. In both instances

[41] Important accounts of Balfour at the Conference include Blanche E. D. Dugdale, *Arthur James Balfour, First Earl of Balfour, 1906–30* (London, 1936), chapter XVI; and Kenneth Young, *Arthur James Balfour* (London, 1963). Both are weak on the later stages of Balfour's career. First-hand observations of Balfour at Washington are by Colonel A. à C. Repington, *After the War* (London, 1922), and Lord Riddell's *Intimate Diary of the Peace Conference and After, 1918–1923* (London, 1933). Riddell's diary is especially illuminating about Balfour's close co-operation with the Secretary of the Delegation, Sir Maurice Hankey, whose brilliant efficiency Balfour acknowledged in glowing terms at the close of the Conference.

he disagreed with his colleagues in London on certain important points. He found himself in the middle of a tug-of-war between his naval advisers in Washington, with whom he was inclined to agree, and the Cabinet and Committee of Imperial Defence. On the naval issue he bowed to Lloyd George and Curzon in a way that raises the entire question of responsibility for naval developments in the inter-war years. On the Far Eastern question he used his discretionary powers to reach agreement on China in a manner that disgusted Curzon, if not the Foreign Office.

The nub of the naval controversy was the proposal for a holiday in ship-building and the issue of submarines. What type of building, if any, could take place during the holiday, and would auxiliary craft such as destroyers and torpedo-boats be included? Accepting the American demand for parity with the British fleet, the Delegation questioned whether the calculation should be based on the number of ships or total tonnage, and what type and age of ships. More important, could British ships be *replaced* during the ten-year holiday? If not, by 1930 the British fleet would be obsolete compared with the American. All new ships would have to be substituted at one time, which, according to Balfour, would cause bursts of feverish shipbuilding at great expense together with violent fluctuations in employment. He reported that the First Sea Lord, Beatty, urged that British ships should be replaced gradually—'slow and steady replacement'. Beatty also insisted that in any disarmament scheme the strength of the French navy would have to be taken into account; so long as France possessed submarines, the British fleet in European waters would be unsafe. The naval view therefore held that submarines should be outlawed altogether.[42]

The Cabinet informed Balfour that the 'sovereign virtue' of the ten-year holiday consisted of the complete cessation of building. There would be no rivalry; the existing fleets would not be made obsolete by the appearance of new and superior capital vessels. But Britain could not accept this programme, however conducive to peace it might appear at first sight, unless the submarine question received 'profound' consideration. With the three naval powers maintaining powerful but

[42] These developments can be traced easily in the last chapter of *D.B.F.P.*, XIV.

obsolete battle fleets, the naval balance of power could be altered unfavourably by the building of submarines and aircraft by minor naval powers such as France, or even Italy or Russia. According to Lloyd George, 'In the duel between fleets of capital ships and flotillas of submarines, the former will remain stationary while the latter will be practically free. The three leading Naval Powers may therefore easily find their whole naval position undermined by the swift development by Powers like France or Russia of large flotillas of far more powerful submarines.'[43] Little could be done about aircraft construction because of the thin line between commercial and military aviation; but Britain might be able to take the lead in the abolition of submarines. If not, the Conference might collapse. According to a Foreign Office minute that went to the heart of the problem:

The submarine may be the rock on which the American proposal may be shipwrecked. We cannot possibly scrap Capital ships whilst all Powers navally inferior to us concentrate on submarines. If this shipwreck is to be avoided America will have to join us in our attempt to restrict or abolish the submarine. I doubt very much whether public opinion in the States will allow this. I am quite sure the French will stubbornly resist any such attempts, even if we were prepared to enter into an Alliance with her, as I think she will always argue that the absence of submarines would place her too much at our mercy and that therefore we should always be in a position to dictate to her.

It seems to me that the Washington Conference will bring it home to us that the advent of submarines and aircraft very seriously impair our natural frontiers, and will reduce us to the position of a continental Power. It would be a curious outcome of this Conference if it forced us to face the problem of having to maintain a large army in order to redress the balance as regards ourselves and France.[44]

In short, with a large submarine fleet, France would hold Britain at her mercy.

The bluster of the French delegate at the Conference, Premier Aristide Briand, aggravated the situation. His swagger alarmed the British Cabinet and caused the Committee of

[43] Curzon to Balfour, communicating the Prime Minister's message, No. 7, Tel. Urgent, 15 November 1921 [A 8510/18/45], F.O. 371/5622.
[44] Minute by Sir William Tyrrell on Hardinge to Curzon, No. 3219, 20 November 1921 [A 8620/18/45], F.O. 371/5623.

Imperial Defence to re-evaluate the entire military situation in Europe. France, now the military cock of the walk, apparently had no serious intention of disarming. The French air force, according to British intelligence, could easily bombard London indefinitely with thirty tons of explosives a day, over three times the amount of the war's worst air raid. By augmenting reserve forces, the French continental army in a matter of years, would have overwhelming superiority. With additional 'nigger army' support from Africa, and with the technological advance in air and submarine warfare, France's military capacity was truly alarming. The submarine itself could bring the Empire to its knees. Geographically, the idea of a French submarine fleet was even worse than a future German underwater threat:

If France has a large submarine force in a future war Great Britain might be cut off for all practical purposes from sea-borne supplies. France dominates the sea approaches to the United Kingdom from the south and could make the English Channel and the Mediterranean impossible for British sea-borne trade by the use of her submarines, even though of the small defensive type.

France has potential submarine bases in Tonquin, West Africa, the Red Sea and on both sides of the Mediterranean, in addition to the bases on the English Channel and the western coast of France, which are all close to British sea routes. Great Britain would consequently in a war with France require a very large force of destroyers and small craft to cope with large French submarine flottilas.[45]

Taking all these alarmist calculations in consideration, the Cabinet gave Balfour stiff instructions not to impair Britain's strength unless France took corresponding measures to disarm.

Balfour replied with supreme irony:

I am to try if possible, to induce the French to agree to a very small battle fleet so as to leave us free to accept American proposals without modification. Having persuaded them to deprive themselves of their form of naval defence I am then to persuade them that they really require no submarines because a war between France and England is unthinkable. This task being successfully accomplished,

[45] Curzon to Balfour, No. 38 Tel., 23 November 1921 [A 8711/18/45], *D.B.F.P.*, XIV, No. 443. For Briand's speech that started this alarmist speculation, see *Conference on the Limitation of Armament, Washington, November 12, 1921–February 6, 1922* (Washington, 1922), pp. 116–35; *Document Diplomatiques: Conférence de Washington, juillet 1921–février 1922* (Paris, 1923).

I am then to ask them to reduce the number of their aircraft seeing that we cannot sleep securely in our beds lest in a war with France, London should be burnt to the ground! For a task so complex as this I fear a trained diplomatist is required.[46]

The Cabinet persevered. In a series of 'Very urgent Personal and Secret' telegrams, Curzon continued to impress on Balfour that France's present policy would lead to a second European war as inexorably as Germany's had precipitated the first war: in bold historical analysis, he wrote, 'the great war was due to the arrogance bred by a sense of overwhelming military superiority and by the desire to destroy every incipient challenge to that supremacy. That situation is being repeated in Europe today and the consequence will inevitably be the same.'[47] Without hoping that France would give way on every point—land, air, sea, and underwater—the Cabinet observed that the French appeared to be entirely intransigent. On the gut issue of submarines, the Committee of Imperial Defence warned that French 'defensive' under-water craft would possess an 'offensive' value against Britain because of geographical proximity. Only a strong British fleet of destroyers and light cruisers could protect Britain from that menace, and for that reason Britain could accept no proposal to limit auxiliary craft unless submarines were abolished. For similar reasons the Cabinet insisted on the ten-year holiday; capital ships over an extended period of time might or might not be able to cope with submarines; in that way imponderable scientific advances complicated the entire issue. In Lloyd George's words: 'We cannot exclude from our minds the possibility that in ten years time the march of science in aviation, in submarines, torpedoes, shells and explosives may render it impossible to construct an inexpugnable capital unit especially within the tonnage limit governing replacements.'[48] Furthermore, there were powerful political and financial reasons for bringing Balfour to heel on the holiday issue. According to Curzon, 'there is no doubt that the

[46] Balfour to Curzon, No. 60 Tel., Urgent, 24 November 1921 [A 8763/18/45], F.O. 371/5624.
[47] Curzon to Balfour, No. 55 Tel., Very urgent, Personal and secret, 27 November 1921 [A 8763/18/45], F.O. 371/5624.
[48] Curzon to Balfour, communicating the Prime Minister's message, No. 66 Tel., Very urgent, Personal and secret, 1 December 1921 [A 8863/18/45], *D.B.F.P.*, XIV. No. 463.

failure of the naval holiday . . . and the financial consequences which it will entail will be severely criticized in the House of Commons.'[49] Balfour yielded. But he thought the French submarine threat chimerical and the holiday scheme both un-workable and dangerous. He rightly surmised that the Conference would be unable to restrict submarines. And had he lived to see the outbreak of the second war, Balfour could have said history proved him right in his plea for an effective, steady replacement of modern naval vessels.

At the Conference, Balfour used his studied politeness as a foil both against his colleagues in London and against his opposite numbers. To Curzon and company he urbanely pointed out that most of Briand's speeches was merely rhetoric and proceeded to ignore the exaggerated issues of French military and naval policy. Most of the alarmist views did in fact evaporate; and the French Premier, Balfour reported, felt thwarted in his effort to play the United States off against Britain. The spirit of Lafayette was running low, he wrote at one stage.[50] Despite the irritation between the British and French delegations, Balfour nevertheless followed Secretary Hughes's lead in working to include France in the Pacific settlement. Though valuable as a sop to French prestige, Balfour endorsed this idea reluctantly because it meant a further dilution of the Anglo-Japanese Alliance.[51] On such issues he worked effectively and on the whole harmoniously with the American Secretary of State. A letter from the Secretary of the British Delegation, Sir Maurice Hankey, reveals some curious features of the negotiations.

Meeting as we have done in Mr. Hughes' private room, and listening to Mr. Hughes' delivering speeches with that strange mixture of high moral purpose and practical bargaining, which I had always thought

[49] Curzon to Balfour, No. 101 Tel., Very urgent, Personal and secret, 9 December 1921, [A 9204/18/45], *D.B.F.P.*, XIV, No. 485.
[50] In London, Curzon was fond of matching Balfour's historical parallels with literary allusions. He once noted: "M. Briand will return to Europe like the Ancient Mariner

'a sadder and a wiser man
He rose the morrow morn'."

[51] Balfour did not have a high regard for the French Delegation, though he no doubt relished some of their blunt remarks to the Americans. See Hankey to Lloyd George, Private and personal, n.d. [Confidential/General/363/21], *D.B.F.P.*, XIV, No. 517.

peculiar to President Wilson, I have to rub my eyes to know if I am not back in the old rooms in Paris [in 1919]. . . . In spite of total physical dissimilarity, Mr. Hughes' mind is in some respects so like President Wilson's that Mr. Balfour nearly always unconsciously refers to Hughes as 'Wilson'. In fact, he does it so often that I have ceased to correct him.

Hughes is a heavy-weight with little subtlety. He delivers terrific speeches with the argument solidly built up, exactly as though he were addressing a jury. It is curious to watch the play between him and Mr. Balfour—rather like a man with a club fighting a man with a rapier. But it is a very friendly contrast and the tone is always quite admirable.[52]

Between the Americans and the Japanese, Balfour played the role of conciliator and respected broker. A few days after the signing of the quadruple treaty, the Japanese delegate told him that he was profoundly grateful for Balfour's dedicated efforts to promote good Anglo-Japanese relations. There is no reason to question the sincerity of Baron Kato's compliment, or the reality of Balfour's reply, that the Alliance from the viewpoint of the two powers had produced 'entirely satisfactory results'.

When Great Britain, Japan, the United States, and France signed the quadruple treaty on 13 December, they attempted to preserve peace in the Pacific; in a further five-power treaty that included Italy, signed on 6 February, they established the naval ratio of 5 : 5 : 3; in the other major treaty of the same date, China, Belgium, Holland, and Portugal joined those five powers to re-affirm the open door in China. The negotiations leading to the conclusion of those treaties were interlocking and complex, and no attempt will be made here to trace what Balfour called the 'endless technical details' of the naval settlement or the multitude of issues in the China problem. But I shall try to indicate briefly how the powers reached agreement, the meaning of the treaties to British security in the Far East, and then general significance of the Washington Conference.

The essential ingredient was an affirmation of the *status quo* and Japanese flexibility. Japan accepted a 5 : 5 : 3 ratio, rather than her initial demand of 10 : 10 : 7, and yielded in China. Historians of American foreign policy have tended to interpret these results of the Conference as a brilliant American diplomatic

[52] Ibid.

victory and a stunning Japanese reverse that was intensely un-popular in Japan.[53] The recently released British documents provide the basis for an interpretation more in line with re-search based on Japanese sources.[54] From the British point of view the Pacific settlement was entirely satisfactory because it did not touch on Australia, New Zealand, or Canada, or the islands adjacent to them, or on the future hub of British naval security in the Far East, Singapore. The settlement appears to have been no less satisfactory to Japan. When the Japanese agreed to the lower naval ratio, they did so on the conditions embodied in the four-power treaty, the non-fortification of the Pacific Islands. They calculated they would retain hegemony in the western Pacific, as in fact, they did. On the Asian mainland, on the other hand, Japan adjusted her policy in accordance with the demands of the western powers. She maintained her position in Manchuria, but eventually withdrew from eastern Siberia and northern Sakhalin and subscribed to these major principles of the nine-power treaty by which the signatory nations agreed:

I. To respect the sovereignty, the independence and the terri-torial and administrative integrity of China;

II. To provide the fullest and most unembarrassed opportunity to China to develop and maintain herself as an effective and stable government;

III. To use their influence for the purpose of equal opportunity for the commerce and industry of all nations through the territory of China;

IV. To refrain from taking advantage of conditions in China in order to seek special rights or privileges which would abridge the rights of subjects or citizens of friendly states and from countenancing action inimical to the security of such states.

After the Conference, Japan, in accordance with her additional major pledge, restored Shantung. In this issue Balfour again, so he thought, played a major role.

Of the many complicated China issues, Shantung was pre-eminent. The gist of the problem, according to one of Curzon's

[53] See, for example, Jean-Baptiste Duroselle, *From Wilson to Roosevelt: Foreign Policy of the United States* (Cambridge, Mass., 1963), pp. 152ff.

[54] See James B. Crowley, *Japan's Quest for Autonomy*, 'Historical Prologue'; and Akira Iriye, 'The Failure of Economic Expansionism, 1918–1931' (unpublished typescript).

pithy summaries, was Japan's continued occupation of the former German territory: 'Briefly stated the Shantung problem resolves itself into the question whether Japan shall or shall not be allowed to remain in sole possession of one of the most important means of peaceful economic penetration into the vitals of China.'[55] British interests were indirectly involved because of the leased territory of Wei-hai Wei. That port, acquired by Britain at the height of the Scramble, was regarded by most British Statesmen as a costly folly but by the Foreign Office as a valuable pawn. In the tradition of imperial diplomacy, if Britain gave up Wei-hai Wei as part of the Chinese settlement, she should receive something in return. Balfour took a more large-minded view. He held that Wei-hai Wei had no value, strategic, administrative, or economic. He furthermore thought that the Washington Conference had met in a genuine spirit of sacrifice. He wrote after the Conference had concluded its work:

The Conference of Washington was no ignoble wrangle for petty gains, where every concession made by a Great Power for a great object had to be paid for by an equivalent fragment of somebody else's rights. It was a sincere attempt to put international affairs, especially in the Pacific Ocean and the Far East, upon a footing at once more friendly and more stable.

He then explained how Japan had agreed to the retrocession of Shantung after long and arduous negotiations and stated that his own position would have been intolerable if Britain clung to the miserable port of Wei-hai Wei.

[H]ow could the British representative effectively urge the abandonment by Japan of a special position in Shantung while he knew that a special position in that province was to be retained by Great Britain? . . . If Great Britain had retained Wei-Hai-Wei after Japan, with the warm approval of Great Britain, had given up Kiaochow, the moral position of this country would certainly have suffered in the estimation of the world, and in my opinion it would have suffered justly. For such a calamity the lease of a hundred Wei-Hai Wei's would have furnished a very insufficient compensation.[56]

For those reasons Balfour took the matter in his own hands and,

[55] Curzon to Balfour, No. 150 Tel., 23 December 1921 [F 4749/833/10], *D.B.F.P.*, XIV, No. 518.
[56] Balfour to Lloyd George, No. 24, 4 February 1922 [F 823/138/10], *D.B.F.P.*, XIV, No. 580.

on 2 February announced to the Conference that Britain would give up Wei-hai Wei to China in full sovereignty. Curzon petulantly noted that Balfour had 'given away' part of the Empire.

Historians will continue to debate the results of the Washington Conference, and indeed to question Balfour's own evaluation when he said, in a lapse from his usual foresight, that the Conference's outcome was an 'absolute unmixed benefit to mankind, which carried no seeds of future misfortune.'[57] One might also question the judgement of the British Ambassador in Tokyo, Sir Charles Eliot, when he wrote that the Conference established the Japanese as 'possessing more or less the same standards and ideas as Europeans.'[58] Another way of putting it might have been to say that the Japanese now played a more important role in international affairs and were regarded as equals. But the opposite point might be made as well. Ultimately the Washington Conference is remarkable not because Britain relinquished her naval supremacy, which no longer existed anyway, nor because the United States achieved a diplomatic triumph over Japan. In the long run, the Conference is significant because it dealt the death blow to the Anglo-Japanese Alliance. With the Alliance the Japanese had been, if not exactly equal, at least friends with the British. Critics of British foreign policy later charged that Great Britain had dropped their friends in 1921–2, and the charge has some ring of truth in it, however unavoidable that course of action appeared at the time. In any case it cannot be disputed that the Washington Conference was a point of new departure in international affairs because of the end of the Alliance. Journalists often have good insights into events of moment, and perhaps this account best sums up the meaning of the Conference. On 13 December, after hearing the clause read out terminating the Alliance, one observer watched Balfour's reaction.

Through the forest of black coats and white collars I could see in profile, motionless and sober, the distinguished head of Mr. Balfour. As the last sentence sounded and the Anglo-Japanese Alliance publicly perished, his head fell forward on his chest exactly as if the

[57] Young, *Balfour*, p. 420.
[58] Eliot to Curzon, Private, 13 January 1922 [Confidential/General/363/18], *D.B.F.P.*, XIV, No. 458.

spinal chord had been severed. It was an amazing revelation of what the Japanese Treaty had meant to the men of a vanished age. It was the spinal chord that had been severed . . . . The head of stereotyped diplomacy had fallen forward—the vital chord severed—and new figures hereafter would monopolize the scene.[59]

Six years later Victor Wellesley evaluated the significance of the Washington Conference and attempted to establish the overriding priorities of British policy. He rebuked those who believed the termination of the Alliance had been a mistake: 'There is a school of thought, increasing in strength, which holds that the abrogation of the Anglo-Japanese Alliance was a great mistake because we have thereby forfeited Japanese co-operation without securing that of America, which has turned out to be a broken reed. I do not share that view. There are matters of higher importance than our policy in the Far East, and one of them is disarmaments. There would have been no naval agreement, if the alliance had remained in being.'[60]

[59] Putnam Weale, *An Indiscreet Chronicle from the Pacific* (New York, 1922), pp. 186–7. Putnam Weale was the pseudonym of Bertram Lenox Simpson, journalist and lobbyist of the Chinese Government. During the Imperial Conference Curzon referred to him as a man 'of doubtful character and antecedents. He is on a sort of roving commission with a very handsome salary paid by the Chinese Government.' I.C.M., 8th Meeting, Secret, 28 June 1921, CAB. 32/2.

[60] Minute by Wellesley, 10 March 1928, F.O. 371/13165.

IV

THE CHINESE REVOLUTION

'TEN years ago', wrote the British military attaché at Peking in 1927, 'there was not an embryo of [a] Communist Party.' He went on to describe the birth of the Party in the era of the Washington Conference and the growth of the movement to the strength of 30,000 Communists who, by their discipline and determination, constituted a danger of the utmost magnitude to foreign interests in the Far East.[1] The extent of this peril came as a revelation in the summer of 1927. At that time a number of Communist documents fell into British hands. They proved beyond doubt that the Nationalist party, or Kuomintang, had been penetrated by Communist agents who were controlled by two respective political and military advisers from the Soviet Union, Michael Borodin and Marshal Galen. So alarming did this evidence appear that some British observers inclined towards the view that Russia had chosen China as the principal battlefield in her worldwide struggle to destroy the British Empire. Even those who regarded the 'Bolshevizing' of China as a myth now became dismayed at the secrecy and thoroughness by which the Communists and their Russian advisers had apparently succeeded in gaining control of the Kuomintang. The British Minister and his staff consequently re-evaluated the Communist movement and

---

[1] Colonel S. R. V. Stewart to Lampson, 5 October 1927, enclosed in Lampson to Chamberlain, No. 1187 Secret, 28 October 1927 [F 9497/3241/10], F.O. 371/12502. The basic British work pertinent to this chapter is the memoir by the Far Eastern Adviser to the Foreign Office from 1925 to 1938, Sir John T. Pratt, *War and Politics in China* (London, 1943). Its scholarly equivalent is by G. F. Hudson, *The Far East in World Politics* (Oxford, 1937), a brilliantly lucid exposition. Two other indispensable companions are Akira Iriye, *After Imperialism: the Search for a New Order in the Far East* (Cambridge, Mass., 1965); and Dorothy Borg, *American Policy and the Chinese Revolution, 1925–1928* (New York, 1968 edn.) The following works are less relevant but need to be mentioned in connection with the central theme of this chapter: Benjamin I. Schwartz, *Chinese Communism and the Rise of Mao* (Cambridge, Mass., 1951); Robert C. North, *Moscow and Chinese Communists* (Stanford, 1953); Allen S. Whiting, *Soviet Policies in China, 1917–1924* (New York, 1954); and Conrad Brandt. *Stalin's Failure in China, 1924–1927* (Cambridge, Mass., 1958).

examined such basic questions as the extent to which intervention by an external power can influence the course of a
revolution. After the ousting of the Russian advisers and the
eclipse of the left wing of the Kuomintang in the spring and
summer of 1927, British alarm at Communism in China subsided. The pattern of thought returned to that of the days of the
Washington Conference. The doctrines of Communism, so held
the British consensus, were alien to China, and the Chinese
people could never be Bolshevized in the Soviet fashion. In a
sense this judgement re-affirmed British optimism about the
peace-loving and lovable Chinese people; in another sense it
reflected despair. The Russians and British alike found it impossible to deal with China, in the recurrent phrase, because of
the age-old Chinese vices of venality and arrogance.

In the five years following the Washington Conference,
British analysts thought that the internal condition of China
was even more confused than it had been after the revolution
of 1911. There appeared to be, in Lloyd George's words, an
'infinite variety of war lords'. Among the more prominent
seemed to be Wu Pei-Fu, who from time to time controlled the
central government at Peking; and one of his rivals, Chang
Tso-lin, whose base of power was Manchuria.[2] Among others,
these two potentates represented Chinese 'feudalism' or
'Tuchunism', characteristically defined by the British as a
system in which militarists grabbed cash boxes and were thus
able to command mercenaries. The struggle between the rival
tuchuns, or military provincial governors, appeared to fit into
the pattern of Chinese history. According to one official, 'long
periods of chaos similar to the present are not unknown in
Chinese history; they occur roughly every 200 or 300 years.'
He explained the purpose of the civil wars in China by applying
the theory of the European balance of power: 'Chinese civil
wars have but one general object—to prevent any single militarist from obtaining undisputed power—and [they] offer no
hope of achieving anything constructive.'[3] Until mid-1925 that

[2] See especially F. F. Liu, *A Military History of Modern China, 1924–1949* (Princeton, 1956), which clearly discusses both the military background and the dominant
political issues.

[3] S. P. Waterlow, 'Memorandum respecting the Problem of China', 13 May
1925 [F 1723/190/10], F.O. 371/10937.

view may be taken as representative of official opinion about the nature of Chinese politics. Between 1925 and 1927, however, the Foreign Office discerned the difference of the civil war from all previous disruptive periods in China's history. Much more was involved than merely the traditional struggle between the north and the south. Canton emerged as the spiritual home of the revolution, the base of the Kuomintang. As the political and military influence of the Kuomintang spread throughout China, British observers attributed this unprecedented effectiveness to Russian organization and staff work. The Acting Consul-General in Canton wrote in November 1926:

[T]he Cantonese have received much help and inspiration from their Russian advisers. Apart from the money and munitions supplied to the Cantonese forces, the Russian military instructors have done wonders in reorganising the army and in turning the unwarlike southern peasant and coolie into a comparatively efficient fighting machine. The rapid and really remarkable progress of the expedition despatched from Canton to the Yangtze, and its subsequent victories over the troops of Wu Pei-fu . . . could not have been accomplished without Russian staff work, and the campaign, unlike all previous civil wars conducted by Chinese troops, is noticeable for the discipline of the southern army and the absence of looting.[4]

As the British watched the simultaneous growth of Bolshevik and Kuomintang strength, they often commented that the Chinese did not realize they were playing with fire.

The 'Chinaman' responsible for the alliance with the Russians was the founder and leader of the Kuomintang, Dr. Sun Yat-sen. He holds a curious place in the history of Britain's relations with China. British officials distrusted him absolutely, regarding him as little short of a lunatic. Typical reports stated that the extravagance of his language and his bitter hostility towards Great Britain seemed to indicate an unbalanced state of mind. After his death in 1925 the story spread that Sun had turned to Russia only after having been rebuffed by Britain and the United States in his efforts to establish democratic institutions in China. The Foreign Office indignantly recorded that the myth of Sun appeared to be triumphing over his historical reality. One of the old China hands, J. T. Pratt, wrote these passages in 1928 in a

[4] J. F. Brenan, 'The Kuomintang', 23 November 1926 [F 229/229/10], F.O. 371/12456.

memorandum that is revealing not only about Sun but also about the British interpretation of the history of the Kuomintang:

It is now generally recognised that Sun Yat-sen was a dreamer and a visionary. He possessed in a marked degree that peculiar magnetic power which, perhaps in one case out of a million, gives a man a strange influence over his fellow-men. In all practical affairs, however, as he himself to some extent recognised, he was hopelessly incompetent. The contrast between the tremendous power he exercised over the minds of his countrymen and his utter failure as a politician to make any practical use of his power for the good of the people greatly irritated the practically minded British and prejudiced them against him. . . .

Pratt then summarized Sun's role in the founding of the Kuomintang:

When the revolution of 1911 proved so unexpectedly successful . . . [he] was elected President of the Republic at Nanking, but soon after resigned in favour of Yuan Shih-kai and busied himself in launching grandiose but quite unpractical paper schemes of railway development. In spite of his popularity with the masses and his visionary fervour, he proved quite unable to guide the revolution; reaction in the person of Yuan Shih-kai reigned supreme.[5]

After tracing the vicissitudes of Sun's attempts to maintain a revolutionary government at Canton, Pratt emphasized the 'secret relations with Japan and Germany, and also with Soviet Russia'. Sun, in an agreement with a Russian envoy, Adolph Joffe, in 1923 had insisted that China was not yet ready for Communism, but accepted the Soviet Union's good wishes in the struggle for national independence.[6] In October of the

[5] J. T. Pratt, 'Memorandum respecting Sun Yat-sen, Moscow and Great Britain', Confidential, 6 February 1928 [F 703/703/10], F.O. 371/13223. In his book Pratt wrote that the myth of Sun turning to Britain for assistance had been 'copied uncritically into almost every recent book on the Far East, and a false picture of the most crucial period in the modern development of China now passes muster as authentic history.' *War and Politics in China*, p. 196. For the Asian perspective, see especially Lyon Sharman, *Sun Yat-sen: His Life and Its Meaning* (New York, 1934); Marius B. Jansen, *The Japanese and Sun Yat-sen* (Cambridge, Mass., 1954); and Harold Z. Schiffrin, *Sun Yat-sen and the Origins of the Chinese Revolution* (Berkeley, 1968).

[6] Text of the Sun-Joffe memorandum is in the *China Year Book, 1928*, p. 318. For detailed discussion see especially Whiting, *Soviet Policies in China*, chapter X. Cf. Leng Shao Chuan and Norman D. Palmer, *Sun Yat-sen and Communism* (New York, 1960).

same year Borodin arrived in Canton. Sun, benefiting from Russian money and guidance, became increasingly hostile to Britain. Critics of British policy charged that, had the Foreign Office countered the Soviet attempt to gain control of the Kuomintang, Sun might have been won over to the west instead of becoming a sort of Chinese Lenin. Pratt pointed out the reality of the situation:

[B]ecause Borodin was able to reorganise the Canton Government, it does not follow that any British subject could have done the same. A British subject rendering such services would have to rely on such salary as the Cantonese might be willing to pay him. Borodin, so far from drawing a salary from the Cantonese, was supplied with unlimited funds from Moscow which he distributed among the persons he was supposed to be serving. Borodin frankly took sides in Chinese domestic politics and helped one side against the other all with the idea of subserving what was conceived to be in the interests of Russia. No one can seriously suggest that this was an example which could be followed by Great Britain.[7]

So far as the Foreign Office was concerned, the conclusion was clear: Sun—'visionary and unpractical as ever'—had been duped by the Communists.

Paradoxically, Sun's three principles of nationalism, democracy, and the people's livelihood did not at all correspond with the doctrines of Communism. One of Sun's subordinates once described him to the British Minister at Peking as a sort of Fabian Socialist.[8] The British Ambassador in Tokyo, reporting Sun's own words indirectly, indicated that Sun attached great importance to American theories of economic development:

Dr. Sun said that, while he was politically in favour of the Soviet Government . . . he disapproved of their economic theories entirely. China was a country, he said, suffering from under-production, and the remedy for this was to be found not in the doctrines of Marx, but in the Ford formula of industrialism and efficiency.[9]

One of the more perceptive British students of 'Sun Yat-senism',

[7] J. T. Pratt, 'Memorandum respecting Sun Yat-sen, Moscow and Great Britain', Confidential, 6 February 1928 [F 703/703/10], F.O. 371/13223.

[8] Macleay to Chamberlain, No. 828 Confidential, 29 December 1924 [F 592/194/10], F.O. 371/10942.

[9] Eliot to Chamberlain, No. 486, 11 December 1924 [F 167/2/10], F.O. 371/10917.

Sir John Brenan of the Canton Consulate, held that there was an ideological similarity with Bolshevism in method but not in content. Sun taught that his three principles could only be achieved in three distinct phases: 'militarism, tutelage, and constitutionalism'. According to Brenan:

[B]y this he meant that military force must first be used to overcome the existing military despotisms in the country; then the people must be subjected to the tutelage of the Kuomintang until they have acquired a political consciousness which will enable them to attain the last or constitutional stage and enjoy a full measure of self-government.

Brenan also stated unequivocally that Sun opposed the theoretical underpinning of Communism, class warfare, and the dictatorship of the proletariat.

There is no indication that Sun Yat-sen was a convert to the Russian theories of Communism and class warfare. In fact, the principles he taught . . . are absolutely opposed to these doctrines, and it is clear that he only accepted the proffered friendship of Soviet Russia because the latter was willing to treat with China on equal terms, and he needed her assistance for the realisation of his own plans.[10]

As a doctrinaire idealist, a nationalist, and a reformer, Sun aimed at the unification of China under civil administration, not a dictatorship of the proletariat. He envisaged the economic development of China along capitalist lines, not Bolshevik. British officials in China therefore regarded it as ironic that after his death on 12 March 1925 he acquired the image of the Lenin of China. They attributed this development entirely to Russian influence. Again in Brenan's words,

Soviet inspiration is . . . reponsible for the elevation of Dr. Sun Yat-sen's memory to a position comparable to that of Lenin's in Russia and for the attempt to give to his writings and wishes the character of scriptural authority, which it would be impious to challenge.[11]

[10] J. F. Brenan, 'The Kuomintang', 23 November 1926 [F 229/229/10], F.O. 371/12456.
[11] Ibid. Brenan's report accurately states that Sun died of a liver ailment. For more typically distorted views reflecting British interpretation of Sun's personality, see for example a memorandum by C. G. Humphrys, Private and Confidential, 23 January 1927 [F 2145/67/10], F.O. 371/12434 (Distributed to King, Cabinet, and Dominions), which accounts for Sun's falling prey to Borodin because 'Dr. Sun's mental equilibrium had already begun to show signs of collapse due to the disease of general paralysis of the insane from which he finally died.'

Despite this ideological association with Lenin, the British community in China during the 1920s persistently believed that the Chinese people desired Sun Yat-senism, not Communism. As one Consul-General summed up the Kuomintang's involvement with the Soviets: 'It ought to be recognised that they were using the Russians for their own ends, and in order to develop a Nationalist Government of China. The movement was not Bolshevik; their doctrine was not Communism, but Sun-yat-senism, and with this no one could quarrel.'[12]

British observers of China had no particular complaint about theoretical Sun Yat-senism. But in practice Sun greatly annoyed them because of his incompetence. He especially irritated them by his charges that Great Britain was responsible for China's chaos and turmoil. His repeated accusations led them to examine, again, the basic question of who and what caused China's disorder. One official answered that question in the following way: 'In China the underlying causes of the present trouble are: firstly, the inherent dislike of the foreigner, which has always existed; secondly, the growth of the student movements and thirdly, Bolshevik influence.'[13] Until the summer of 1927 the Foreign Office regarded the first two elements as more important than the last. Students in particular lashed up anti-foreign sentiment against the British. The Vice-Consul in Canton wrote in June 1925:

It is Great Britain with her subject peoples and her history of conquest in India and Egypt, who is constantly denounced in the press and by the student body as 'arch-imperialist' and the oppressor of China. She is the butt of most of the attacks, owing to her strong attitude and lack of sympathy with advanced political ideas.

He went on to describe the principal characteristics of Chinese students.

The average Cantonese student or graduate can only be described as a half-educated product. He has learnt but a smattering of Western culture, along with scraps of the most extreme Social-Democratic principles, and the leaven of new ideas rising in his

[12] Remark by Sir James Jamieson, 'Notes on a Discussion on China between Sir E. Wilton and Sir J. Jamieson', 28 June 1926, enclosed in Lampson to Chamberlain, No. 935, 31 December 1926 [F 1330/2/10]. F.O. 371/12401.
[13] Memorandum by Newton, 25 June 1925 [F 3008/194/10]. Printed for the Cabinet, Most Secret, F.O. 371/10943.

mind, with its new-felt consciousness of national pride, has created within his heart a burning indignation at the inequality of China among the nations.[14]

Vice-Consul Scott then analysed the way in which the Kuomintang attempted to manipulate student and other groups:

The Executive Committee of the Kuomintang, which took control after the death of Dr. Sun, has, among other activities, fostered the establishment within the past year of an Anti-Christian Alliance, an Anti-Imperialist Countries League, a Union of Soldiers, Students, Workers and Agriculturists, and a General Labour Federation of all artisans and organised labour in Canton, Hong Kong and Macao.[15]

With Russian assistance in gaining support through those organizations, the Kuomintang transformed itself from 'a sect to an effective political party'. But British consuls remained quite sceptical about the chances of the Kuomintang to unite all of China. In the months following Sun's death, opinion split between those who believed the Kuomintang would disrupt because of internal factions and disputes over domestic issues, and those who believed that the Kuomintang might lead China to her salvation. Within a year and a half after Sun's death, the latter view prevailed. The Consul-General of Shanghai wrote in late 1926: 'In my opinion there can be no doubt that the K.M.T. is destined to rule China, and the only question is whether that rule, when it comes, is to be that of the right or left wing.'[16] In short, as the strength of the Kuomintang grew, Sun's disciples presented his ideology as the central idea

[14] 'Memorandum respecting the Political Situation at Canton, by Mr. A. L. Scott, Vice-Consul at Canton', 30 June 1925 [F 2699/2/10], F.O. 371/10920. To put it mildly, the British generally despised Chinese students. Here is another typical example: 'The Chinese student is the result of the zeal of the foreigner for bringing the Chinese up to modern requirements, and I think the very large bulk of the foreigner now regrets his arrival. . . . The student, usually a wretched half-baked creature who argues like a small child without fear of correction, has no solid basis of education to help him. He picks up a smattering of foreign learning, which enables him to pose without difficulty as a superior being among his own people, who therefore fear him, whilst before the foreigner he realises his inferiority, causing him a loss of face and turning him to anti-foreign feelings at heart.' 'Notes on the Chinese Student by the Late Brigadier-General G. E. Pereira' (received in Foreign Office, 24 July 1924) [F 2497/174/10], F.O. 371/10270.
[15] Scott's memorandum cited in the preceding footnote.
[16] Barton to O'Malley, 6 November 1926, enclosed in Lampson to Chamberlain, No. 935, 31 December 1926 [F 1330/2/10], F.O. 371/12401.

of Chinese nationalism; but both right and left wings of the Kuomintang claimed Sun's principles as their own. Who would prevail? And should Britain give outright support to the more moderate branch of the Kuomintang? There lay the dilemma: 'In proportion as we kowtow to the implacable hostility of the left wing, so we discourage the moderates of the right wing, and thereby delay even if we do not frustrate that broadening of the basis of the Nationalist Government which will enable anyone who supports it to be sure that he is really supporting the bulk of reasonable Chinese opinion.'[17]

The suggestion that Britain should intervene or take sides in China's civil war flew in the face of the Foreign Office's traditional attitude, but not the Colonial Office's. The Foreign Office persistently took the line that Great Britain should remain aloof from the internal struggle and continue to recognize whatever 'legitimate' government held sway at Peking. To understand the rationale of this policy, it is first necessary to identify the factions controlling various parts of China in the mid-1920s. Now as then, this is no easy task. The political map of China changed like a kaleidoscope, and the 'inscrutable' Chinese protagonists were often difficult to tell one from another. Nevertheless the Foreign Office valiantly scrutinized Chinese politics and the British Government was probably better informed about the domestic situation in China than any other nation save Japan. The following excerpts from the Foreign Office's confidential 'Who's Who in China' for the year 1925 describe the principal parties and personalities as seen through British eyes. There were four main political or military groups:

ANFU.—The bulk of the members of the present Provisional Government [at Peking] are drawn from this party, of which the President or Chief Executive of the Republic, Tuan Chi-jui, is the head. The present Government has been in office since the latter part of 1924, when the Chih-li Government supported by Wu Pei-fu was crushed by Chang Tso-lin, with the help of Feng Yu-hsiang, who deserted Wu Pei-fu at the critical moment. The Anfu party is pro-Japanese. It has no military forces of its own and has, since taking office, depended chiefly upon the military support of Chang Tso-lin, the head of the Fengtien or Mukden group, and of Feng Yu-hsiang, who has relations with the Kuo Min Tang.

[17] Ibid.

CHIH-LI.—The Chih-li military party were in office between 1920, when the Anfu party were driven from power, and September 1924, when Wu Pei-fu was crushed by Chang Tso-lin, and the Anfu party again took office. The most powerful adherents of the party are Wu Pei-fu [and numerous other Tuchuns]. . . . The Chih-li party is more nationalist in tendency than the Anfu party, but has always been anti-Bolshevik.

FENGTIEN (the Chinese name for Mukden).—Describes the military group headed by Chang Tso-lin, nominally Director-General of Military Reconstruction in Fengtien, but for all practical purposes the independent ruler of Manchuria. The Fengtien group have never held office in Peking, but have wielded great influence on successive Governments from their headquarters at Mukden. The group is strongly anti-Bolshevik and is largely in the hands of Japan.

KUO MIN TANG.—The Radical party, of which the late Sun Yat-sen was the leader. It is strongly nationalist and its left wing is deeply infected with Bolshevism. Its headquarters are at Canton, where it has set up a semi-Bolshevik Government, which is under the influence of the Soviet Government. . . .

The next part of the report dealt with the territorial distribution of the parties:

ANFU.—Having no military power, this party itself controls no territory. It is a clique of politicians and simply holds ministerial office in Peking.

CHIH-LI.—The area at present under Wu Pei-fu's influence includes . . . Central China generally. Present headquarters, Hankow.

FENGTIEN.—Chang Tso-lin controls, in addition to Manchuria, . . . North-Eastern China generally—with headquarters at Mukden.

After commenting on the Kuomintang's grip over southern China, the 'Who's Who' discussed, among others, these personalities:

CHANG TSO-LIN has for many years been ruler of Manchuria, with headquarters at Mukden, the capital. Mukden is also known as Fengtien; hence one sees references to the Fengtien party (as opposed to the Chih-li party under Wu Pei-fu), the Fengtien army. &c.

FENG YU-HSIANG is known as the Christian general; has a great reputation as an able soldier and able administrator; formerly as a general in Wu Pei-fu's army he greatly contributed to the defeat of the Anfu Government in 1920 and of Chang Tso-lin in

1922. Subsequently he nursed a grievance against Wu Pei-fu and took his revenge by deserting in the middle of the campaign against Chang Tso-lin in October 1924. He expelled the President from Peking and installed Tuan Chi-jui as Chief Executive. He then withdrew to Kalgan, in the northwest, and under Bolshevik influence adopted a violently anti-British attitude. . . .

TUAN CHI-JUI, President of the Republic. Is the head of the Anfu party, which was long kept in office by Japanese influence, and is justly charged by Chinese public opinion with having sold China to Japan. Nevertheless, Tuan Chi-jui *personally* is held in great respect.

WU PEI-FU, chief supporter of the Chih-li party. Keeps his soldiers efficient and well disciplined, but he fails in handling large bodies of troops and in higher strategy. He is also a great failure as a politician and administrator. He is genuinely opposed to Bolshevism, and has suppressed labour movements with a firm hand. Honesty of purpose and strong nationalism give him a strong hold on the Chinese. Utterly defeated last autumn, he has just emerged again as the head of a confederation of Yang-tsze provinces opposed to Chang Tso-lin and the present Chief Executive and Cabinet in Peking.[18]

Two years later the 'Who's Who' contained these entries for the two principal Russian advisers in China:

BORODIN.—Soviet Commissioner at Canton. . . . He is said to be a Lettish Jew, about 45, and to have been the chief factor in the training and equipment of the Cantonese army. . . . His real name is Michael Grusenberg. . . . In 1919 he worked on Communist propaganda in Spain and in 1920 in Mexico, where he used a Mexican passport to enter the United States freely. When in England in 1922 he was quite definitely assisting the British Communist party here under instructions from Moscow.

GALLENT [sic].—Chief military adviser to the Nationalist army, Borodin being chief political adviser. Though less in the limelight than Borodin, his influence is possibly as strong, and is directed to the same end. His aim is to keep Chiang Kai-shek well under his control and to eliminate him if he tries to manage the situation independently.

The entry for Chiang Kai-shek reads:

Commander-in-chief of the Cantonese armes. . . . Organiser of the

[18] 'Who's Who in China', 26 October 1925 [F 5218/5218/10], F.O. 371/10957; C.P. 12991.

Cantonese forces, which he used to secure a dominating force in Canton. Is reported to be an extreme Nationalist, but impatient of Bolshevik control.[19]

Throughout the 1920s, the Foreign Office maintained a stance of theoretical non-intervention towards these diverse parties and personalities, and, indeed, made no direct move against the Soviet agents. In practice the Foreign Office recognized that strict neutrality did not exist. British policy in effect supported what the Minister at Peking in 1924 called 'the saner and more conservative elements in the country represented by statesmen such as Tuan Ch'i-jui.'[20] But such support fell far short of the Colonial Office's proposal to supply arms and ammunition to anti-Red forces in the south.

As Communist strength in southern China grew along with the Kuomintang's influence, anti-British sentiment intensified in Canton. Boycotts and strikes disrupted British trade not only there but also in the neighbouring colony of Hong Kong. This anti-British agitation could be discussed at length in the chronological context of the revolution, but the main point is that in the spring of 1927 one of Chiang Kai-Shek's subordinates, General Li Chai-Sum, pacified Canton. Li opposed the Communists. The Colonial Office (along with the Consul at Canton) urged that he be given arms and ammunition from Hong Kong. In an 'Immediate and Secret' despatch to the Foreign Office, the Colonial Office stated:

In the last resort, all Governments depend on force, and when, as in this case, an authority has at last succeeded in tranquillising a disturbed district in which a neighbouring British Colony has a vital interest, it would appear illogical to handicap that authority by placing obstacles in the way of the supply of the arms and ammunition necessary for the maintenance of peace and good order while the forces of disorder are liberally furnished with arms by the Soviet.[21]

Leopold Amery, the Colonial Secretary, argued that to supply

[19] 'Who's Who in China', 10 February 1927 [F 1398/1398/10], F.O. 371/12473; C.P. 13313. For Borodin, see especially Jonathan Spence, *To Change China* (Boston, 1969), chapter 7.

[20] Macleay to Chamberlain, No. 773, 8 December 1924 [F 357/2/10], F.O. 371/10917.

[21] Colonial Office to Foreign Office, Immediate and Secret, 11 May 1927, C.P. 13304.

arms to Li would not violate the British policy of non-intervention because the purpose was merely to police Canton. Therefore the Arms Embargo Agreement of 1919 would not be compromised.[22] Amery also pointed out that the Foreign Office had approved a delivery of Vickers airplanes to Chang Tso-lin, and that this action thus created a precedent for aid to anti-Communist forces in the south.

[T]he supply of these aeroplanes has now been sanctioned, but . . . while it is clear that they will, in fact, be used for military purposes, they have been described as commercial, in order that there may be no conflict with the terms of the China Arms Embargo Agreement. If the supply of aeroplanes to a Northern general under a specious disguise of this nature is not regarded as improper, Mr. Amery can see no reason why the despatch of arms to a Southern general for police purposes should not be regarded as equally legitimate.[23]

In short, the Colonial Office thought it folly not to assist the Chinese anti-Communists.

The Colonial Office's accusation of a double standard greatly annoyed the Foreign Office. In reply the Foreign Office said it would be much more reasonable to supply arms and ammunition to 'an old-established and well-known' leader, Chang, than to 'a comparative new-comer', Li. In fact the Foreign Office refused Chang the supplies he requested, even though he represented China's main bulwark against Bolshevism. Responding to the airplane issue, the Foreign Office pointed out the difference between sanctioning a delivery of commercial aircraft to Chang and giving arms to Li:

[I]n view of the fact that other embargo Powers were supplying aeroplanes to the Chinese in spite of our attempts to tighten up the

---

[22] There is a vast correspondence on this subject that is most easily traced through the Confidential Print series. Here is an interesting evaluation of the arms embargo: 'It has certainly not prevented, and does not on the face of things appear to have seriously handicapped, civil warfare in China. Nevertheless, there is little doubt that it has prevented enormous dumping of surplus war material in China during the post-war years, and thrown the Chinese back on the resources of their own arsenals (which have, on the other hand, been correspondingly developed). On the whole, therefore, the embargo has probably served a useful purpose, while its moral effect on both Chinese and foreign public opinion has doubtless been very good.' (Teichman to Newton, 3 August 1925 [F 3737/1/10], F.O. 371/10916.

[23] Colonial Office to Foreign Office, Immediate and Secret, 11 May 1927, C.P. 13304.

embargo under this heading, we decided not to regard aeroplanes for commercial purposes as coming within the scope of the embargo. It is in view of this last decision that we have recently declined to intervene in order to prevent Messrs Vickers from carrying out an order for aeroplanes for Marshal Chang Tso-lin.

The supply of arms and munitions to General Li is on quite a different footing. The question of including aeroplanes in the embargo was a point on which the embargo Powers were not agreed; but the supply of arms and munitions would be in flat contradiction to the Embargo Agreement, and we could scarcely be so cynical as to remain parties to the Agreement. No doubt other Powers would follow our example, but upon us would rest the odium of breaking down an arrangement which, although partially ineffective, has certainly, to some extent, prevented a general scramble to supply the Chinese with arms, and has stood as a visible sign of the Powers' refusal to take sides in the Chinese civil war.[24]

Regardless of the justification for delivering aircraft to Chang, there was a real danger of supplying arms to any Chinese militarist. 'In China military leaders rise and fall; their professions of friendship are quite unreliable.' If Britain supplied arms to southern generals, there could be no guarantee that they might not be used against pro-British warlords in the north. Even worse, 'they might be used for an attack against British troops in the Shanghai area.' There thus was a good case for British neutrality—at least until it could be ascertained who would win. When the 'psychological moment' arrived, or, in other words, when 'a fairly stable government' acceded to power, Britain would supply arms to China's central government—but only then.[25]

The Foreign Office also carefully considered the question of direct intervention against the Russian Bolsheviks in China. In

[24] 'Memorandum on the Arms Embargo and Supply of Arms to Canton', with important enclosures, 16 May 1927, C.P. 13304.

[25] Ibid. The Foreign Office would then nullify the embargo act by a neat twist of imperial logic: 'We would proceed to replace the Arms Embargo by a policy of applying to British subjects the Chinese law prohibiting the import of arms and ammunition, *i.e.*, we would supply arms only to the Central Government of China and their nominees.' During the era of the revolution, it does appear that the British adhered to the embargo. The Colonial Office, for example, complained: 'This arms embargo has been faithfully observed by the British Government, but it is notorious that other Governments have not been so strict. . . .' The British documents thus make curious reading if compared with works based on Russian sources such as Brandt, *Stalin's Failure in China*, *passim*.

perhaps the most important analysis of the issue, one of the China experts, Basil C. Newton, speculated that Bolshevism in Asia would destroy itself as it had in most of Europe. Writing in June 1925, he surveyed the course of Bolshevism in Europe and predicted its fate in the Far East.

If we look back over five years we find a vast change in the influence of Bolshevism throughout Europe. For a period after the war the spectre of Bolshevism loomed large and threatened to cause greater ruin than the war itself. But once contact was established with the actualities of Bolshevism, its influence, which was based on discontent and vague suggestion, and on no constructive realities, began to wane, and Bolshevism was found to be its own best antidote. In Hungary and in Italy there was an overdose of inoculation, and the reaction has been correspondingly severe. . . .

   Turning to Asia we find in Turkey and Persia instructive examples of the growth and subsequent decline of Bolshevik influence. . . . Bolshevik doctrine, once properly understood, was revealed as being repugnant to the whole tradition and outlook of the country. The Soviet agents were soon treated as they deserved, and their creed definitely discredited. Bolshevism is even more repugnant to the thought and feeling of China, so much so that the Soviet agents dare not themselves reveal the full doctrine of Communism. But it is bound to come out, and the more its true inwardness and Dead Sea fruit can be made known the better.

Left to themselves in China, Newton went on, the Soviet agents would eventually compromise their own work. The Chinese themselves would see that 'the crazy mischief-makers of Moscow are not merely futile, but are positively ridiculous. Their end as a world force will then come of itself without any external attack.' By entering the field against the Bolsheviks, Britain would revitalize the force she sought to destroy. 'If we launch a general attack on Bolshevism we shall, in my judgement, be misjudging the real forces at work in China. . . . Mere force is more likely to aggravate than heal such a scourge, for which the true remedy . . . is to expose the treachery, criminal insanity and the sterility of Bolshevism, whenever and wherever we can.'[26] One might observe that this emotional language conveys a sense of frustration; with the constitutional and increasingly

---

[26] 'Memorandum by Mr. Newton', 25 June 1925 [F 3008/194/10]. Printed for the Cabinet, Most Secret, F.O. 371/10943.

democratic checks on the Foreign Office and other governmental branches, Britain could not match Soviet intervention either in trained agents or in aid, even had it been thought desirable. But Newton's remarks also illustrate the conviction held by most British officials in the mid-1920s: that China's revolution must occur without undue foreign intervention, and that the Chinese themselves would eventually turn against the Soviet agents.

Revolution or no revolution—and regardless of the extent of Russian intrigue—the Chinese sorely tried British patience whenever they disrupted foreign trade and commerce, not to mention when they endangered British lives and property. To understand the paramount problems posed to Great Britain by the revolution—and also to comprehend some of the major issues of the revolution itself—it is necessary to establish the chronological framework in which British policy developed. There are four critical dates in four crucial years. 1. 30 May 1925—the Shanghai incident—after which time an anti-British strike and boycott spread through southern China and Hong Kong. 2. 9 July 1926, at which time the Kuomintang launched its northern expedition and British officials began to reassess Chiang Kai-shek as a national leader. 3. The Nanking incident of 24 March 1927, when the British Consul and a military officer were wounded, two British subjects killed, and the Consulate, in the British Minister's phrase, treated like a pigsty. 4. The Kuomintang's seizure of Peking on 19 July 1928, marking the advent of the Nationalist Government and placing Britain's relations with China on a new footing.

The crux of the Shanghai incident, and of the Shakee-Shameen shooting in Canton in the following month, on 23 June 1925, can be stated simply as police reponse to mob demonstrations. In late May of that year Chinese students protested against the killing of a Chinese labourer in a Japanese cotton mill in the International Settlement. On the 30th the municipal police arrested three students for making inflammatory anti-Japanese speeches. A crowd then assembled at the Louza police station in Nanking road and began shouting 'Kill the foreigners'—meaning the five British policemen at the station. Inspector Edward W. Everson ordered the crowd to disperse. When they rushed the station, he gave the order to fire. Seven Chinese were killed instantly, and many others wounded. This incident became the subject of a lengthy and contentious investigation, but from the British point of view the major issue was clear from the beginning: the police acted in accordance with their mandate to maintain public order; they had not, according to Bolshevik propaganda, callously shot students carrying on a peaceful demonstration. In the words of the British Minister, 'the action of the police was fully justified by the events with which they had to deal. . . .' According to the Consul-General at Shanghai:

[F]ar from acting in a hasty or brutal manner, the police made every endeavour, first by persuasion and then by baton charges, to induce the threatening mob to disperse, and it was only when the small body of police at the station gate was about to be overwhelmed, and the station with its armoury captured, that a volley was fired.

The courage, patience and good temper of the handful of foreign constables, who for an hour tried to stem the infuriated crowd, and who were assaulted and even knocked down and yet refrained from using their fire-arms, were deserving of all praise.[27]

The British press depicted Everson as a hero in the best imperial tradition. In the widely quoted words of an eyewitness, the Inspector appeared in the guise of a 'Chinese' Gordon at Khartoum:

The situation became tense, and it seemed as though the mob would again enter the station. Banners and pennants filled the air. The students slapped their knees with open hands, struck their chests and arms, and worked themselves into a mechanical frenzy through psychological methods unknown to Westerners, but typical of the Indian dervish and the primitive American Indian medicine man. They shouted in thin, raucous tones their favourite slogan, forgetting meanwhile all else but . . . 'Kill, strike, down with him!' &c. It seemed like a mass drill of murder, for as they shouted they moved their hands in a wild rhythm, as though they were striking with a knife.

The police fell back to within a few yards of the gate. Then

[27] Palairet to Chamberlain, No. 396, 8 June 1925 [F 2685/194/10], F.O. 371/10943; Barton to Palairet, No. 104, 4 June 1925, enclosed in the above despatch. Accounts vary about the number killed and wounded. The principal documentary source is *Report of the International Commission of Judges Appointed to Inquire into the Causes of the Disturbance at Shanghai, May 30, 1925* (Shanghai, 1925). For a scholarly treatment, see especially Borg, *American Policy and the Chinese Revolution*, chapter II.

Inspector Everson, commanding at the half-closed gate, who saw the futility of batons and fists, but cool as the ex-naval man that he is, at last gave the order to shoot.

One can find countless examples of similar British restraint in Asia and Africa in the nineteenth century and first two decades of the twentieth. But they are beside the point. Bullets provided no answer to the wave of anti-British sentiment developing in southern China in the mid-1920s. However heroic the circumstances, the use of British force usually recoiled against British interests.

Only in the last resort, to protect lives, and, to a lesser extent, property, did British officials in China believe that force of arms should be employed. They clearly recognized that times had changed since the nineteenth century, when Britain's commercial empire in China was established by force and secured by the fleet. British diplomacy in the 1920s aimed to adjust Britain's relations with China in accordance with changing circumstances of the growth of Nationalism and the threat of Communism. Indiscriminate use of force played into the hands of the Bolshevik agents, who then had opportunity to denounce the brutality of British imperialism. If necessary, however, Britain would employ force to defend British nationals and their commercial interests. This was the message conveyed by the Consul-General in Canton to the Chinese authorities when he learned that student demonstrators would attempt to capture the Shameen concession in Canton in protest against the Shanghai incident. He warned the Chinese officials:

[I]n the course of a patriotic demonstration . . . the student element intend to make martyrs of themselves by attacking the bridges leading on to Shamien. . . . any attempt to penetrate on to the British concession on Shamien will be resisted by force of arms. . . .

I write in this serious strain so that it may not be said hereafter that brutal Imperialist rifles wantonly massacred unoffending Chinese youth.[28]

When the 'monster demonstration' occurred on 23 June, the Consul-General and Naval Commander proved firmness of intent to protect British integrity. In response to shots from the

[28] J. W. Jamieson to Chao Chu Wu (Chinese Department of Foreign Affairs), 23 June 1925, enclosed in Palairet to Chamberlain, No. 484, 11 July 1925 [F 4118/194/10], F.O. 371/10947.

Chinese side, the defence force of the British and French concessions opened fire, killing over fifty Chinese and probably wounding over twice that number. The Consul-General stated vehemently that the Chinese started it:

I can, from the evidence of my eyes, make a statement on oath that the firing was first started by the Chinese. As it was, the British senior naval officer and myself, who were standing unarmed by the bridge for the special purpose of guarding against any precipitate or nervous action on the part of the defenders, only escaped with our lives out of the hail of bullets which was directed at us. It was only then that, in self-defence, fire was opened from this side.[29]

The Consul-General and Naval Commander believed that the Russians were ultimately responsible for the slaughter. According to the naval officer: 'There is no doubt that the soldiers who started the firing belonged to that section of the Cantonese army trained by Russians.'[30] The Russians and their dupes, the Chinese Communists, thus incited Chinese hatred towards the British 'foreign devils'.

In the months following the Shanghai and Shameen shootings, an anti-British boycott quickly extended through southern China and Hong Kong. In Canton British trade stopped. In Hong Kong strikes paralysed the harbour and disrupted the entire city. According to a Hong Kong intelligence report:

The Hong Kong police received information on the 22nd June [1925] that ten of the leading strike agitators are Bolsheviks. Some of them have been to Russia this year, and it is reported that the Russians have given 600,000 dollars to the various labour unions in Hong Kong and Canton to go on strike. Eight of these are executive officers of the Chinese Seamen's Union. It is also reported that some

[29] J. W. Jamieson to Civil Governor, Canton, 24 June 1925, enclosed in Jamieson to Chamberlain, No. 5, 25 June 1925 [F 3473/194/10], F.O. 371/10946.

[30] M. Maxwell Scott, Commander, *H.M.S. Tarantula*, to Commodore, Hong Kong, 30 June 1925, enclosed in Admiralty to Foreign Office, 4 September 1925 [F 4367/194/10], F.O. 371/10948. In retrospect Sir John Brenan wrote that the incident was a triumph for the Bolsheviks. The nature of the student demonstration precluded any serious attempt to seize the concession, and its defenders, 'strung up to a pitch of anxiety by rumours of impending trouble' too hastily returned the volley from the Red agitators. 'The whole affair was disastrous, and not the least regrettable aspect was the disproportionate number of casualties among the Chinese demonstrators, the majority of whom could have had no thoughts beyond a somewhat provocative display of patriotism.' Memorandum by Brenan on the Kuomintang, 23 November 1926 [F 229/229/10], F.O. 371/12456.

members of the Dare-to-Die Society have been or will be sent down from Canton to set fire, throw bombs, &c.[31]

In the words of the Governor: 'The strike which has been organised in Hong Kong is entirely due to these Communist agitators in Canton.'[32] On the mainland the situation was even worse. Communists terrorized Chinese friendly to Britain. British prestige as well as trade suffered. For example, from Swatow, one of the principal ports, a correspondent of the *Morning Post* reported 'there is no end to the tale of indignity and insult' to Great Britain.

British activity in the port has been attacked by the Chinese with amazing ferocity. Trade ceased entirely . . . Chinese in the employ of British subjects, in whatsoever capacity, were forced to strike, British property was destroyed and residences, offices and clubs were burgled and looted. . . .

No reason has been given for this atrocious treatment except the vague cry of 'British Imperialism.' The game still goes on. . . . Both strike and boycott are pursued with unabated vigour and intensity. Loyal and friendly Chinese have been imprisoned, tortured and even murdered.

The continued strain has broken up nearly every British home in the place. All this is the work of agitators, Bolshevik-trained and taught in Moscow and Canton. These people have a 'Red' military Government behind them. They are the people with the guns and therefore have the power.

This scum on the surface of a great and kindly people is the only articulate element. The mass of decent, friendly Chinese have no voice, for woe unto any who, by word or action, show sympathy for the British. We who live out here are faced to-day with one of the most ghastly and tragic muddles in human history.[33]

With such reports appearing in the leading London newspapers, the Foreign Office somehow had to counter Bolshevik activity or face the possibility of hostile Parliamentary criticism.[34]

[31] Hong Kong Monthly Intelligence Summary No. 7, 1925, enclosed in the Admiralty despatch cited in the preceding footnote.

[32] Sir R. E. Stubbs to Amery, Confidential, 26 June 1925, enclosed in Colonial Office to Foreign Office, 5 August 1925 [F 3668/194/10], F.O. 371/10946.

[33] *Morning Post*, 18 January 1926.

[34] See for example *Parliamentary Debates*, 5th series, vol. 191, 10 February 1926, c. 1008–13. Most of the questions put to the Foreign Secretary in the House of Commons implied failure to defend Britain's commercial interests, but occasionally

Convinced that the Russians were at the heart of Britain's troubles in southern China, the Foreign Office in late January 1926 considered courses of action against them. There were five possibilities: force, blockade, assistance to anti-Bolshevik forces, pressure on Moscow, and conciliation.[35] All except the last proved too dangerous or difficult. When asked by the Foreign Office whether Canton ought to be given an ultimatum and the Russians expelled by force—'if necessary, by aerial bombardment'—the British Minister at Peking replied that war with Canton would imperil future trade relations and would cause 'a fresh outburst of anti-British feeling all over China.'[36] The Consul at Canton stated, 'As war would leave a legacy of hatred and might unite the rest of China, I deprecate it emphatically.'[37] Even the Governor of Hong Kong stopped short of recommending war: 'the time has gone by for warlike action to be undertaken . . . by Great Britain alone, except at the risk of jeopardising our future economic relations with China'.[38] The second option, blockade, was dismissed because it would be unworkable and because of international complications with the other treaty powers. The third possibility, giving aid to a powerful anti-Red leader, the Foreign Office ruled out by its own rhetorical question, 'where is he to be found?' The fourth, pressure on Moscow would probably be futile unless Britain threatened to break off relations with Russia, which, among other things, would probably merely advertise Britain's failure against the Bolsheviks in China. Moreover, there was no reason to believe that the Russians could be trusted in any case. Only the last course, conciliation, seemed

---

Labour M.P.s took the opposite tack. For example: 'Has it never dawned upon the Foreign Secretary that the troubles we are having in China are the result of the capitalists of this country going out to China to exploit the Chinese because of their cheap labour, and that the Chinese have now revolted against the conditions that we were imposing? . . . Is [the Foreign Secretary] prepared to go to war to force the Chinese to buy British goods?' (Mr. David Kirkwood, Labour). The questions were ruled out of order because they were 'argumentative'.

[35] Tyrrell to Macleay, No. 35 tel., 29 January 1926 [F 375/1/10] (drafted after extensive minutes and correspondence with M.P.s and C.O.), F.O. 371/11620.

[36] Macleay to Chamberlain, No. 39 tel., 30 January 1926, in annex XVIII of 'Memorandum respecting Canton' by Ashton-Gwatkin, Secret, 3 February 1926 [F 513/1/10] F.O. 371/11621. Circulated to the Cabinet.

[37] Jamieson to Chamberlain, No. 5 tel., 2 February 1926, in annex XVIII, ibid.

[38] Governor of Hong Kong to Secretary of State for Colonies, tel., 6 February 1926, annex XIX, ibid.

both practicable and constructive. The Minister at Peking summarized the over-arching reason:

This policy of patient conciliation has borne abundant fruit in restoration to a great extent of friendship and goodwill between British and Chinese and resumption of normal commercial relations throughout China except in a few areas, such as, notably province of Kuangtung [Canton] which are controlled by external influences violently and openly hostile to Great Britain.[39]

In another telegram he explained the practical rationale for a policy of conciliation: 'our wisest course is to hold our hand and to see it patiently through in the hope that impending events in China will lead to a weakening of Bolshevik influence in Canton and to the ascendancy there of a more moderate party.'[40]

There were in fact precious few indications that the Kuomintang would purge itself of extremists. When Chiang Kai-shek began his drive to the north in the summer of 1926, the Communist stranglehold seemed as strong as ever. The only ray of hope came from reports that Chiang himself was not a Communist at heart. But the British did not know what to make of him: to some observers he appeared to be an utterly unscrupulous opportunist, while others depicted him as that *rara avis* of Chinese politics, a man of principle and character. Though not a Russian stooge, Chiang apparently could not control the rabble or fanatics in his army. Consequently, as the Kuomintang marched northwards, the British faced potential encounters with the Nationalist troops similar to the confrontations at Shanghai and Shameen. A handful of agitators could provoke defence forces at British concessions and settlements to fire on otherwise peaceful demonstrators. British lives and property had to be protected; but if Britain found herself at war with Nationalist forces, she might be playing the game of the Bolsheviks.

The first test of the dilemma of force versus appeasement came on 3 January 1927 at Hankow. John Bull escaped from a dangerous situation by the skin of his teeth. When a mob, under the influence of the left wing of the Kuomintang, attempted to break into the British concession, British marines kept it at bay without firing. The marines were pelted with bricks and stones,

---

[39] Macleay to Chamberlain, No. 42 tel., 1 February 1926, annex XVIII, ibid.
[40] Macleay to Chamberlain, No. 39 tel., 30 January 1926, annex XVIII, ibid.

and, in the opinion of the British Cabinet, had every justification for the use of their weapons. When the riot continued on
the 4th and 5th, Nationalist troops proved incapable of maintaining order. The crowd could not be held back indefinitely
except by firing. By order of the Consul and the Senior Naval
Officer, the marines withdrew. The local British authorities
abandoned the concession. The Minister at Peking angrily
informed London that Britain's position in China had been
undermined.[41] The Cabinet met to consider what could be
done about this humiliating situation. The more they thought,
the more they believed that a calamity had been avoided.
According to the Foreign Secretary, Sir Austen Chamberlain:

At first the withdrawal of the naval forces from the Hankow
Concessions had given the impression of a grave blunder. Later
communications, however . . . indicated that the action of the Rear-
Admiral and the Consul had averted a great disaster. The mob at
Hankow (probably incited by the Nationalists) had been so violent
as to be controllable only by the use of firearms. But the military
forces of the South China Nationalist Government were at hand, and
it was probable that, if fire had been opened they would have joined
the mob, with incalculable consequences.[42]

British subjects had been saved from a massacre and were
permitted by the Nationalists to resume control of the concession a few days later. Responsibility to protect life and property now rested with the Kuomintang. Hankow thus became
the test case of the Chinese responsible government under the
Nationalists.[43] That was the positive side of the incident.
Negatively, it warned the British that similar situations might
develop at places such as Shanghai, where Britain would have
no choice but to fight. According to a highly secret report by
the Chiefs of Staff on 11 January 1927:

In the last few months the situation has very much deteriorated. . . .
The Nationalist Government, working to a considerable extent under
Bolshevist influence, has obtained control of the greater part of
China south of the Yangtse. . . .
    We recognise that the magnitude of our interests at Shanghai and
the reaction of a disaster there on our interests and prestige in other

---

[41] For summary, see 'Weekly Summary of Events in China', by F. Gwatkin,
7 January 1927 [F 1085/27/10], F.O. 371/12419.
[42] Cabinet Minutes, Secret, 12 January 1927, CAB. 23/54.
[43] Discussed below in detail, chapter V.

parts of China and of the whole East may be such as to compel us to an active defence. We admit the possibility also that by showing a bold front at Shanghai we may stop the rot. But we feel bound to point out that our attitude may lead to a war, the consequences and magnitude of which cannot be foreseen.[44]

To protect British lives and interests, 12,000 troops were despatched to China. When asked how the Kuomintang would respond to the British re-enforcement of the Shanghai and other settlements, Chiang Kai-shek replied: 'The attitude adopted by Great Britain towards China up to the present is exactly as if she were dealing with her own Colonies, and proves that she does not understand China.' Perhaps to clarify his warning, he added that full-scale British intervention might jeopardize the success of the revolution;[45] it might tip the balance in favour of the world revolutionaries rather than the moderate nationalists.

The decisive series of events began on the morning of Thursday 24 March 1927, in China's historic southern capital, Nanking. About 9 a.m. Nationalist troops began to sack the city. The soldiery, running amok, pillaged the British, American, and Japanese consulates. They killed three British subjects and wounded the Consul General. They even desecrated English womanhood. As the Foreign Secretary, Sir Austen Chamberlain, later explained to an indignant House of Commons: 'Foreign women, including Mrs. Giles, the wife of His Majesty's consul-general, were thoroughly searched and rudely stripped of valuables. Many had their clothes torn off them, and two American women were saved from violation.'[46] The American

---

[44] 'Situation in China, January 1927', Report by the Chiefs of Staff, C.O.S. 59, 11 January 1927, CAB. 24/184. Though labelled only 'Secret', the Secretary of the Cabinet requested that all copies be returned to the Cabinet Office because of its especial sensitivity.

[45] Copy of interview enclosed in Tilley to Chamberlain, No. 88, 14 February 1927 [F 2664/2/10], F.O. 371/12403.

[46] *Parliamentary Debates*, 5th series, vol. 204, 6 April 1927, c. 2144. For an important analysis of foreign reaction in Shanghai and other places to the Nationalist take-over, see that classic of classics on the revolution by Harold R. Isaacs, *The Tragedy of the Chinese Revolution* (New York, 1966, second revised edition), pp. 148–50. The dominant British attitude appears to have been '*Irritated*: "The first thought that comes to one is the bother of it. To have one's home turned upside down, to have to hastily lump a few belongings into a trunk or two and a suitcase and leave the rest behind to be looted or whatnot, is an unadulterated bother"' (p. 148).

community, treated almost as violently as the British, was able
to signal the American and British men-of-war in the Yangtze.
At 3.45 p.m. His Majesty's Ship *Emerald* and two American
destroyers bombarded the city. The ravage ceased immediately
and a landing party evacuated the British consular group the
next day. 'I have not the slightest doubt,' the Foreign Secretary
stated, 'that the timely communication with the warships and
their timely action alone saved the lives of citizens of British and
American nationality.'[47] In this instance no one disagreed that
British force of arms had been properly employed. The question
was whether Britain should retaliate for the Nanking and
Hankow outrages. The members of the Cabinet gave sustained
attention to the matter.[48] They reached no conclusion. A
memorandum by Winston Churchill (then Chancellor of the
Exchequer) explains part of the reason. Writing a month after
the Nanking incident, he grumbled: 'To fire off Naval
cannon at obsolete Chinese forts, or worthless Chinese arsenals
or ludicrous Chinese warships cannot lead to any lasting
advantage.' He caught the mood of the British Cabinet,
Government, and public when he stated in angry frustration,
'Punishing China is like flogging a jellyfish.'[49]

The British did not act, partly because no effective action
could be taken, partly out of fear that full-scale intervention
might precipitate another Boxer uprising. Moderate inaction
saved the day. To British eyes the Nanking incident ruptured
the Kuomintang. Chiang Kai-shek ruthlessly purged the
Communists. According to Sir Austen Chamberlain, speaking
in the House of Commons:

The Nanking affair had precipitated a long impending split within
the Nationalist ranks. The looting of foreign property at Nanking
and the shooting of foreigners were the culmination of a continued
policy of agitation, rapine, terrorism and murder; the tools of this
policy were the unpaid soldiery of the Nationalist armies and the

[47] *Parliamentary Debates*, 5th series, vol. 204, 28 March 1927, c. 850–52. There is a
poignant account by the British Consul, Bertram Giles, 'Nanking Outrages', 9
April 1927 [F 4899/1530/10], F.O. 371/12481, in which he stated: 'My chief dread
was that the soldiers would kill the men first, after which the women would undoubtedly have been raped.' Cf. the vivid account by Borg, *American Policy and the
Chinese Revolution*, chapter XIV.
[48] See Cabinet minutes in CAB. 23/54.
[49] Memorandum by Churchill, 'Sanctions', Confidential, C.P. 133 (27), 25
April 1927, CAB. 24/186.

mobs of the great cities, but its organisation and driving force were borrowed, directly or indirectly, from the Third International.

He explained how British restraint had foiled Russian intrigue and conspiracy.

This [Communist] policy had failed to create an anti-British incident at Hankow in January. It had been unable to seize Shanghai owing to the protective presence of the Defence Force. By March it was becoming directed against the Nationalist generalissimo, Chiang Kai-shek, of whose power the Communists were jealous. The organised side of the Nanking outrages appears to have been an attempt to embroil Chiang Kai-shek with the foreign powers.

Chiang Kai-shek overnight had become the saviour of Britain in China. 'The real offenders—the Chinese agitators—have been punished by the Chinese Nationalists themselves with an effectiveness of which no foreign Power was capable.' Retribution at last, Chamberlain stated.

The outrages at Naking have already reacted in China in a dramatic and, to their authors, an unwelcome manner. . . . Nanking . . . has split the Communist wing from the Kuo Min-tang party, and—most important of all—it has deeply discredited the Communists and their foreign advisers in the eyes of all China.[50]

Not all Members of Parliament shared Chamberlain's jubilation. One M.P. immediately attacked his speech as 'flamboyant and melodramatic.' Others demanded action. In a confidential interview with the Parliamentary 'China Committee', this exchange took place:

Sir Robert Waley Cohen complained of the 'tolerant and supine action' of His Majesty's Government.

The Secretary of State asked whether the despatch of 12,000 troops was a supine action? He was sure that violence advocated by Sir Robert was not the basis for future relations. Maybe we are now suffering from the past.

Sir Robert replied that the propertied section in China would be pleased by vigorous action.[51]

[50] *Parliamentary Debates*, 5th series, vol. 206, 9 May 1927, c. 19–23.
[51] Foreign Office Memorandum, 31 May 1927, C.P. 13304. According to this memorandum, written only five days after Britain's severance of diplomatic relations with the Soviet Union, Chamberlain was reported to have drawn a curious parallel between the attitude of the 'propertied class' in Russia during the civil war and the disposition of the Chinese bourgeoisie. His conclusion about the

Chamberlain's antagonist had at least a minor point. Despite the purging of the Communists and the emergence of Chiang as the champion of the bourgeoisie, firms such as the British Cigarette Company in Hankow remained closed. Whatever the justification for the Foreign Office's policy of restraint, no one could deny that the Russians had injured British trade. In the words of a report from Peking: 'The Soviets have caused direct and indirect financial losses to foreign capitalism, in particular to Great Britain, the chief victim of their attacks. No estimate need be made here of the losses. Suffice it that they are certainly enormous.'[52]

After the expulsion of the Russians in the summer of 1927, anti-foreign agitation subsided. China in a sense returned to her normal muddle. The dominant theme of British despatches ran: 'Chaos reigns on all sides.'[53] The British Government sympathized. Whatever wrongs done to British trade, the consequences for the Chinese themselves were infinitely greater. 'It is China and the Chinese which are the first and greatest victims of the anarchy which prevails,' Chamberlain said in a public speech. His orations are good representations of British interpretations of the confused military and political situation in China. For example:

China is accustomed to armies. There are I know not how many generals at this moment in China, I know not how many armies, for no sooner do they unite than they break up and reform in different groups. But the armies to which China is accustomed are armies which are a terror to the peaceful population, whose passage is marked by ruin, looting and outrage.[54]

purpose of British policy is also bizarre. 'No doubt there were in China, as there had been in Russia, many inhabitants of the country anxious that we should intervene to protect their property, but that was not our business. His Majesty's Government tried to keep their eyes on the long future.'

[52] Memorandum by W. R. Connor Green, 10 June 1927, enclosed in Lampson to Chamberlain, No. 629, 17 June 1927 [F 6820/3241/10], F.O. 371/12501.

[53] See for example Lampson to Chamberlain, No. 1076, 1 October 1927 [F 8922/959/10], F.O. 371/12470.

[54] Chamberlain went on to praise the fairness and discipline of the British garrisons who, in good public-school spirit, carried on the midst of turmoil by playing football: 'The small British force was a disciplined force such as they [the Chinese] had never seen, was a friendly force with no object but to preserve the peace and defend the settlements. It paid for everything it took. It played football and did other human things such as our soldiers are accustomed to do even when they are on active service if they get the opportunity.' *Birmingham Post*, 20 January

In the north, British observers watched the ebbs and flows of the fortune of Chang Tso-lin, whose raid on the Soviet Embassy in Peking in April 1927 helped to precipitate the uprising against the Communists by the capture of documentary evidence that revealed the extent of their conspiracy. In the south, the Communists entrenched at Hankow denounced Chiang Kai-shek as a militarist, counter-revolutionary and traitor to the Kuomintang. Chiang continued to exterminate the Communists and to reaffirm 'true Kuomintang principles'. His momentary resignation in August 1927 further confused the situation. It seemed to be a matter of which Kuomintang faction could eliminate the other, and, even should the right wing triumph, anyone could bet with equal odds that it would degenerate into a tuchun regime in the south or would develop as a national movement. One thing was clear—the Russian plot had failed, at least temporarily. The British Minister reported in August:

As I read the situation, this reaction against the Russians and their dupes, the so-called Chinese Communists, represents a genuine revulsion of feeling amongst the Chinese, and especially, so far as the leaders are concerned, amongst the military chiefs, who must have been perfectly aware that labour agitation and mob rule were incompatible with the maintenance of their position. The Russians overreached themselves, and the tide has, for the moment, set in against them.[55]

With a mixture of fascination, relief, and even a little admiration and sympathy, British observers watched the movements of Borodin, who, broken in spirit and health, returned to Russia in late July.[56] British China hands cheered the battle cry of the moderate Nationalists, 'Nationalism purged of Communism and Russians'. Englishmen in China believed, on the whole, that they witnessed not merely another civil war, but a revo-

---

1928. Chamberlain probably did not mean to imply that British soldiers preferred fornicating to fighting, not to mention footballing. See Richard H. Ullman, *Britain and the Russian Civil War: November 1918–February 1920* (Princeton, 1968), footnote addendum inadvertently omitted from the text of chapter one.

[55] Lampson to Chamberlain, No. 904, 22 August 1927 [F 8096/959/10], F.O. 371/12470.

[56] Understandably enough, Borodin on his way back to Russia remarked: 'When the next Chinese general comes to Moscow and shouts: "Hail to the World Revolution!" better send for the G.P.U. .... all that any of them wants is rifles.' Isaacs, *Tragedy*, p. 275.

lution—a revolution Chinese style. As one official wrote after the Nanking incident in a summary remark that holds true generally for British judgement of events in China in 1927: 'It is a strange and incalculable mixture of revolution, Bolshevism, youthful idealism and crime.'[57]

In finally evaluating the salient themes of China's history from the time of Borodin's arrival in 1923 to that of his expulsion in 1927 and the takeover of Peking by the Nationalists in the following year, there are two major British interpretations, one explaining the Russian failure, the other accounting for the Nationalists' success. Ultimately they both boil down to the question of the Chinese national character, which both pleased and exasperated Russians and Englishmen alike. The complexity of this idea is perhaps best expressed by two key words, 'lovable' yet 'arrogant.' The first word conveys optimism and faith in the positive features of the Chinese character. Sir James Jamieson, the Consul at Canton, once expatiated on the sterling qualities of the Chinese in connection with the Russian question:

They had turned to the Russians, not out of love for the Russians, but because the Russians were the only people who had, however bad their motive, treated them as friends. The Chinese had no respect for the Russians, and they had very great respect for us, and would be our friends if we took the right steps. There was no greater or more lovable race than the Chinese, and they and ourselves could work together, and old relations could be re-established, if the right policy were now adopted.[58]

The consensus of British opinion held that the 'right policy' consisted of a policy of non-intervention, a course of action that reflected the hope that somehow or other the Chinese would be able to sort things out themselves. Though willing to admit that the Russians hastened the 'tempo' of the revolution, British observers believed that external interference would probably backfire. The Foreign Office lamented the disruption of trade and the jeopardy of British subjects, but persistently held that the Bolsheviks would fail because the doctrines of Communism were alien to Chinese culture. Except for a brief Red scare

[57] Teichman to Lampson, No. 33, 7 April 1927, enclosed in Teichman to Chamberlain, received 24 May [F 4906/1530/10], F.O. 371/12481.

[58] 'Notes on a Discussion on China between Sir E. Wilton and Sir J. Jamieson', 28 June 1926, enclosed in Lampson to Chamberlain, No. 935, 31 December 1926 [F 1330/2/10], F.O. 371/12401.

following the seizure of the Soviet documents in Peking in April 1927, the pattern of British thought remained the same as at the time of the Paris and Washington Conferences. As the financier, Sir Charles Addis, expressed the basic idea in 1925:

If by Bolshevism is meant Communism and anarchy, then I have no fear of the Soviet propaganda ultimately being successful. I cannot imagine any soil less favourable in which to plant the seeds of these pernicious doctrines than China, the distinguishing characteristic of her industrious population being a high degree of innate respect for law and a determined resolution to hold on to what they have.[59]

There was also a negative aspect. The Russians failed, in the British view, not only because of the unsuitability of doctrines of Communism, but also, again, because of the other side of the Chinese national character. According to the Military Attaché in Peking:

That the national army should now in 1927 have reverted to a con-glomeration of units loyal only to their immediate commanders, and have slipped back into pre-Soviet ways, can only be laid to the charge of the Chinese character; since once the army was too big to be leavened by the small numbers of Soviet advisers, the innate venal-ity and rapacity of the Chinese militarist could not be checked.[60]

In short, Borodin and Galen were the victims of double-crossing, fanatical Chinese militarism. They got their deserts, but they also built a powerful Chinese army. 'The advance from Canton into Shantung of this army of poor material is a great achieve-ment, for which Borodin and Gallen [sic] should take the credit.'[61]

Only Russian training could explain the Nationalist army's triumphal entry into Peking in June 1928. But this was far from the total explanation. In the end the success of the Nationalist movement had to be attributed not only to Russian organi-zation but also to the political make-up of the Kuomintang. In attempting to explain this complex phenomenon, British analysts described it as essentially a bourgeois organization whose influence extended *throughout* China. As a correspondent

[59] 'Speech by Sir Charles Addis at a Banquet given to the Council of Consortium for China, by Mr. T. W. Lamont at the Metropolitan Club, New York, on October 19, 1925', enclosed in China Consortium to Foreign Office, 2 November 1925 [F 5323/190/10], F.O. 371/10941.

[60] Steward to Lampson, 20 August 1927, enclosed in Lampson to Chamberlain, No. 896, 22 August 1927 [F 8094/87/10], F.O. 371/12440.

[61] Ibid.

for the *Manchester Guardian* put it in May 1927, 'the Kuo Min-
tang influence is almost as strong in the North as in the South,
and is the one *force* to be reckoned with throughout China.'[62]
When Chiang successfully broke with the Communists, the
reasons, according to a knowledgeable British official, 'can be
summed up in the words "revolt of the *bourgeoisie*".'[63] To
Chiang belonged the credit of crushing the Communists, but
the methods he used scarcely differed from the terrorism of the
Cheka. Nor did the British approve of the tactics of the
Nationalist army. In evaluating the reasons for its successful
advances, the British Minister wrote that the victories of the
southern armies over their northern opponents were as much
due to bribery, extortion, and other typical forms of Chinese
corruption as to any real military superiority.[64] There lay the
nub of the problem. Ultimately, in British eyes, the Chinese
possessed certain faults of character that offset their more
favourable characteristics. Their *naïveté* made them fail to see
that a ruthless minority could rule in China as in Russia. Their
corruption did not augur well for stable and responsible
government, and their xenophobia threatened to retard
economic contact with the west. British opinion divided over
the question whether the Chinese fundamentally were lovable
or arrogant, but on the whole the judgement tended to be more
negative than positive. Probably most British observers of
China in the 1920s would have agreed with this statement made
by the British Minister in 1924. There was, he wrote,

conceit, venality and lack of real patriotic spirit of China's governing
classes. . . . it is a distressing fact that the governing classes in China,
since the Revolution of 1911, have shown themselves incapable of
producing men with sufficient pride of race, honesty and patriotism.[65]

In other words, the Chinese lacked the cardinal virtues of the
English race.

[62] 'Record of Conversation between Mr. Mounsey and Mr. Ransome, of the
"Manchester Guardian"', 2 March 1927, C.P. 13304.
[63] 'Memorandum on Communism in China', by A. D. Blackburn, 5 August
1927, enclosed in Lampson to Chamberlain, No. 933 Secret, 26 August 1927,
[F 8515/28/10], F.O. 371/12422.
[64] See for example Lampson to Chamberlain, No. 904, 22 August 1927 [F 8096/
959/10], F.O. 371/12470.
[65] Macleay to MacDonald, No. 220, Confidential, 15 April 1924 [F 1914/237/
10], F.O. 371/10274.

V

THE UNEQUAL TREATIES

THE British responded to the challenge of Communism with two fundamental and conflicting evaluations of the situation in China. The first calculation was that a successful Nationalist movement, with foreign assistance, might be able to provide stable government with sound finances that would thwart Bolshevism. The second view held that official corruption would frustrate the western powers as well as the Bolsheviks. Public depravity rendered the situation almost hopeless and left China, in the phrase of the principal authority, Sir Victor Wellesley, stewing in her own juice. In Britain the latter view, on the whole, predominated until the triumph of the Kuomintang in 1928; thereafter, until the Manchurian crisis of 1931, moderate optimism prevailed. Throughout this era Britain proceeded on the assumption that China might be convinced of English goodwill by revision of the unequal treaties, thereby restoring sovereign rights and tariff autonomy. No one denied the enormity or complexity of readjusting Britain's political and economic relations with China, which interacted with the imperialisms of all foreign powers in Asia. One thing at least was clear in British eyes: if Britain could not end the age of exploitation symbolized and sustained by the treaty system, no power could. Britain had no territorial or 'imperialistic' aims in China, merely the desire for Free Trade, an idea entirely compatible with that of a united and prosperous China. With a sense of moral superiority, and at the same time with a sense of despair at the deficiencies in the Chinese national character, the British attempted to lead the Chinese into the twentieth century. Militarily powerless to coerce China, Britain attempted to achieve through diplomacy the reforms necessary to preserve British influence and prestige, to counter Bolshevism, and to prevent a split between the white and yellow races. The British drew their strength in this monumental endeavour from the founts of English morality. 'Once we fall from our traditional standard of fair play and straight dealing.' Wellesley wrote, 'then we are lost.'[1]

As in the case of the Bolshevik agents, the problem of reform raised the issue of the extent to which Britain could successfully intervene. So far as countering Communist activities was concerned, it was easier not to act than to imitate the Russians' game. With the unequal treaties, however, Britain and the powers in Asia were compelled to take reformist action, if for no reason other than that Soviet Russia had renounced the diplomatic instruments of the Czarist regime, including extraterritoriality, and could claim with considerable force to treat China as an equal. The western powers and Japan, furthermore, had bound themselves at the Washington Conference to deal with the question of China's finances. Britain and the United States, with charity and commiseration, would help China to find her salvation along western lines. By abolishing or at least modifying the treaty system, the British and the Americans would prove that they, not the Russians, were the true friends of China. More sarcastically, in Wellesley's words, 'At the Washington Conference the Powers tumbled over each other in their anxiety to bestow undeserved benefits on China, and one of the most pernicious results of their labours was the China Customs Tariff, which promises China a $2\frac{1}{2}$ per cent increase of the tariff.'[2] In short, at Washington the great powers had agreed to act in concert with the Chinese Government to work towards tariff autonomy. After delays caused by the ratification of the Washington treaties, the Chinese accordingly issued invitations for a Special Tariff Conference to convene in Peking in October 1925. In preparation for that Conference the British reviewed their China policy and calculated the extent to which Britain should, or indeed could, free China from the shackles of the treaty system.

The main participants in the China policy debate of the

---

[1] Memorandum by Wellesley, 20 August 1926 [F 3456/8/10], F.O. 371/11653. In addition to the books by Borg and Iriye cited in chapter IV, note 1, the most useful work on the subject of this chapter is by Wesley R. Fishel, *The End of Extraterritoriality in China* (Berkeley, 1962). For a contemporary analysis, see G. W. Keeton, *The Development of Extraterritoriality in China* (London, 1928).

[2] Wellesley, 'Memorandum on British Policy in China', 1 March 1925 [F 952/190/10], F.O. 371/10937. The Chinese Customs Treaty is printed in *Cmd. 1627* of 1922, pp. 47–52, along with the resolution respecting extraterritoriality, pp. 53–4.

mid-1920s were Sir Victor Wellesley and another member of the Far Eastern Department, S. P. Waterlow. Wellesley, who prided himself as a realist, drove into British policy a hard line emphasizing the necessity for the Chinese to help themselves and put their own house in order before effective international action could be taken. Waterlow, more optimistic about the Chinese than Wellesley, believed in a forward course of action. Their attitudes did not entirely diverge: both regarded the internal situation of China as so tumultuous that the western powers might be paralysed, however benevolent their intent.

Wellesley's pessimism derived from his analysis of power politics in the Far East as well as from his study of the internal situation in China. Whereas Britain desired the Open Door and a unified China, 'Japan, for very intelligible reasons, does not want a strong and united China.' Whereas Britain wanted to co-operate with the United States, the Americans, who were jealous of British influence in the Far East, also failed to understand the true nature of the financial problem in China. He chose the ideas of Senator Oscar W. Underwood to illustrate his point about American misconception:

The avowed object of the Washington Conference was to place the Chinese Government in funds, because, as Senator Underwood expressed it at the time, 'a Government without funds cannot govern.' In the abstract this is, of course, true of all Governments, but he apparently failed to see that it does not follow that, because a Government is in funds, it will necessarily govern. In fact, in China, in the present state of affairs, it is more likely to lead to the negation of government. . . .

[U]ntil all the leakages are stopped, which implies a comprehensive reorganisation of China's financial and fiscal system, to place the Chinese Government in funds is like pouring water into a bottomless tank.[3]

To restore the credit of the Chinese Government, Wellesley concluded, would be merely 'to wipe the slate clean for them

[3] Ibid. For China's foreign finances, Charles F. Remer, *Foreign Investments in China* (New York, 1933); and, by the same author, *A Study of Chinese Boycotts* (Baltimore, 1935). For more specific British information, generally though not always in line with Remer, see E. M. Gull, *British Economic Interests in the Far East* (London, 1943). See also G. E. Hubbard, *Eastern Industrialization and its Effect on the West, With special reference to Great Britain and Japan* (London, 1935); and Albert Edward Hindmarsh, *The Basis of Japanese Foreign Policy* (Cambridge, Mass. 1936).

to indulge in a fresh orgy of loans and to encourage them in their "rake's progress".' The solution to the problem of China's economy was infinitely more complex than mere funding. How could Britain subsidize a warlord faction at Peking without antagonizing other warlords, or for that matter the Nationalist movement in the south, where British interests were substantially greater? He gave this answer: 'We must draw a sharp distinction between "putting China's financial and fiscal system in order," which of course involves a comprehensive scheme, and putting the Central *Government's* finances in order, ... which in practice revolves itself into a debt-funding operation.'[4]

Only a comprehensive plan dealing with the whole of China might cure the ills of the economy. The mere thought apparently made Wellesley's mind boggle. Nevertheless the British did produce a far-reaching scheme. The 'Teichman Plan', named after its author, Chinese Secretary to the Legation in Peking, contained these major elements:

1. To free trade in all goods, Chinese or foreign, from all forms of vexatious and uncertain internal taxation.
2. To consolidate the foreign and domestic debts.
3. To provide both Central and Provincial Governments with reasonably adequate revenues.
4. To make the scheme attractive not only to the Central Government, but to the Tuchuns.
5. To provide adequate guarantees for effectiveness.[5]

Though praising the plan as 'a masterly piece of work ... [that] reflects the greatest credit on Mr. Teichman's abilities', Wellesley thought it entirely impracticable.

There are so many imponderable factors in the situation, psychological as well as financial and political, that it is impossible to say

[4] Wellesley, ibid.

[5] As analysed by Wellesley, ibid; Teichman's memorandum attached. Teichman was the expert in Peking whose grasp over the intricacies of Chinese politics contributed greatly to the continuity of British policy. After the negotiation of the Extraterritoriality Treaty of 1931, the Minister appropriately commented on Teichman's work: 'It is no exaggeration to say that without his ingenuity, his unfailing patience and his unflagging energy and resource we should never have achieved the results that we have done.' (Lampson to Henderson, No. 806, 8 June 1931 [F 4057/34/10], F.O. 371/15462; *D.B.F.P.*, Second Series (all references to *D.B.F.P.* in this chapter are to the Second Series), No. 460. See Sir Eric Teichman, *Affairs of China* (London, 1938).

anything positive except that the difficulties in the way of its acceptance and application are legion. . . . In any case I cannot bring myself to believe that the centuries-old fabric of Chinese 'squeeze' and corruption is, like the wall of Jericho, going to fall before the blast of Mr. Teichman's trumpet.[6]

In Wellesley's judgement the only way in which the corrupt Chinese finances could be reformed would be by foreign control, which meant, in effect, foreign rule. Foreign rule in turn meant domination by force.

The truth is that, in all probability, nothing short of complete foreign control, by which I mean foreign Government control, of China's financial and fiscal system would bring about the rehabilitation, in the true sense of that word, of that unhappy country. That, of course, implies control of the sources of revenue, which in turn presupposes a unified China. To control the sources of revenue ultimately rests on force. Such a policy is intervention pure and simple, and to be successful depends essentially on the sympathy and goodwill of the people. It is only necessary to mention these implications in order to rule out at once the possibility of any such idea coming within bounds of practical politics,[7]

He reluctantly concluded that 'a policy of inaction' was the only wise course open to Britain. 'From whatever angle I approach the problem I always come back to the conclusion that the really right policy is to let China work out her own salvation, at any rate, up to a point.' Any discussion of China's rehabilitation would only stir up an international hornet's nest because of the divergent and conflicting aims of the great powers in Asia. The issues at stake, for both Chinese and foreigners, were so great that no agreement could be reached, and the China situation would become worse than ever.[8]

The other trend in British official thought at this time held that the Special Tariff Conference would provide an opportunity not merely to solve the problems of China but also to advance the industrial position of Great Britain. According to Wellesley's colleague, S. P. Waterlow:

In the whole range of international politics there is no problem of which a settlement would be of greater or more rapid material

[6] Wellesley, 'Memorandum on British Policy in China', 1 March 1925 [F 952/190/10], F.O. 371/10937.
[7] Ibid.   [8] Ibid.

benefit to this country. We are dealing with a quarter of mankind, not rivals in industry but producers of raw material. By incredible toil the Chinese contrive to make good the ravages of civil war and bandit raids, to meet every kind of exaction for the upkeep of useless armaments and hordes of armed coolies, and yet to have something over to exchange for our manufactures.[9]

He went on to speculate more specifically how the Chinese could benefit the British economy:

Imagine the consequences if the surplus wealth produced by these docile and industrious millions were to become available for exchange in the markets of the world, instead of being squandered in the aimless strife of self-seeking individuals. Iron and steel, railway material and ships, piece goods and hardware—China would want them all in vastly increased quantities. And the expansion of demand would be quick.

It is not a question of the slow development of an uncivilised country with no commercial equipment or traditions. For twenty-five years the natural instinct of the Chinese for trade and industry has been thwarted by circumstances, and to give them some measure of stable government would mean a sudden bound forward, an increase of exports and an improvement of credit, which would react immediately upon our own unemployment problem. It would be like the bursting of a dam. There is no region of the world except China where we can reasonably hope for that large and rapid expansion of the foreign market that our industries urgently require to-day.[10]

In all the evaluations, by whichever British official, the theme of the Chinese national psychology intertwined with those of politics and economics. Again to use Waterlow's ideas as an example:

We are not dealing with Russia or Mexico. We are dealing with a people essentially reasonable, but constitutionally averse from taking the initiative. Their peaceful, industrious character, their capacity for business, their anxiety to do business with us, all this makes them singularly responsible to a lead, provided it is at once strong and sympathetic. But it must be a strong lead; there can be no satisfactory result unless the Chinaman is convinced that the foreigner is determined and that he has force somewhere in the background which, at the worst, will be used.[11]

[9] S. P. Waterlow, 'Memorandum respecting the Problem of China', 13 May 1925 [F 1723/190/10], F.O. 371/10937.
 [10] Ibid.   [11] Ibid.

Here Britain held the advantage over the other powers. 'Personality, especially British personality, counts enormously in China.' Prestige carries with it responsibility. Britain, in Waterlow's mind, not only had a magnificent opportunity but also a moral obligation to 'rehabilitate' the Chinese. 'We can no longer shut our eyes and repeat the incantation that "China must work out her own salvation".' Specifically, Britain should seize the opportunity of the Tariff Conference to tackle the problem of China's economy as a whole, and should adopt the existing customs machinery to promote the unification of China along federal lines. Unless this were done, and unless the other powers were blocked in their efforts to earmark increased revenues to satisfy their own financial appetites, East would become permanently alienated from West. Waterlow thus argued vigorously against Wellesley's policy of 'inaction'.

We should go into the Tariff Conference prepared to offer to China a large scheme of reconstruction on the lines indicated—namely, the introduction of a financial system sufficiently elastic not to be thrown out of gear by whatever relation between the central Government and the provinces may eventually be evolved, and including machinery for payment to the provinces by results.[12]

Whichever attitude one took, either Wellesley's or Waterlow's, it was clear that the China situation was desperate. On the eve of the Special Tariff Conference the mood of the British China community wavered between feelings of futility and hope. The Conference loomed as Britain's remaining chance to save China in concert with both the Chinese and the Washington powers. At a luncheon given by the China Association in honour of the departing British Delegates, the Foreign Secretary, Sir Austen Chamberlain, reminded his audience of the grave challenge ahead in the East. He spoke *in memoriam* of Sir John Jordan, whose recent death cast a pall over the meeting but whose lifelong work in China for over fifty years provided inspiration for the future. Chamberlain recapitulated the history of Britain's relations with China. He recalled Napoleon's gibe, that England was a nation of shopkeepers. In China that was true, for all that Britain desired was trade.

[12] Ibid. The train of thought is also interesting because it illustrates the tendency of British officials to conceive of the evolution of China's government along federal rather than centralized lines.

I wish that I could persuade some Chinaman of historical knowledge, of statesmanship, and of authority with his own people to explain that all this system of the unequal treaties was not of our choosing. We did not desire it; it was the minimum that we could ask of a China that repelled the foreigner, that would not give him justice in his own courts, or secure for him the ordinary advantages of civilised and orderly government. (Cheers.)

It was largely British policy which opened China through that and subsequent treaties to international trade, and it was first and foremost British enterprise which showed the way to other nations, and proved to them how great a market was open now to them and us and the Chinese, to the mutual advantage of us all.

Times change and circumstances alter. We are ready, and our history shows it, to adapt ourselves to new conditions.[13]

The meeting of the Tariff Conference, Chamberlain said, would give China an 'unrivalled opportunity' to take her place among the ranks of the great modern, progressive, and civilized nations. 'Will China take the chance that is open to her? Will she seize the opportunity as it passes? Ah! gentlemen, I do not know. The salvation of China can come only from the Chinese (cheers).' Having thus developed the main idea propounded by his principal China adviser, Wellesley, the Foreign Secretary fused it with Waterlow's grand design: Britain was willing to deal comprehensively and liberally with China's finances in return for effective guarantees of British commercial rights. Concluding, Chamberlain drank to the health of the delegates.[14]

In reply, Sir Ronald Macleay, British Minister in Peking and principal representative to the Conference, stated in sombre and forthright tone that no one should deceive himself about the gigantic and peculiar nature of the task.

There was one peculiarity of China which was not thoroughly appreciated by the outside world. That was the existence simultaneously of two practically distinct Chinas. There was the new China, the China of the treaty ports, which was mainly controlled by the young element, and there was also the old-world China, which, in its civilisation, was in the position which we were in in the 16th century. These two elements interacted upon each other, and made the problem a very difficult one.

The Conference would not provide a panacea for China's ills, Macleay said, nor would it usher in the millenium. But it might

13 *The Times*, 19 September 1925.   14 Ibid.

achieve valuable results and help to cement the friendship between China and the foreign powers.[15]

Even Macleay's guarded optimism proved unwarranted. When the Conference opened on 26 October 1925, civil war had again broken out and the precarious regime at Peking threatened to collapse during the proceedings. Nor was that the only difficulty. At a conference that symbolized the concert of the Washington powers convened to establish a new order in the Far East, the British, American, and Japanese delegates found themselves hopelessly at odds.[16] The British delegate from the beginning fought a rearguard action. Instructed to follow the fundamentals of the Teichman scheme, Macleay sought to obtain from the Chinese effective guarantees for free trade in return for the gradual establishment of tariff autonomy. The nub of the entire transaction lay in a most complicated system of taxation, *likin*, defined narrowly by the British as the levy of tolls on merchandise in transit. As Wellesley summarized the problem, 'the li-kin stations all over China are innumerable, and the charges, delays, arbitrariness and other vexations constitute a heavy incubus on trade.' In a broader sense, *likin* embraced consumption and other taxes and comprised many forms of internal taxation on foreign and domestic trade.[17] As described by Macleay in the Conference, *likin* consisted of 'all taxes on goods from the point of import or production up to the point of consumption in the shop'.[18] The entire British position was predicated on the effective abolition of *likin* in return for the granting of the Washington surtaxes of $2\frac{1}{2}$ per cent on ordinary dutiable articles and 5 per cent surtax on luxuries. Without the cessation of *likin*, the Foreign Office saw little point in proceeding to discuss such issues as tariff autonomy and debt consolidation.

[15] Ibid.

[16] See especially Borg, *American Policy and the Chinese Revolution*, chapter 6; and Iriye, *After Imperialism*, chapter 2. For the proceedings of the Conference, *Special Tariff Conference on the Chinese Customs Treaty (October 1925–April 1926)* (Peking, 1928).

[17] Wellesley, 'Memorandum on British Policy in China', 1 March 1925 [F 952/190/10], F.O. 371/10937.

[18] This and other developments described in 'Memorandum by Mr. Wellesley on the Chinese Situation', 27 November 1925 [F 5662/190/10], F.O. 371/10941; circulated by the Foreign Secretary to the Cabinet, 28 November 1925, CAB. 24/176.

The representatives at the Conference refused to fall in with what they considered to be a basically conservative British position. On 17 November Macleay reported that he had resolved along with the other representatives (1) that tariff autonomy would be granted by 1 January 1929; and (2) that he would accept the pledge of the Chinese Government that *likin* would be abolished simultaneously.[19] In other words, Macleay acquiesced in the proposition that tariff autonomy was not necessarily *conditional* on the abolition of *likin*. The Foreign Office, without charging that Macleay had been derelict, observed that it would be indeed difficult for him to deliver the goods. When notified that he should not be lulled by mere assurances into a false sense of security, Macleay replied that China after all was committed to abolishing *likin* prior to achieving tariff autonomy. The Foreign Office nevertheless felt that the entire British programme had been undermined. Britain might wind up having to grant tariff autonomy in return for paper guarantees that amounted to nothing. What then should Britain do? Macleay could be instructed to withdraw, thus aborting the Conference; or he could continue to try to make the best of a bad situation. Wellesley analysed the possible consequences of the first alternative, break-up:

1. We should reap the odium of all concerned, the other Powers as well as China.
2. Rightly or wrongly, we should be regarded by China as the one Power which has broken its bond entered into at Washington.
3. Our interests in China would be exposed to the full blast of Chinese wrath and the boycott might be intensified.
4. The Chinese might take the bit between their teeth, tear up the treaties and make a direct attack on the Customs Administration. This would be fatal.
5. We should be playing directly into the hands of the Bolsheviks.[20]

He reckoned that Britain could not afford to take those risks. But the other choice was almost as objectionable.

The other alternative means granting tariff autonomy and agreeing to a settlement of the unsecured debt in return for practically nothing. This course is neither free from serious objections nor from considerable dangers. In the first place tariff autonomy will not be

[19] Ibid.   [20] Ibid.

without its effect on our trade, but it need not in itself affect us vitally if we can secure proper safeguards.

If it be remembered that the Chinese do not want tariff autonomy for protective but for revenue purposes—they are simply out for more money to squander—then they will very soon find out that prohibitive duties will kill the goose that lays the golden eggs.

Wellesley nevertheless considered the second alternative by far the lesser of the evils. The Chinese had at least agreed on paper to abolish *likin*, even if there were no guarantees that they would do so. 'Even a paper abolition will be *some* good,' Wellesley wrote. 'It will be a simplification and a move in the right direction.'[21] With that consoling thought, the Foreign Office allowed the Conference to continue.

The delegates met intermittently until April 1926, when the Conference ended with each of the powers reproaching the other for its failure. The Foreign Office publicly had rebuked the State Department by stating that Britain would be prepared to grant the Washington surtaxes unconditionally and with no attempt to exact guarantees.[22] The Conference did not act on the suggestion. The only tangible accomplishment was the declaration that tariff autonomy would be established by 1929, an unexpected and unwelcome outcome for Great Britain. Having received nothing concrete at the Conference, the British expected but little from the Chinese in the future. 'Gratitude is not a Chinese virtue,' one official once wrote. Nevertheless one of the Chinese delegates hailed the tariff declaration as 'a milestone for fair play and just dealings between China and the friendly powers'. At least the Far Eastern powers had proved that they desired to perpetuate 'the spirit of the Washington Conference', to benefit China, rather than to demand a pound of Chinese flesh. On the major problems of debt consolidation and surtaxes, however, the Conference ended inconclusively and with recrimination. With the background of the civil war, it is doubtful whether the delegates could have resolved those

21 Ibid.
22 See the note of 28 May 1926, published with the memorandum of 18 December 1926, in *Survey of International Affairs, 1926*, pp. 488–94. The note was in response to a pointed American inquiry about the attitude of the British towards the Conference. The historian of American policy in China, Professor Dorothy Borg, refers to it as an 'attempt to break through traditional ways of thinking and [to] place the negotiations on a level more in keeping with ideas of international equality'. *American Policy*, p. 120.

issues even with the best of will and in the friendliest of spirits; as it happened the British Government regarded it as deplorable that Japan and the United States attributed to Britain motives of economic imperialism that caused the Conference's collapse. In an attempt to set straight the history of the Conference and to clarify British motives and policy, a Foreign Office memorandum concluded:

[T]he Tariff Conference came to its inconclusive end (1) because of the attitude of certain Powers, notably Japan and the United States, who, in their eagerness to obtain payment of their unsecured debts, were determined to perpetuate as regards the additional revenues the vicious system ... by which the customs revenues were impounded under the control of the Inspector-General of Customs for the service of the foreign obligations; and (2) because the course of the civil war made it impossible for the Chinese to present anything like a representative delegation.[23]

After nine months of consultation with her oppressors, China retained the status of a semi-colony. In the first and last effort by the Washington Powers to reconstruct the economic order of the Far East, the unequal treaties remained basically intact. Great Britain reverted to an independent policy of reform.

The fiasco of the Tariff Conference caused critics of the Foreign Office increasingly to condemn Britain's strategy in China as unsound, weak, and leading to disaster. Those critics included the British Minister in Peking, the Delegation to the Conference, the Shanghai and other important Chambers of Commerce, a large section of the British community in China, most of the persons in England interested in China, certain officials in the Consular as well as the Diplomatic service, and even some dissenters in the Foreign Office itself. They held that Britain overdid her attitude of goodwill: far from bringing kudos, generosity brought only scorn from the Chinese, who regarded it as a sign of weakness. The more Britain yielded, the more China demanded. Unless Britain envisaged the situation with greater determination and firmness, resisted the vociferous extremists and stopped the flow of customs revenues into civil wars, China would continue to degenerate.

[23] Foreign Office memorandum on 'British Policy in China', 8 January 1930 [F 6720/3/10], F.O. 371/14667; *D.B.F.P.*, VIII, No. 1; circulated to the Cabinet 8 January 1930, CAB. 24/209.

So strident did the criticism become after the disintegration of the Conference that the high-priest of British China policy, Sir Victor, paused to reflect. After carefully examining the pros and cons of a 'get tough' policy, Wellesley concluded that the critics of the Foreign Office were totally wrong. They erred fundamentally by failing to see that, although Britain intended to act benevolently in China, the Foreign Office had no desire to be weak.

Weakness is, however, unfortunately inherent in the situation, for our liberty of action is strictly limited, firstly, by the fact that a gunboat policy is no longer possible if only by reason of the existence of the League of Nations. . . .

Lastly, though by no means least, the undisguisable fact [is] that from military and naval points of view we are more or less powerless to deal with such an amorphous mass as China; and this rules out anything in the nature of coercion, except possibly naval demonstrations in conjunction with the other Powers. Weakness is, as I say, inherent in the situation, but I agree . . . that we need not go out of our way to emphasise it and thus encourage the Chinese to flout us. . . . But our policy is not entirely made up of weakness. I hope and trust that there is an element of prudence if not of justice.[24]

Wellesley admitted the force of the argument that the release of customs revenues might feed the civil war and that China might deteriorate to the extent that foreign intervention might be necessary. But he asked, did not the continuing foreign control of China's finances provide a short rather than a long-ranged solution? 'Shall we not be piling up for ourselves infinitely greater trouble in the future against the day when China may become strong enough to assert herself once more, and will not the storm, if and when it does burst, be ten times worse?' After all, the revenues raised in China belonged legitimately to the Chinese, not to the foreign powers. If the Chinese frittered away their resources in civil war, did Britain have a moral obligation to prevent them from doing so? 'Is not this really rather hypocritical because behind it is not so much the welfare of the Chinese as the fear that further deterioration will affect our interests?' And did not the opponents of the Foreign Office misjudge the nature of the Nationalist movement?

[24] Memorandum by Wellesley, 20 August 1926 [F 3424/8/10], F.O. 371/11653.

We are told that the Nationalist movement should not be taken too seriously. It is not governed by any high ideals or noble aspirations for the further regeneration of China such as similar movements in other countries frequently are, for such qualities as patriotism, self-sacrifice, etc., which are a necessary concomitant, are alien to the Chinese character. This may be true and, if so, it follows that very little can be expected of it as regards the regeneration of China, but none the less it is capable of infinite mischief, or it is principally actuated by xenophobia.

Whatever the internal dissensions may be which divide Chinaman from Chinaman, there can be no more potent rallying cry than: 'Let us oust the foreigner and be rid of the unequal treaties.'[25]

Wellesley urged that Britain, at least, should treat China as an equal; the Foreign Office should side with the Chinese in such issues as debt consolidation and prevent the other powers from using foreign control as a tax collecting agency. 'The embodying of debt consolidation and control in a new agreement would be adding yet one more to the list of "unequal treaties".' By blocking the efforts of the United States and Japan to extract monies from unpaid accounts, Britain would demonstrate to the Chinese the morality of fair play and there might at least be some chance for amicable relations with China in the future. 'If we keep our hands clean,' he wrote, 'there is always the hope that with patient and tactful handling matters will in the end come right.' Thus in Wellesley's mind the only policy offering any chance of success was one which was 'morally unimpeachable'. He therefore argued that, regardless of the reaction of the other powers, Britain should publicly declare her intention to abolish the unequal treaties. 'We cannot maintain the "unequal treaties" indefinitely. . . . Our policy in China must be one of treaty revision; the question is how and when such revision must come, and what course it is to take.'[26]

The milestone was laid on 18 December 1926, with the famous public memorandum of that date. Britain expressly disclaimed all intention to perpetuate imperialism in China. She declared her willingness to grant unconditional tariff autonomy, to free all revenues from foreign control, and to implement the recommendations of a report submitted by an

[25] Ibid.   [26] Ibid.

international committee on extraterritoriality[27]—in brief, to
help the Chinese to establish their sovereignty. The memorandum was published on Christmas Day. In ringing words,
Britain pledged to meet 'the legitimate aspirations of the
Chinese people'.[28]

The strategists of the time disputed the significance of the
'Christmas message', and historians have been unable to agree
on the meaning of the subsequent events at Hankow on 3–5
January 1927.[29] In a sense the memorandum appeared as a
colossal miscalculation. 'I confess that I am getting a little
alarmed at the pace at which we are going ever since our
declaration of policy was made,' Wellesley wrote.

That declaration set out clearly the lengths to which we were
prepared to go in order to meet the Chinese aspirations. It is quite
clear now that instead of it being interpreted as an act of generosity
and good-will towards China it is being generally looked upon as an
act of weakness prompted by fear not only by the Chinese but also
by some of the other Powers. As the Secretary of State is aware, my
fears of a general statement always were that the Chinese would say
'mere words; we want deeds'.[30]

Like the pious declarations of self-determination in 1919, the
idealistic rhetoric of the Christmas message of 1926 carried
words that returned to bite their authors. When the leftist
faction of the Kuomintang seized the concession at Hankow, the
British had to prove that they genuinely believed in China for
the Chinese, or to eat those solemn words.

In the opinion of some, the December memorandum pre-

---

[27] Printed in Cmd. 2774 of 1926. The recommendations included these points:
   1. That the courts be protected against unwarranted interference, civil or
      military.
   2. That judicial codes, etc., be completed and put into force.
   3. That laws be enacted, etc., under a uniform system.
   4. That the system of modern courts, prisons, etc., be extended.
   5. That adequate financial provision be made for courts, prisons, etc.
   6. That prior to compliance with the above recommendations, but after the
      principal items had been carried out, some progressive scheme for abolition
      of extraterritoriality be considered.
   7. That the extraterritorial powers should make certain modifications in the
      existing system, e.g. by applying Chinese laws in consular courts. . . .
   (As summarized in *D.B.F.P.*, VIII, No. 1.)

[28] Memorandum of 18 December 1926 cited in note 22.
[29] The Hankow incident is described above, pp. 130–1.
[30] Minute by Wellesley, 7 January 1927, F.O. 371/12398.

pared the ground for the Chinese to demonstrate that Britain lacked a spine. In the view of many more, the surrender of the concession proved it. The seriousness of that 'abject capitulation' can best be emphasized by stating the nature of the concessions. They were unique to China. In the complex British imperial system of Dominions, Colonies, Protectorates, and other title gradations of territories under the rule of the Crown, the China concessions held a place of their own. They were virtually slices of territory, or enclaves, granted by treaties imposed on China, mainly between 1842 and 1876, in a port or other trading centre in which the foreign power held absolute rights of extraterritoriality and local self-government. The four most important British concessions were Shanghai (technically an International Settlement rather than a concession), Tientsin, Canton, and Hankow.[31] With the principal exception of Shanghai, these concessions, even to most Englishmen, seemed to be anachronisms in twentieth-century China. To the Chinese these foreign enclaves were visible proof of the humiliation and servitude to which China had been subjected by the imperialist powers. Britain, of course, was the apotheosis of western imperialism. In the words of Eugene Chen, the Nationalist Minister for Foreign Affairs at the time of the Hankow incident:

The system of international control in China, known as foreign imperialism, has necessarily involved such limitation of Chinese sovereignty, economic, judicial and political, that anything like real and full independence has not been enjoyed by China since England imposed on her the Treaty of Nankin, which inaugurated the system.

In a very real sense, therefore, it is historically true to state that the British, having defeated China in the opium wars, deprived her of her independence. Englishmen of the present generation born since that dark transaction may not remember; but Nationalist China with the old iron of defeat in its flesh must needs remember. This is the Nationalist view; and unless it is grasped, one of the dominant aims of Chinese nationalism will not be understood.[32]

Chen's message was clear: any attempt to restore control over

---

[31] For a discussion of the concessions, see especially Westel W. Willoughby, *Foreign Rights and Interests in China* (2 vols., Baltimore, 1927), I, chapters 19 and 20.

[32] As paraphrased by the Chinese Information Bureau, 25 January 1927, Confidential Print 13313.

Hankow would be regarded by the Chinese as an atavistic return to the methods of the nineteenth century. Britain now had a chance to prove her good intentions. But there was another way to view the problem. Letting the Nationalists retain their illegitimate seizure would amply demonstrate that the British paper tiger could not defend its interests.

No one worked harder to prevent Britain's position in China from being undermined than the Minister who arrived in China on the eve of the Hankow incident, Sir Miles Lampson. During the critical era from late 1926 through the time of the Manchurian crisis, he acquired the reputation of one of Britain's hardest-working and most skilful diplomats. A man of robust energy and intellect, he and Sir John Jordan were the two truly distinguished China hands of the twentieth century. Lampson believed ultimately that Britain should pursue a policy of force if all other methods proved futile. 'What Sir Miles Lampson says,' Wellesley once wrote when analysing the differences in opinion between the Legation in Peking and the Foreign Office, 'amounts in fact to this: if the Chinese refuse to come to heel we must once more have recourse to the gunboat policy.'[33] In fairness to Sir Miles, it must be said that he never advocated forcible means unless British lives and property were at stake. He believed in a policy not of retreat but retrenchment. He once wrote:

There is only one way in which to do real business with them in the long run. Conciliation is merely regarded as a sign of weakness; but let them realise that whilst we are fully prepared and only too anxious to do the right and fair thing by them, yet, if they refuse conciliation, and if driven too far, we will without question stand up for our rights.[34]

Despite the moderation of that statement, the difference between his approach and that of the Foreign Office experts was profound. They usually took the line that the use of coercion in matters other than to prevent murder would destroy any hope of amicable relations between Britain and China. Lampson thought, on the other hand, that if the Chinese were allowed to take over with impunity such concessions as Hankow, one

[33] Minute by Wellesley, 2 March 1927 [F 1913], F.O. 371/12402.
[34] Lampson to Chamberlain, No. 170, 28 February 1927 [F 3563/959/10], F.O. 371/12470.

British concern after another would fall until even Shanghai would be threatened. That was the main point of the Hankow controversy. In his view the Consul General and Naval Officer blundered by giving the concession to the Nationalists; having surrendered it, the British should at least receive something substantial in return. But Lampson characteristically reserved final judgement. And in analysing the issues, he showed greater grasp of the nuances and splits developing in the Nationalist movement than did his colleagues twelve thousand miles away in London.

[T]he verdict must depend on the attitude adopted towards us by the Hankow and Nanking Governments. If they continue to attack our whole position in China until we are driven somewhere to make a stand, then it will be shown that they have had no desire to get on terms with us, and we might as well have made our stand at the start as be driven to do so at a much later stage when we have suffered enormous losses.

If, on the other hand, the moderate section of the Nationalists even now recognises that the measures adopted at Hankow were indefensible and is prepared to settle by negotiation the questions outstanding between China and Great Britain, the sacrifice of the Hankow concession will have achieved its purpose.[35]

He thus clarified one of the two major issues of the Hankow incident. The other issue was the attitude Britain should take after the Nationalist *fait accompli*. Lampson urged that Britain should decline to negotiate, leaving the Nationalists in unlawful possession until they saw the error of their action. The Foreign Office refused to follow Lampson's lead and instructed the Legation to come to terms. On 19 February 1927 Eugene Chen of the Hankow faction of the Kuomintang signed an agreement with the Counsellor of the Legation, Owen O'Malley.[36]

The Chen–O'Malley agreement essentially granted Chinese control over the Hankow concession. From one point of view it represented a step forward in the readjustment of Britain's treaties with China, and from the other it meant a jump

[35] Lampson to Chamberlain, No. 723, 1 July 1927 [F 7382/2/10], F.O. 371/ 12409. This is probably the dispatch that best presents Lampson's interpretation of the Hankow incident and his objections to Foreign Office policy.

[36] Printed in Cmd. 2869 of 1927, *Papers respecting the Agreements relative to the British Concessions at Hankow and Kiukiang.*

towards disaster. Lampson was the leading exponent of the latter opinion. The main complaint against the agreement, he wrote, 'is that it represents a complete surrender to Chinese extremist demands, and it set a precedent which has not been confined to Hankow, but has shaken the whole British position in China.'[37] After Hankow, the Nationalists seized the smaller concession of Kiukiang. The process would not stop, according to Lampson, until Britain stood up for her rights, and this would not be done until the Foreign Office and Cabinet recognized the true significance of the concession system. The basic misapprehension of the China experts in London, in Lampson's opinion, was that they failed adequately to see that these enclaves conducted almost the entire foreign business of China. Even in the midst of civil war, trade could flourish because the concessions permitted banks to function and protected foreign nationals under systems of municipal government. Lampson wrote:

Once the areas revert to Chinese control foreign merchants have no doubt, protestations to the contrary from all Nationalist China notwithstanding, that it can only be a question of time before the administration degenerates and malpractices in connexion with trade occur, which make it impossible for banks to give the banking facilities they hitherto have done.[38]

The concessions in effect protected the foreign trade of China, and to prevent China's commercial destruction the Chinese had to be protected against themselves by preventing them from illegally seizing such places as Hankow. Lampson summarized the crux of the matter by interpreting the Chinese 'national psychology' in this regard. As they themselves would say: 'Firmness is what we Chinese understand, firmness with justice.'

Stung by criticism of the Chen–O'Malley agreement, the Foreign Office rebutted.[39] According to the most comprehensive defence of British policy towards Hankow, one of the main points of the Christmas message had been the assurance that the concessions would ultimately revert to Chinese control. 'Such

---

[37] Lampson to Chamberlain, No. 723, 1 July 1927 [F 7382/2/10], F.O. 371/12409.
[38] Ibid.
[39] See especially the minutes and memoranda in F.O. 371/12436.

useless concessions as those at Amoy, Chinkiang or Kiukiang could be abandoned immediately or the Chinese authorities might be asked to assume the responsibility for them. In Shanghai, at the other end of the scale, Chinese control could only be admitted slowly and cautiously, and there was the added difficulty that the settlement is international and not British.'[40] In between those two extreme types of concessions came Hankow. There the Chinese had already established municipal councils in the former Russian and German areas. Britain's goal had been to amalgamate all the foreign spheres into one district under a single municipal council, on which foreign representatives would ensure the proper control of finances. When the events of 3–5 January overtook that plan, the Foreign Office faced the choice of negotiating a settlement, or of applying a policy of force. The former course was chosen, in part because cruisers could not reach Hankow until the higher waters of March and April. But it was not entirely because of military impotence that Britain opted to negotiate. Even the left-wing faction of the Kuomintang held out the hope of establishing a municipal council along the lines of the former German concession. In the event, O'Malley obtained, at least on paper, a complicated municipal council system in which the British ratepayers together with representative Chinese authorities would regulate the finances and management of the district. Moreover, the agreement even included guarantees for surrogate extraterritoriality and consular jurisdiction. Admittedly the entire transaction was a gamble because in January 1927 it was impossible to know the extent to which the Russians controlled the Hankow faction of the Kuomintang. But at least the agreement passed the onus of responsibility to the Chinese, who would be put to the test. Their response in Hankow would determine British action in other concessions. Theoretically Britain had acquired safeguards for justice, property, and trade. 'Mr. O'Malley . . . had, in fact, carried out the original intention of our December memorandum and treaty alteration proposals. It is difficult to see how this can be described as a humiliating surrender.'[41]

With the Nationalist movement in full swing and the

---

[40] 'Memorandum respecting the Hankow Agreement', 7 June 1927 [F 5349/67/10], F.O. 371/12436.   [41] Ibid.

collisions between contending armies in central China, British trade continued to deteriorate. For that reason it is difficult to assess the Hankow settlement. It did not check the loss of life or decline in trade, but neither can it be said that it substantially improved Britain's position. It did not bring about a cessation of anti-British agitation, nor did it immediately prove that foreign trade could prosper under Nationalist rule. Critics of the Hankow agreement therefore argued that it should be torn up and the concession reoccupied. The Chinese would learn, by force if necessary, that British rights could not be flouted. Whatever the merit of that idea, however, there were grave military and commercial arguments against it. Reoccupation of the concession would probably have meant war with at least a major faction of Nationalist China in a location where gunboats could be effective only part of the year. British trade would be boycotted; and after all Hankow was a *minor* rather than a *major* British interest. The leading British firms at Hankow were not even in the concession area. '[T]he four largest British business establishments in Hankow, namely, the British-American Tobacco Company, Messrs. Butterfield and Swire, Messrs. Arnhold Brothers, and the International Export Company, are all *outside* the British concession.'[42] Retaking Hankow therefore would involve the occupation of districts beyond the concession in order to protect British firms; for, if only the concession itself were reoccupied those businesses obviously would be endangered. For sound commercial reasons the Foreign Office thus justified the Hankow settlement.

In the following months of turmoil the Chinese did keep the concession in better order than the British anticipated, and trade, though in relative decline, continued. In a visit to Hankow following the Nanking incident, when Anglo-Chinese relations reached their nadir, a British naval officer noted the following number of merchant steamers on the Yangtze:

British	27
American	3
Japanese	8
French	2
German	2
Norwegian	1

[42] Ibid.

The Foreign Office judged that the Hankow settlement had allowed Britain to maintain her commercial supremacy on the Yangtze. And, by declining to use force to protect her commerce, Britain achieved the advantage of being able to disclaim charges of imperialism. 'To sum the matter up, it seems a fair statement of the case to say that the Hankow Agreement has placed us in a position of moral and tactical advantage.[43]

At the same time of the Hankow crisis, Britain in January 1927 launched a concrete programme of treaty revision. The proposed reforms were manifold, including the recognition of Chinese law in British courts, the payment of Chinese taxes by British subjects, and the modification of the concession privileges. There was a twofold negative purpose. The Chinese would have less cause to denounce British imperialism; and they might see that alteration of the treaty system would prove so difficult for them to work out in detail that they would prefer at least some aspects of the *status quo*. The positive aspect of the programme was the hope that relations with China should and perhaps could be put on a more equitable footing.

In the turbulent months of the first half of 1927, the treaty revision programme made little progress. After the Nanking incident in March, negotiations virtually ceased. Britain's attitude was that the Nationalist government must prove its bona fides by appropriate apology for Nanking. After Chiang Kai-shek's victory over the Hankow faction and the rout of Russian influence, relations between Britain and the Kuomintang became more friendly. The two governments closed the Nanking incident by exchange of notes in August 1928.[44] They began more intensive negotiations about the unequal treaties. The scope of those complex transactions is far beyond the compass of this commentary. But it is important to see at least the main outlines in order to comprehend the nature of the problem facing Britain after the establishment of the Nationalist Government at Nanking. Jumping ahead chronologically, here is an official Foreign Office summary of what had been accomplished by January 1930:

1. *Recognition of modern Chinese law courts as the competent courts for*

---

[43] Ibid.
[44] See Cmd. 3188 of 1928, *Papers relating to the Settlement of the Nanking Incident of March 24, 1927.*

cases brought by British plaintiffs or complainants without attendance of a British representative.—This is now in force.

2. *Recognition of a reasonable Chinese Nationality Law.*—A carefully studied solution for this complicated question—which vitally affects the 'Anglo-Chinese' of Hong Kong and Malaya—has now been evolved, and is the subject of negotiations with the Chinese Government; a working arrangement is actually in force in South China.

3. *Application in British courts in China of the modern Chinese civil and commercial codes, etc.*—No progress has been made, since when these codes, etc., came to be examined they were found to be incomplete and unsuitable for application in the British courts, with the singular exception of the trade-mark law.

4. *Payment of regular and legal Chinese taxation by British subjects.*—As a matter of fact British firms pay most, if not all, of the various consumption taxes, stamp taxes, etc., which are now being levied in a haphazard fashion on Chinese and foreign goods alike. We have not, however, made this taxation legally enforceable in the British courts. . . .

5. *Application in British courts of the Chinese Penal Code.*—The Provisional Criminal Code of 1912 has only recently been replaced by a new code, which came into force on the 1st September, 1928. . . .

6. *Modification of municipal administrations of British Concessions:*—

(a) *Hankow.*—Restored to Chinese control under the Chen-O'Malley Agreement of 1927, which is now working satisfactorily.

(b) *Kiukiang.*—Restored to Chinese control by the Chen-O'Malley Agreement of 1927.

(c) *Chinkiang.*—Has been restored to Chinese control under similar arrangements as at Kiukiang. Chinese are granting perpetual leases to former tenants of His Majesty's Government.

(d) *Amoy.*—No change.

(e) *Canton*, i.e., *Shameen.*—No change.

(f) *Tientsin.*—Constitution of the British Concession has been modified so as to allow Chinese to vote on equal terms with foreigners, and to provide for increase of Chinese representation on the Municipal Council; these arrangements are working satisfactorily. . . .

7. *Special treaty privileges possessed by British missionaries.*—These have been, or are in course of being, surrendered.[45]

---

[45] Foreign Office memorandum on 'British Policy in China', 8 January 1930 [F 6720/3/10], F.O. 371/14667; *D.B.F.P.*, VIII, No. 1; circulated to the Cabinet 8 January 1930, CAB. 24/209.

From those summary comments, it should be clear that by 1930 Great Britain had indeed made progress in the revision of the unequal treaties that surpassed all but the most optimistic forecasts of a few years earlier. One could go on to discuss in the context of all of China the gargantuan problem of extraterritoriality, and other subjects such as the Commercial Treaty, the Maritime Customs Administration, the Wei-hai Wei and Boxer Indemnities, and the Salt-Gabelle. But those topics will provide the basis of doctoral dissertations and monographs, which alone can give them adequate treatment. To evaluate the general significance of the multiple aspects of the unequal treaties, this chapter turns to the geographical vortex of almost all troubles that confronted Britain in China—Shanghai.

British residents in China looked upon Shanghai as one of the glories of Britain's informal Empire. Men of English stock had transformed it from a mudhole into the greatest port in the Far East, the fourth largest in the world. In a technical sense, of course, it was not part of the Empire, as was Hong Kong, but an International Settlement. But British influence and control prevailed. Compared with 2,000 Americans in Shanghai, there were 6,000 Englishmen. The Japanese had a population of 20,000. But, of the members of the municipal council, or governing authority, five were British (including the chairman), two were American, and two were Japanese. Two British firms, Butterfield & Swire & Jardine, and Matheson & Company dominated Shanghai's shipping and trade. The principal utility companies—the Shanghai Waterworks Company and the Shanghai Gas Company—were British. So also were the largest manufacturing firms, the Ewo Cotton Mills, Ltd. and the British-American Tobacco Company. The Hong Kong & Shanghai Banking Corporation, and the Chartered Bank of India, Australia & China, exercised preponderating control over Shanghai's finances. In round figures, of the total British investment of approximately £200 million in China about 1930, roughly £150 million was in Shanghai. In other words, Shanghai was Britain's financial, commercial, and industrial base on the Asian mainland.

To those who attempted to plot Britain's long-range strategy, all the concessions or other interests in China were marginal compared with Shanghai. Recognizing that the force of the

Nationalist movement would probably diminish all foreign influence, the Foreign Office's grand design—as conceived in particular by Sir Victor Wellesley—was to plan an orderly retreat throughout China and to hold the main line of defence of Britain's interests at Shanghai. Britain would systematically equalize the unequal treaties by such measures as handing over the concessions and abolishing extraterritoriality in the interior —*in return* for safeguards at Shanghai. If Britain proved her good faith by redressing the inequities of the treaty system, China in justice would have to recognize the legitimacy of Britain's position in the major port.

Shanghai was exceptional not only because of the extent of foreign interests, but also because of the powerful and deep-seated belief of the British community in China that Shanghai had not been created by the Chinese but by foreigners.[46] As Lampson described the attitude of the British in Shanghai: 'From their own point of view the plain fact is that until the foreigner came Shanghai was a mud flat. Its present position as the fourth largest port in the world is entirely due to foreign— and mainly British—enterprise.'[47] If, as in other parts of China, the foreigners were asked to hand over to the Chinese what the foreigners themselves had built up, it would be as unjust as the unequal treaties seemed to the Chinese. The British residents had every reason to assume, Lampson wrote, that Chinese control would be 'corrupt and incompetent'. And the Chinese had no right to demand 'self-determination.' So far as the whites were concerned, the yellow men had moved into the settlement to find a haven from the turmoil of China and to enjoy the benefits of the prosperous trading community. 'The foreigners now happen to be outnumbered in their own settlement by Chinese who have flocked there simply to get protection or share the prosperity which foreign administration ensures!'[48] With that sort of attitude, the residents of Shanghai had ac-

---

[46] When Sir Austen Chamberlain once emphasized this point in the House of Commons, one M.P. interrupted to ask whether 'God had nothing to do with it?' Chamberlain replied that the observation 'is rather ribald.' *Parliamentary Debates*, 5th series, vol. 204, 6 April 1927, c. 2143. Of the numerous books on Shanghai, the most lucid exposition of the complexity of the problem, in my opinion, is by F. C. Jones, *Shanghai and Tientsin with Special Reference to Foreign Interests* (London, 1940).

[47] Lampson to Mounsey, 4 November 1927 F.O. 371/12419.

[48] Ibid.

quired the reputation of being among the most reactionary Englishmen abroad. At the same time that the Chinese increasingly demanded equal rights, the Shanghai 'diehards' became equally determined to retain their special privileges. Hence the magnitude of the task facing any responsible British Minister. 'I have to pursue a double policy out here,' Lampson once wrote.

On the one hand I am trying to create the proper atmosphere for His Majesty's Government's policy of conciliation. That is to say, that I have to bring the Chinese along, and the British community in China along, to a meeting point from which some sort of settlement may eventually start. On the other hand, it is my duty to preserve and defend vested British interests in China to the best of my ability. It's a ticklish business—rather like tight rope walking.[49]

Even in Shanghai, Britain's position could not be defended at any cost. There as in all of China, any long-range accommodation would depend on the attitude of the Chinese; but in Shanghai the Foreign Office encountered the staunchest opposition against any revision of the unequal treaties.

The Foreign Office warned that the Shanghai group might jeopardize themselves by refusing to meet legitimate Chinese aspirations. In a poignant letter to Lampson, one of the members of the Far Eastern Department, George Mounsey, discussed at length the lamentable fact that the Shanghai community had done nothing, and that, if they persisted in their refusal to co-operate in the revision of the treaty system, the British Parliament and public, and perhaps the world at large, would join the Chinese in liquidating the Shanghai problem at the expense of the foreigners. He dwelt on the central point: the bullheadedness of the foreign community. He wrote that it was 'most disheartening' to find no evidence whatever that the Englishmen of Shanghai wished to improve relations with the Chinese. He challenged the historical interpretation that the Chinese had moved into the settlement after the trading community had already been developed.

Surely, in the first place, while it is true that foreign enterprise has turned Shanghai from a mud flat to the fourth harbour of the world, the fact remains that Shanghai has never ceased to be

[49] Ibid.

Chinese soil, and that its prosperity must in the long run depend on good relations and friendly co-operation with the Chinese.

Moreover, is it not more than questionable whether it could ever have reached its present state of prosperity had the original intention been maintained of excluding all Chinese from the settlement? Chinese were in fact admitted at first partly owing to their seeking refuge there from the chaos outside, and partly because their presence was profitable and served to enhance the value of the land. Once voluntarily admitted, their presence ought to have been recognised and the new situation resulting therefrom taken into due account; and the foreign community have themselves to blame to a great extent for their failure to meet the situation as it developed and make some concessions to the Chinese both inside and outside the settlement, on whose goodwill the building-up and preservation of their own fortunes primarily depend.[50]

In summary, the principal foundation of Shanghai was the International Settlement, 'efficient but parochial, and in the administration and public life of which the Chinese who have been admitted in large numbers have no share.' So far as the reactionary Englishmen of Shanghai were concerned, that situation could only be improved by politically severing the International Settlement from China and creating an International City on the model of Danzig.[51]

Great Britain did make substantial progress between 1928 and 1931 in both reconstructing the attitude of the Shanghai community and in redressing Chinese grievances. One person deserves the principal credit, Minister Sir Miles Lampson. His unflagging efforts to strengthen the Chinese voice in Shanghai's administration and his tireless negotiations with the Chinese Government took much of the sting out of the epithet 'British Imperialism'. By 1930–1 the five British members of the Municipal Council were balanced by five Chinese representatives. During this same time Lampson began negotiations with the Nationalist Government that led to the surrender of most of Britain's rights of extraterritoriality. These negotiations lasted for over a year and a half and culminated in the Extraterritoriality Treaty of June 1931. The Treaty was never signed, but it

---

[50] Mounsey to Lampson, 18 January 1928 [F 9426/25/10], F.O. 371/12419.

[51] See for example the memorandum submitted to the Foreign Office by R. Huntley Davidson (Editor of the *Shanghai News Bulletin*), dated February 1929, F.O. 371/13946; *D.B.F.P.*, VIII, No. 13 note 2.

represents Britain's abandonment of the unequal treaties and her tangible recognition of China as a responsible nation.

Lampson's mere summary of those negotiations contains seventy-one separate entries and occupies over forty pages in the *Documents on British Foreign Policy*.[52] The discussions ranged over all aspects of Anglo-Chinese relations: jurisdiction, taxation, arbitration, shipping, companies, reserved areas, and so on. From the beginning Lampson achieved a tactical advantage over his counterpart, C. T. Wang, by getting him to discuss detailed and relatively uncontentious issues rather than dealing with general principles such as extraterritoriality, which Britain might have been forced to yield at the outset. The two parties thus were able to build up common ground by resolving minor problems, while reserving debate on the major issues and areas. From Britain's point of view there were four principles at stake, and four major areas. There was a close inter-connection. The principles were, in order of ascending importance: evocation, foreign co-judges, criminal jurisdiction, and excluded areas. The areas were, again in order of ascending importance: Canton, Hankow, Tientsin, and Shanghai. Lampson's strategy was to retreat gradually from the first of the principles and areas, and to hold on to extraterritoriality in Shanghai at all costs, at least for a period of years. The negotiations followed roughly that pattern. They were characterized by endless argument and manoeuvre, and several times Wang came close to being repudiated by his Government for giving way too much to Lampson. In May 1931 party leaders of the Kuomintang challenged Chiang's control of the party, and the negotiations threatened to collapse because of a change of government. In the same month the People's Convention, in honour of Sun Yat-sen's death-bed admonition to abolish the treaties as soon as possible, unilaterally declared a series of articles governing extraterritoriality. The Government nevertheless continued the negotiations. After almost endless wrangling, the two parties finally reached agreement on the crucial point: extraterritoriality would continue for a maximum of ten years not only in Shanghai but also for five years in Tientsin.[53]

The Treaty lapsed and Britain and China did not resume negotiations. Without the Treaty Britain was able to perpetuate

[52] *D.B.F.P.*, VIII, No. 460.   [53] Ibid.

her stronghold over Shanghai with no specific timetable for abolition of extraterritoriality. At the same time, the Chinese now had demonstrable proof that Britain 'in good faith' was prepared to alter the treaty system with even extraterritoriality in Shanghai reverting to China after a transitional period. Lampson commented after the close of the negotiations:

[W]hatever the future may hold in store, we have, at any rate, on record, as accepted by the Minister for Foreign Affairs of the National Government and myself, a fair and reasonable draft treaty settlement of the vexed question of jurisdiction on which we can take our stand and with which we can meet any future threats of uni-lateral abrogation of our extraterritorial rights. In the meantime we can sit back and await developments in the internal political situation.[54]

And so the British continued to follow their customary line. They made concessions to Chinese Nationalism by driving hard bargains in the toughest tradition of British diplomacy. The negotiation of the Extraterritoriality Treaty placed them, in Lampson's words, 'in a moral and tactical' advantage *vis-à-vis* both the Chinese and the foreign powers. It was now up to the Chinese to prove that their government was stable enough to accept the transfer of extraterritorial responsibilities, now up to the United States and Japan to follow Britain's lead in the revision of the treaty system. Had the Far East not been dis-rupted by the Manchurian crisis, the unequal treaties might eventually have been abolished. As it happened they merely remained in abeyance.

Writing today, in 1970, it appears that the intricate negotia-tions between the British and the Nationalist Government are open to two different interpretations. The usual English view has been that Britain's diplomacy set an example in the recognition of the Chinese national consciousness.[55] On the other hand, there is an air of futility about the entire venture of attempting to bring China into the mainstream of the western world. Students of China's history could certainly argue that the British fought against forces they hardly understood and sought to achieve goals that today appear unrealistic in the

[54] Ibid.
[55] See for example the introduction by Rohan Butler to volume VIII of the *D.B.F.P.*

extreme. The British worked to modernize China along western lines and to inject into Chinese culture Anglo-Saxon traditions of law, finance, and government. The more optimistic of them envisaged the emergence of a federal government, a China ruled by parliamentary democracy. The more perceptive saw that those traditions were alien to the Chinese, who merely absorbed foreign ideas and techniques in Chinese fashion. The Consul-General in Shanghai once wrote:

> The Chinese are an arrogant race, with a firm belief in the superiority of their own culture and civilisation. They may absorb ideas and methods laboriously introduced from outside, but they transmute them to their own uses and the resulting product is likely to astonish the progenitors.[56]

Lampson, one of the keenest observers of China, believed that any attempt dogmatically to impose Anglo-Saxon traditions would end in failure. He preferred to move ahead pragmatically. When he did venture analogies, he saw the future of China more along European than Anglo-Saxon lines. Writing of the central problem of Shanghai, that of municipal government, he commented:

> [I]t is, perhaps, too much to expect that the Chinese will ever be educated up successfully to the theory and practice of independent municipal government as we understand the term; . . . the Chinese conception of municipal government, as now being developed all over China, is the continental rather than the Anglo-Saxon one, i.e., an official municipal administration with an elected council whose powers are limited to a measure of legislative and financial control, something on the lines of our own Crown Colony Governments; and a solution of the Shanghai problem may conceivably in the distant future lie along these lines.[57]

According to the prevalent British view of the mid-inter-war years, the Chinese were incapable of being educated in the tradition of Anglo-Saxon government, and the ultimate reason was a 'moral defect' in the Chinese national character. The Chinese, then as now, would no doubt consider that interpretation as arrogant; it was precisely the quality of arrogance that the British saw as the root cause preventing a satisfactory

---

[56] Brenan to Henderson, No. 835, 18 June 1930 [F 4961/61/10], F.O. 371/14689.
[57] Lampson to Foreign Office, 7 June 1929 [F 3797/250/10], F.O. 371/13930.

12—B.S.F.E.

revision of the unequal treaties and stirring up international trouble. Sir Miles Lampson wrote in February 1929: 'The trouble is that the Chinese remain an unbelievably arrogant race, and they will not face the fact that sooner or later they must be on terms with Japan.'[58]

[58] Lampson to Chamberlain, No. 21 Confidential, 4 January 1929 [F 1054/3/10], F.O. 371/13889.

VI

THE MANCHURIAN CRISIS

WITH the wealth of unpublished as well as published documentary evidence now available, one could study the events in the Far Eastern affairs of 1931–3 from any number of vantage points—though at the risk of repeating major commentaries, some written over a decade ago.[1] None the less the subject demands reinvestigation, if only because the new British sources clarify a number of important details and provide an opportunity of re-evaluating the significance of the crisis in relation to the origins of the Pacific war. The two preliminary questions that have remained unanswered are, through British eyes: did Chinese troops actually attack the Manchurian railway line prior to the Japanese occupation of Mukden on the night of 18–19 September 1931? And, could the confrontation have been localized? Those questions were answered similarly by the Legation in Peking and the Embassy in Tokyo, but the meaning of the events were interpreted differently by the Foreign Office, the Delegation to the League of Nations at Geneva, and the Embassy in Washington. Britain's reaction to the crisis ultimately gave rise to further and more important questions: could closer co-operation between Britain and China, Britain and Japan, and, above all, Britain and the United States, have eliminated one of the causes of the

[1] Notably, R. Bassett, *Democracy and Foreign Policy: A Case History, The Sino-Japanese Dispute, 1931–33* (London, 1952, 1968 edn.), one of the best books on British foreign policy in the inter-war years. The clearest account of the first part of the crisis is by Sara R. Smith, *The Manchurian Crisis 1931–1932: A Tragedy in International Relations* (New York, 1948)—balanced, but contentious in the argument that everything that happened after December 1931 was 'anticlimax', which certainly is not true for Great Britain. See also Irving S. Friedman, *British Relations with China, 1931–39* (New York, 1940). For further references see the select bibliography in Crowley, *Japan's Quest for Autonomy*, also the extensive list in Dorothy Borg, *The United States and the Far Eastern Crisis of 1933–1938: From the Manchurian Incident Through the Initial Stage of the Undeclared Sino-Japanese War* (Cambridge, Mass., 1964), the first chapter of which is a penetrating review of the Manchurian episode. From the western side the affair is now receiving exhaustive treatment by Christopher Thorne, *The Limits of Foreign Policy* (forthcoming).

Pacific war? And was Great Britain, as the principal supporter of the League and the greatest western power with a stake in the Far East, responsible for 'the failure of collective security'? This chapter addresses itself to those problems, but first it reconsiders Britain's general position in the Far East before the crisis, and the geo-political situation in Manchuria.

In China, Britain had partly managed to revolutionize the treaty system, thus, in the British view, contributing to the stability of the Asian mainland. Despite the great depression and the continued internal strife, the Chinese Government at the beginning of the Manchurian crisis appeared more secure than at any time since the revolution of 1911. Sir Miles Lampson reported:

We find President Chiang Kai-shek once more victorious and his enemies discomfited. It would be idle to deny that formidable dangers still exist, including the menace of the Communists and of further military rebellions. . . . But, as each year passes, and they survive and suppress rebellion after rebellion, the Nationalist Government, though financially exhausted, grow ever stronger in military and political prestige; while each rebellion crushed renders a further successful outbreak against their authority more difficult of accomplishment.[2]

Anti-foreign agitation continued; but the more 'enlightened' of the Chinese leaders appeared willing to co-operate with Britain in the treaty revision programme and to recognize the legitimacy of Britain's trading interests. The pendulum of fortune seemed to be swinging back in Britain's favour. By comparison with Lampson's gloomy views during the tumultuous months after his arrival in China in late 1926, his outlook by 1930–1 had become one of restrained optimism. In his letters he frequently developed the idea that, with patience and considerable good luck, Britain might maintain and develop her commercial position in China—barring any unforeseen difficulty in 'the North'.

In Japan, Sir Francis Lindley arrived to assume his ambassadorial responsibilities only a month before the beginning of the crisis. In July 1931 he presented to the Foreign Office an

---

[2] Lampson to Henderson, No. 1927, 23 December 1930 [F 860/69/10], F.O. 371/15472.

evaluation of Britain's role in the Far East compared with the time when he last served in Japan 23 years earlier. He observed above all that Great Britain had been reduced from a major to a minor power, and that the influence of the United States had increased to a degree that astonished any Englishman who remembered the days when the Japanese played cricket, not baseball.[3]

It is difficult to imagine a greater change from this state of affairs than exists at the present moment. The events of the war, the abolition of the alliance, the financial difficulties in London, the reduction of the British navy, the serious situation in India, the enormous development of Japanese industry and, finally, the earthquake of 1923, which completely destroyed Yokohama, have combined to reduce our predominant position to one of a very modest character; and there can be no doubt that the country which now looms far larger in Japan's eyes than any other is the United States of America.[4]

Lindley went on to comment that through industry and self-discipline the Japanese had raised themselves to the status of a major power. They had assimilated modern ideas; they believed that Britain's goodwill and the Alliance accounted in part for their successful adjustment to the modern world.

[T]hey are now told ... that alliances are evil things and that great Powers shall count for no more than small. Whether they will assimilate these new ideas as they did the old in another fifty years remains to be seen. All that can be said now is that they have not done so yet; and that the new indecision and extreme caution of their world policy is due. ... to a very perplexity as to where their true national interests lie. In common parlance, they don't know where they are.[5]

The Japanese, in Lindley's estimate, were confused about their relations with the western powers and uncertain about their policy towards 'the growing truculence of the Chinese' in Manchuria.[6]

[3] 'One of the most remarkable changes which may have considerable influence on the race. ... [is] the great popularity of game playing. Baseball, which I never saw in Japan when I was last here may now be called a national game. ... Cricket is, I am sorry to say, in a somewhat less satisfactory condition than it was twenty-five years ago; and the decline of the British colonies has unavoidably reduced the interest in our national game.' Lindley to Henderson, No. 392, 23 July 1931 [F 4555/1975/23], F.O. 371/15521; *D.B.F.P.*, Second Series (all subsequent references in this chapter are to the Second Series), VIII, No. 495.
[4] Ibid.   [5] Ibid.   [6] Ibid.

Through a combination of historical and geographical circumstances, Manchuria had become the cockpit of East Asian rivalries. In this area of 36,000 square miles, one-fourth the size of China, clashed the demographic and economic thrusts of three major powers, Japan, China, and Russia. As an international issue involving the western powers, Manchuria had only recent antecedents, dating at earliest from the nineteenth century; as a location of geo-political importance, Manchuria was the route of historical invasion of China. According to typically British sweeping interpretations of the problem written either before or during the course of the crisis, from Manchuria came the Manchu conquerors, to Manchuria came the Russians in search of a warm-water port, the Chinese seeking settlement and refuge from the chaos of China, and the Japanese in search of raw materials and foodstuffs. By the early twentieth century Manchuria had thus become a microcosm of the modern world's problems. Though Russia ceded her warm-water port as a consequence of the Russo-Japanese war of 1904-5, she retained her Manchurian ambitions because the shortest route from Moscow to Vladivostok ran through Manchuria. Throughout the entire Manchurian crisis loomed the spectre of Russia—a chilling vision to the Foreign Office because a wrong move might incite the Chinese to turn again to the Bolsheviks. China herself viewed Manchuria as part of her domain, an attitude not shared, of course, by Japan. To the British Manchuria was, to use the recurrent analogy, a sort of Asian Alsace-Lorraine, a problem defying a straightforward or satisfactory solution. Of China's total population, less than 6 per cent occupied Manchuria; but the Chinese population substantially outweighed Japan's in numbers of at least ten to one. With standards of living higher in Japan and the harsh climate of Manchuria, Japanese peasants refused to emigrate. Yet Japan controlled Manchuria's economy, and to Japan belonged the *entire* credit, according to the British view, of Manchuria's development of industries such as timber, iron and coal. One British North China Consular officer summarized the problem:

As a whole, this vast territory is bound, at least for some years to come, to be drawn more and more within the economic orbit of Japan. Of the three protagonists for the predominance over it,

Russia has hitherto been actuated mainly by the spirit of adventure that drove our own forefathers overseas, while China is naturally eager to retain within her dominion a region so rich in resources which offers a ready refuge to her harassed population in case of need, but for Japan the control of those resources is a matter of grim necessity, and necessity knows no law.[7]

On the whole British sympathies lay with Japan, perhaps above all because of the power of analogy. In the words of Lindley's predecessor, Ambassador Sir John Tilley: Japan 'estimates the importance of Manchuria to herself as Great Britain does that of Ireland or Egypt.'[8] Perhaps a sense of justice also determined the predominant British attitude. Again in Tilley's words, 'Japan feels deeply that she is not allowed to send her surplus population to Australia, Canada or California, and it is well that her activities should not be too much criticised in Manchuria.'[9]

The crux of the struggle between Japan and China for Manchurian hegemony was railway construction. In analysing the development of this explosive issue, British China hands identified its immediate origins in the years 1925–9, but historically they saw it arising in the aftermath of the Sino-Japanese war of 1894–5. They held that the root of the problem stretched back to China's 'folly' in granting permission to Russia to build across Manchuria the Trans-Siberian Railway, of which the section in Chinese territory was known as the Chinese Eastern Railway. From Harbin, in northern Manchuria, the Russians constructed two branch lines to Port Arthur and Dairen. This was the major cause of the Russo-Japanese war. Via those railways, Russia threatened to absorb Korea, the vital line of Japan's defence. Japan declared war on Russia and victoriously acquired the Southern Manchurian Railway. It became the economic spine of Manchuria. Between 1925 and 1929, however, a further branch connected the Chinese Eastern Railway and Peking, greatly facilitating the transport of Chinese to Manchuria. In 1905 there were three million Chinese in Manchuria; in 1930 there were approximately

---

[7] P. Grant Jones to Lampson, No. 113, 7 October 1928, enclosed in Lampson to Cushendun, No. 1399, 14 November 1928 [F 34/2/10], F.O. 371/13388.

[8] Tilley to Cushendun, No. 451, 31 November 1928, F.O. 371/13173.

[9] Ibid.

thirty million.[10] On the other hand, Japanese economic development proceeded apace, with interests valued at about £200,000,000.[11] According to Sir Victor Wellesley:

In South Manchuria, Japan has developed her sphere with notable success, transforming that uneconomic waste into some semblance of a civilised country. Towns such as Dairen and Mukden have become important trading centres with both Japanese and European establishments. The more these interests develop, the greater is the call upon the local administration for the maintenance of order and protection. The Chinese authorities who are nominally in control of the province are quite unable to meet this demand; not only so, but they have been actively engaged in circumventing the Japanese, e.g., by establishing railway competition with the S. Manchurian railway ... and thereby jeopardising the earning capacity of the Japanese line.[12]

With the Chinese attempting to 'strangle' the South Manchurian Railway by building lines parallel to it, and with the increasing number of Chinese subjects, China and Japan by the late 1920s seemed to be on collision course. The clash occurred at Mukden, which was the nucleus of the complex southern Manchurian system.

In the historiography of the inter-war period, the occupation of Mukden by Japanese troops on the night of 18–19 September 1931 has been subject to two radically different interpretations, those by political left and right. The former holds that the League's inability to check Japanese aggression encouraged further aggressions commonly associated with the causes of the Second World War. Had Britain stood firmly by the Covenant, so the argument runs, the League in co-operation with the United States might have reversed the disastrous chain of events in the Far East; by failing to apply sanctions, the League caused the collapse of collective security, and the principal party

[10] Memorandum by Pratt, 12 October 1931 [F 6118/1391/10], F.O. 371/15495; *D.B.F.P.*, VIII, No. 621. For other characteristic interpretations see memorandum by F. H. Roberts, 'Sino-Japanese Relations in Manchuria and the Mukden Negotiations on Manchurian Railway Problems', 27 July 1931 [F 4123/10/10], F.O. 371/15446; and memorandum by N. Charles, dated October 1931 [F 5614/1391/10], F.O. 371/15492. Cf. Harry L. Kingman, *Effects of Chinese Nationalism upon Manchurian Railway Developments, 1925–1931* (Berkeley, 1932).

[11] Memorandum by Wellesley, 1 February 1932 [F 654/1/10], F.O. 371/16143; *D.B.F.P.*, VIII, No. 239.

[12] Ibid.

responsible for that failure was Great Britain. In other words, 'the pathway to the beaches of Dunkirk lay through the waste of Manchuria.'[13] The opposite or 'Tory' interpretation predominated among those Englishmen who viewed the League with suspicion and lamented the lapse of the Anglo-Japanese Alliance. At the time of the crisis they took the line that Britain should have given full-hearted support to Japan, and later maintained that Britain's betrayal of her old ally weakened the Japanese moderates and strengthened the 'diehard'. The Tory criticism of the government was more mute than the left's, but it nevertheless holds an important place in the mythology of the affair. Ultimately the two theories amount to the same thing: if Britain had taken a firm stand one way or another, either with the League or with Japan, war might have been averted. Both theories have the advantage of being straight-forward and clear cut, and take the Manchurian crisis as the great watershed of the inter-war years. If one reconstructs the events and issues as they were seen by the Foreign Office at the time, however, the historical circumstances become considerably more complex.

From Britain's vantage point there were two major chronological divisions of the crisis, one following the occupation of Mukden in September, the other after the Japanese bombing of Shanghai in January 1932. The principal events and dates of the first period are these. When the Japanese seized Mukden and other key points, they did so alleging Chinese attack and executing a carefully prepared plan.[14] On 21 September China appealed to the League.[15] On 30 September the League Council adopted a resolution taking note of Japan's statement that troops would be withdrawn as soon as the lives and property of Japanese nationals could be guaranteed. Following

[13] Sir Geoffrey Mander, quoted by Bassett, *Democracy and Foreign Policy* p. 5.

[14] See especially Sadako N. Ogata, *Defiance in Manchuria* (Berkeley, 1964); and Crowley, *Japan's Quest for Autonomy*, chapters two and three; also Robert H. Ferrell, 'The Mukden Incident: September 18–19, 1931', *Journal of Modern History*, 27 (1955), 66–72; and Richard Storry, 'The Mukden Incident', *St. Antony's Papers* (Far Eastern Affairs, No. 2, 1957), 1–12.

[15] The most convenient reference work on the League and Manchuria is by Westel W. Willoughby, *The Sino-Japanese Controversy and the League of Nations* (Baltimore, 1935); other standard works dealing with the problem are by Alfred Zimmern, *The League of Nations and the Rule of Law* (London, 1936); Charles K. Webster, *The League of Nations in Theory and Practice*, (London, 1933); and F. P. Walters, *A History of the League of Nations* (2 vols., London, 1952).

Japan's failure to withdraw, the Council resolved further on 24 October that Japan should evacuate within three weeks. Japan cast the only dissenting vote. On 10 December the Council decided to appoint a Commission of Enquiry to investigate the circumstances threatening 'to disrupt peace between China and Japan'. In January of the next year began the Shanghai incident, which marks the beginning of the second part of this story.

All those events took place of course, against a background of worldwide economic depression, with Britain being forced off the gold standard and—of special importance to the Empire —of unrest in India.[16] The Foreign Secretary who presided over Britain's policy during the first six weeks of this critical juncture, Lord Reading, scarcely had time to master the onerous details of the Foreign Office before the reorganization of the Government.[17] After the general election of 27 October 1931 he was replaced by a Liberal statesman of long judicious experience, Sir John Simon. His handling of the Manchurian affair holds an unfortunate place in the historiography of the period. His critics were vicious and libellous, especially about the abrogation of the Anglo-Japanese Alliance; there were Tories who believed that Britain in these crucial years, 1931 as well as 1921, should have cultivated friendship with Japan rather than have fawned on the United States. The criticism from Labour circles, then as later, was just as scurrilous. As John Strachey of the *Left News* later stated the case, Simon used the 'full strength [of] his immense forensic powers, and . . . by using the whole influence of Britain, stopped the League from taking action.'[18] The Foreign Secretary thus encountered hostile criticism from those on the right who would befriend Japan as well as from those on the left who would stand by the League, the United States, and China. As a politician who had, in Lloyd George's phrase, 'sat on the fence so long that the iron

[16] 'The Indian conundrum is as urgent as the Manchurian conundrum and if it goes wrong will lead to appalling consequences on a scale as big as China itself.' Simon to Cecil, 26 November 1931, *D.B.F.P.*, VIII, No. 789.

[17] Smith, *The Manchurian Crisis*, p. 7, makes some perceptive remarks about the difference in British policy under Reading and Simon.

[18] Quoted by Bassett, 625. Bassett's goal is to destroy such myths, and he ruthlessly succeeds. There is no satisfactory biographical study of Simon. See Carl E. B. Roberts, *Sir John Simon*, (London, 1938), and Simon's own juiceless autobiographical account, *Retrospect* (London, 1952).

has entered into his soul', Simon now attempted coolly and rationally to reconcile China and Japan, to uphold the principles of the League, and to work closely with the United States. It was perhaps the most thankless task of his career.

The permanent officials of the Foreign Office had already laid the basis of Simon's policy before his arrival. Their initial response to the Mukden incident was to avoid involvement at all costs. Various minutes by those monitoring telegrams from Tokyo and Peking were unanimous in the view that it was uncertain whether the Japanese had acted in retort to military action on the part of the Chinese forces, or without provocation. Nor was it clear whether the Japanese military commanders in Manchuria had brushed aside the restraining influence of their superiors in Tokyo, or whether the latter merely professed to deplore this decisive takeover. On the one hand, the crisis could be interpreted as the result of a Japanese military conspiracy; on the other, the government might be conniving to strengthen Japan's position in Manchuria. What was obvious was that if Great Britain expressed a view one way or the other, she would reap the ill will of either China or Japan. 'It would be the height of unwisdom for us to interfere,' wrote Sir Victor Wellesley.[19] Thus was born a policy of neutrality out of prudence. Until the facts of the incident could be clarified, the Foreign Office would remain impartial, and in any case would wait for full reports from Peking and Tokyo.

In Peking, Sir Miles Lampson judged that two crucial points were open to doubt: the way in which the crisis originated and the future intentions of the Japanese Government. In one of his initial and most lucid reviews, he asked whether Chinese troops actually had attacked the railway line and thus created a 'critical situation', and whether the incident could have been 'localized'. He thought it would never be definitely known whether the Japanese had been provoked. But he was sceptical.

Frankly, I admit that I am extremely sceptical, and my doubts are shared by many. It is clear, I think, that the Chinese had for some time been genuinely afraid of the aggressive temper of the Japanese troops in Manchuria . . . and, in the circumstances, such an outrage on their [the Chinese] part seems wildly pointless.

[19] Minute by Wellesley, 21 September 1921 [F 5031/1391/10], F.O. 371/15489; other important minutes in the same file.

Personally, if the Japanese story is not a complete fabrication, which no one who knows their character will, I think, rule out as impossible, the most that I am disposed to believe is that suspicious persons approaching the railway line may have been fired on by the railway guards, which gave the alarm to the Japanese troops.[20]

Could the crisis have been localized? Lampson continued:

My own answer . . . which I give with some confidence, is that the Japanese army did not want to localise the incident, even if the incident was not of their own fabrication. The rapidity and precision with which their operation were carried out are remarkable.[21]

As to the responsibility of the authorities in Tokyo, Lampson wrote: 'All I need say is that the facts as I have described them can all be conveniently interpreted on the theory that the army acted in the first instance on their own initiative . . . and without the knowledge of the Japanese Foreign Office, who were thus faced with the necessity of adapting their policy to an entirely different situation.'[22] The interpretation of the British Minister in China thus accords generally with the judgement of the affair by prominent scholars of Japanese history.[23] Lampson further guessed that the Japanese would attempt to use their military hold over Manchuria to settle to their advantage long standing issues with the Chinese; and that the extent to which Japan would be more or less moderate in her demands would depend on internal developments in civil and military circles and the nature of external pressure brought to bear on them. In a long-range forecast of the future, he hazarded this prediction: 'In the course of years Japan will come to realise that her political adventures in Manchuria have cost her more "blood and treasure" than they have been worth and have impeded rather than advanced her progress towards the economic supremacy of the Far East for which she seems marked out.'[24]

In Tokyo, Sir Francis Lindley on 17 September, the day before Mukden, also proved himself a prophet by gloomily

[20] Lampson to Reading, No. 1429 Confidential, 27 September 1931 [F 7189/1391/10], F.O. 371/15446.
[21] Ibid.
[22] Ibid.
[23] See Iriye, *After Imperialism*, chapter 9; Crowley, *Japan's Quest for Autonomy*, chapters 2 and 3.
[24] Same as footnote 20.

indicating the probable course of events in Manchuria.[25] He reported a decline in popularity of the Minseito Government's policy of conciliation with China and a rise in support of the army's tendency towards independent action.[26] After the beginning of the crisis he noted that it was impossible exactly to determine the extent to which the military controlled Japan's policy, but that any external pressure would cause civil and military authorities to close ranks and form a united front. He warned above all that any mention of direct intervention by the League would have catastrophic results for Japan's relations with the western powers. The Japanese were determined to deal with China alone, and Lindley believed that if left alone they would hold true to their pledges repudiating territorial ambitions. They would brook no interference whatever in Manchuria, any more than Britain or France would tolerate subversion in their colonies. He wrote that the position of Japan in Manchuria was unique, and probably misunderstood by those in the west.

[T]he exasperating attitude of the Japanese Government and the blunders of their soldiers might lead the Council [of the League] to lose sight of the essential facts that Japanese rights in Manchuria were considered by the whole nation as somewhat sacred, and that the present crisis was due to the deliberate policy of the Chinese of undermining those rights and fostering anti-Japanese feeling by all means in their power. . . .

It is easy to argue that the Japanese are unreasonable, that they should behave like other people, that they should accept the verdict of public opinion when it goes against them and that, if they don't, they must be induced to do so by some effective form of pressure. The answer is that, unfortunately, the Japanese are not reasonable when they believe their vital interests are involved; and that the mere hint of pressure, so far from rendering them more reasonable, makes them see red.[27]

[25] 'A most interesting & accurate prophecy.' Minute by N. Charles, 13 October, on Lindley to Reading, No. 459 Confidential, 17 September 1931 [F 5636/1391/10], F.O. 371/15492.

[26] 'This loss of prestige by the Minseito Govt. has strengthened the hands of the Army in their independent action in Manchuria & prevented the former from regaining real control of the situation.' Minute by F. H. Roberts, 13 October 1931, ibid.

[27] Lindley to Reading, No. 512, 30 October 1931 [F 7122/1391/10], F.O. 371/15502.

After numerous attempts during the course of the crisis to urge moderation to the Japanese, Lindley concluded that representations—the diplomatic term for complaints—did more harm than good. He observed with despair that in proportion to mounting international indignation, so rose the Japanese 'passionate belief in the justice of their own cause.'[28] Lindley persistently pleaded with the Foreign Office to pursue a cautious path, lest Britain help drive Japan down the road of aggressive expansion and military dictatorship. At one stage he reported that 'the active part of the nation has been brought into a state of violent war psychology, resembling that in Germany in 1914.'[29] In those circumstances the British Ambassador found himself in a most difficult situation: if he sided with the dominant view in the League, that Japan was guilty of aggression, he faced growing antipathy of the Japanese Government and further deterioration of Anglo-Japanese relations; if he sympathized with Japan, he received criticism from Peking and Geneva. Damned either way, Lindley interpreted his preeminent duty as Ambassador to remain as friendly as possible with the Japanese. He was rebuked by British representatives at Peking and Geneva. In reply to criticism by Sir Miles Lampson, that the Embassy in Tokyo had done little to mitigate the dispute, Lindley bitterly wrote: 'The trouble all through has been that we have been trying to make the best of a bad job, whereas Sir M. Lampson has been seeking a much better solution which our knowledge of the present Japanese feeling convinces us is impossible of attainment while crisis lasts except at the price of world war.'[30]

If Lindley and some of the Foreign Office officials such as Sir Victor Wellesley showed undue sympathy towards the Japanese, Lord Robert Cecil viewed Japan's action as 'pure militarism of the worst type'.[31] Cecil, who more than any other

[28] Lindley to Simon, No. 588, 12 December 1931 [F 367/1/10], F.O. 371/16141.
[29] Lindley to Simon, No. 80 Confidential, 11 February 1932 [F 3298/40/23], F.O. 371/16242.
[30] Lindley to Simon, No. 132 tel., 25 February 1932 [F 1698/1/10], F.O. 371/16152. Armin Rappaport, *Henry L. Stimson and Japan, 1931–33* (Chicago, 1963), p. 201, records Lindley's complaint to the American Ambassador in Tokyo, that the Foreign Office laid down 'dogmatic theories without regard to facts'. On the whole, the Foreign Office judged that Lindley viewed British policy towards Japan too much in isolation. See for example *D.B.F.P.*, X, No. 64.
[31] Cecil to Simon, 8 December 1931, *D.B.F.P.*, VIII, No. 831.

Englishman had helped to found the League and who now headed the Delegation at Geneva, blamed 'Japan and Japan alone' for creating a crisis that threatened to destroy his life's work. To him there was no question of guilt: the Japanese had no business in Manchuria and by late October had flouted the League, indeed the entire civilized world, by refusing to get out. Cecil held that the central doctrine of the Covenant was to make aggression an international crime, and he had no doubt that Japan was an aggressor. He became the leading advocate of the use of embargoes against Japan, and, at least in retrospect, of force. He later became one of the more prominent critics of the government by repeating the phrase 'we did nothing', in other words, as one of the keenest critics of the Manchurian affair has pointed out, nothing coercive.[32] In his autobiographical account written in 1941, Cecil stated that 'force alone would have turned her (Japan) from her purpose.'[33] He thus took an entirely different approach to the problem from the Ambassador in Tokyo, whom he regarded as subverting the League. 'May I submit', Cecil wrote to Sir John Simon in December 1931, 'that the attitude of Sir F. Lindley right through this dispute has been quite inadequate? ... What an attitude for a British representative! Can nothing be done to spur him into some sort of activity?'[34]

Sir Victor Wellesley quickly came to Lindley's defence, and the role of Sir John Simon in the controversy illuminates his basic approach at a crucial juncture of the Manchurian affair. In late December 1931, after the League had decided to send a Commisssion to the Far East, and on the eve of the Japanese takeover of Chinchow (one of the remaining Chinese strongholds in south eastern Manchuria), Wellesley observed that Lindley's position in view of the impending arrival of a Commission with a British chairman was 'painfully difficult'.

[32] Bassett, *Democracy and Foreign Policy*, p. 596. The evolution of Cecil's views is more complex than has been assumed. At the beginning of the crisis apparently he was convinced that force would be neither necessary nor desirable. About January 1932 his attitude hesitantly began to shift. But only years later, after the publication of his autobiography (*A Great Experiment*, London, 1941), did he emerge as the champion of forcible action. For insight into these points I am indebted to Christopher Thorne, who has a forthcoming article on the subject in the *Historical Journal*.

[33] Cecil, *A Great Experiment*, p. 332.

[34] *D.B.F.P.*, IX, No. 17 note 4; cf. F.O. 371/15507.

One of the distinctive features of the Sino-Japanese dispute has been that Japan has been regarded in some quarters as 'flouting', 'defying' or 'challenging' the League. It is obvious, therefore, that Sir F. Lindley had no easy task in reconciling the evident contradictions of his two functions. . . .

No blame for this unfortunate state of affairs can be attached to Sir F. Lindley, but on him fell the duty of remedying it, and especially of restoring as far as he might the good relations between his country and Japan which had suffered unprecedented damage in a few weeks.[36]

Wellesley went on to say that the Japanese attacked Great Britain more bitterly than any other power because of the assumption that the British representative at Geneva had sponsored anti-Japanese resolutions. In those circumstances Wellesley judged that Lindley had displayed great tact in partially restoring friendly relations with Japan. 'Sir F. Lindley has deserved well of his country for his conduct in the dispute,' he concluded.[37] On those comments by Wellesley, Sir John Simon wrote the following minute, which well indicates how Simon saw the complexity of the problem and Britain's dilemma of Japan and the League:

No one proposes that we should pick a quarrel with Japan, & Sir F. Lindley has of course shown great diplomatic discretion. . . . The important question now is as to the outcome. Supposing Chinchow is attacked & taken & the League Comsn. arrives to find a Japanese Protectorate *de facto* in Manchuria? If this is what is in store, we may expect (1) trouble at the League Council in January (2) challenge in the H[ouse] of C[ommons] and a demand to know what representations we made to stop it. I quite agree that good relations with Japan are of the first order of requisites, & must be safeguarded: but we must, consistently with this, play our part as a member of the League, and use such influence as we have.[38]

Foreseeing trouble in every direction, Simon encountered it: in England and Switzerland, from Japan, China, and, not least, from the United States.

The events are well known. Less than forty-eight hours after the League's decision on 10 December 1931 to send a committee

[36] Memorandum by Wellesley, 22 December 1931 [F 7766/1391/10], F.O. 371/15507; *D.B.F.P.*, IX, No. 21.
[37] Ibid.   [38] Ibid.

of inquiry to Manchuria, the liberal Japanese Cabinet fell. Hopes of conciliation between Japan and China diminished. By 2 January Japanese forces had captured Chinchow, thus destroying the last major foothold of the Chinese in Manchuria. As Japan consolidated her hold, however, an anti-Japanese boycott spread throughout China, with disastrous effects on Japanese trade. On 18 January five Japanese nationals, including two priests, were attacked and injured by Chinese on the northern boundary of the International Settlement at Shanghai. The Japanese Consul-General demanded reparations. On 24 January Japanese naval reinforcements arrived. Hostilities between Chinese and Japanese forces commenced within the city, plunging Britain into the second major part of the Manchurian crisis: Sino-Japanese antagonism now disrupted Britain's trade at the heart of commercial China, Shanghai.[39]

The proclivity of British statesmen during these crucial months was to appease Japan and work in concert with both the League and the United States. This proposition can be amplified by the addition of two corollaries. First, with the principal exceptions of Lord Robert Cecil and Sir Alexander Cadogan of the Geneva delegation, British officials during the Manchurian part of the dispute were profoundly anti-Chinese and pro-Japanese.[40] This predominant attitude changed to one of alarm at Japan during the Shanghai incident. Second, Simon and his Foreign Office staff saw their paramount duty as cooperation with the League and viewed the policy of the United States with all of the distrust and misgiving that had characterized Lord Curzon and his colleagues a decade earlier. These sentiments have perhaps never been adequately described and are not fully reflected in the *Documents on British Foreign Policy*. It is important to understand them in order to grasp the underpinning of Britain's position, and the hopes and despairs of her statesmen who shaped Far Eastern policy.

[39] For the Shanghai incident, see especially Payson J. Treat, 'Shanghai: January 28, 1932', *Pacific Historical Review*, 9 (1940), 337–43; and Robert H. Ferrell, *American Diplomacy in the Great Depression: Hoover-Stimson Foreign Policy, 1929–1933* (New Haven, 1957) chapter 11; for British attitudes, Bassett, *Democracy and Foreign Policy*, Part II.

[40] Another exception might be Sir Victor Wellesley. He had little use for either the Japanese or Chinese and once described them both as 'puerile, deceitful, cruel and savage'. Memorandum by Wellesley, 1 February 1932 [F 654/1/10], F.O. 371/16143.

Simon himself frequently used the words 'wretched' or 'foolish' to describe the Chinese. His staff for the most part shared his views and believed that the Japanese had a better case than they themselves made in Geneva. If one traces the evolution of official British thought through the Foreign Office files from the beginning of the crisis to the time of the Shanghai incident, one comes across the recurrent idea that Japan might have acted impetuously but not without provocation. The Japanese looked upon Manchuria as a vital national interest, one that had to be respected as other nations respected Britain's interests in India or Egypt. The following minutes by Foreign Office officials of various rank illustrate this and other points.

They [the Japanese] are not likely to move an inch from this position. They have the moral and physical strength. They have a weak inefficient & troublesome neighbour. Manchuria is next door to Japan and touches her vital interests. Anything but the most tactful outside interference may encourage her to do something rash.[41]

On the question of Japanese guilt and the Chinese attempt to twist the situation to their advantage:

It is pretty clear that the Japanese brought matters to a head. But the existence of the League as a possible damper on Japanese wrath may have stimulated the natural Chinese propensity to encroach & obstruct.[42]

On top of the arbitrary action of the Japanese, their inept defence at Geneva made a bad case even worse. They were outwitted by the Chinese: 'modern Chinese have facile tongues while Japanese are notoriously inarticulate.'[43] As Simon explained to the Cabinet: 'The Japanese representative at Geneva had not put his country's case very well.' This made Britain's dilemma worse.[44] If the Chinese managed to use the League to prosecute Japan, the League would lose one of its most powerful supporters and Britain would lose a friend. If the Chinese succeeded in their game of embroiling Britain and Japan, Britain's position in all of the Far East would be undermined.

---

[41] Minute by N. Charles, 13 October 1930 [F 5611], F.O. 371/15492.
[42] Minute by C. W. Orde, c. 22 October 1931 [F 5950], F.O. 371/15494.
[43] Minute by C. E. Whitemore, 3 November 1930 [F 6271], F.O. 371/15495.
[44] Cabinet Minutes, Secret, 11 November 1931, CAB. 23/89.

Such ideas can be followed through the first three months of the dispute and perhaps were put in most comprehensive form by Sir John Pratt. He wrote after the commencement of hostilities at Shanghai:

The trouble at Shanghai arises directly out of the trouble in Manchuria, but the action taken by the Japanese at Shanghai faces us with a set of considerations of a different order to those which were raised by Japanese action in Manchuria. In Manchuria the Japanese, as regards the fundamental issues at stake, had a great deal of right on their side. The Chinese were almost entirely in the wrong. By their corruption, incapacity and blind conceit they were reducing to ruin one of the wealthiest regions in the world, thus going a long way towards undoing the good work of the Japanese who had made prosperity possible by keeping Manchuria free from civil war. They ignored both Japan's treaty rights and the historical justification for Japan's position in Manchuria. They regarded the policy of patience and conciliation pursued by Japan as a sign of weakness, and met Japan's efforts to reach a working agreement on the railway question —the fundamental of all the questions at issue—with an exasperating policy of evasion and procrastination.[45]

Pratt went on to explain further why the situation in Shanghai differed fundamentally from that in Manchuria. His analysis is a good example of the shift of British official opinion *after* the Japanese attack at Shanghai. In Manchuria, the Japanese had legitimate reasons to act; but the move into Shanghai could be prelude to a Japanese attempt to control all of China. There was nothing illegal about the anti-Japanese boycott, Pratt wrote, and it was the only weapon the Chinese possessed; but the Japanese had responded to it with brute force, bombing civilians, burning bridges, and killing large numbers of non-combatants. If Japan continued unleased, 'The British will have to retire altogether from the Far East,' and perhaps, he warned direly, even from India.

[I]f we stand aside and leave Japan to work her will unchecked upon China British commercial interests may suffer severely from Japanese arrogance and Chinese xenophobia. A Far East where Japan was dominant and supreme and also perhaps contemptuous of Great Britain would not be a favourable sphere for the development of British trade and industry. . . .

45 Memorandum by Pratt, n.d. but *c.* 1 February 1931 [F 654/1/10], F.O. 371/16143.

If it is decided that we must check Japan certain preliminary measures could be adopted—such as rupture of diplomatic and economic relations—but in the end Japan can only be checked by force. Ultimately, we will be faced with the alternatives of going to war with Japan or retiring from the Far East.[46]

The question of *war* inevitably raised the issue of Anglo-American co-operation.

Pratt's cogent summary was analysed by his immediate superiors, Sir Victor Wellesley and the Permanent Under-Secretary, Sir Robert Vansittart. Wellesley wrote: 'The dangers to which Sir J. Pratt calls attention are undoubtedly very real ones the more so since we now know that the Japanese Naval and Military Authorities are completely out of hand and the Japanese Government more or less impotent.'[47] Vansittart's serial minute indicates the extent of the Foreign Office's alarm, and illustrates the uncertainty of attitude towards the United States:

(1) If Japan continues unchecked & increasingly, as she indeed seems bent on doing, our position & vast interests in the Far East will never recover. This may well spread to the Middle East. The Japanese victory in 1904 was the beginning of trouble there.

(2) *We* are incapable of checking Japan in any way if she really means business and has sized us up, as she certainly has done.

(3) Therefore we must eventually be done for in the Far East, unless

(4) The United States are eventually prepared to use force.

(5) It is universally assumed here that the U.S. will never use force.

(6) I do not agree that this is necessarily so. The same was said of the U.S. in the Great War. Eventually she was kicked in by the Germans. The Japanese may end by kicking in the U.S. too, if they go on long enough kicking as they are now.

(7) The Japanese are more afraid of the U.S. than of us, and for obvious reasons. At present, however, they share our low view of American fighting spirit.

(8) By ourselves we must eventually swallow any & every humiliation in the Far East. If there is some limit to American submissiveness, this is not necessarily so.

Vansittart went on to conclude that Britain could have no firm

---

[46] Ibid.

[47] Minute by Wellesley, 1 February 1932 [F 1263/1/10], F.O. 371/16148.

policy in the Far East until the American attitude could be determined.[48] Simon, characteristically keeping an open mind and being reluctant to commit himself, merely initialed the minutes.

In some ways historical myths assume an importance as great as the historical reality. This is the case of Sir John Simon's action—or inaction, depending on the interpretation—during the winter of 1931–2, which has become one of the great myths in Anglo-American relations. From the American side the myth has been exploded, or at least explained.[49] From the British side, however, the evidence has remained fragmentary until the opening of the British records in 1969. There are two points at issue, as charged by the American Secretary of State, Henry L. Stimson. First, that the Foreign Office rebuffed the State Department following the declaration on 7 January 1931 of the 'Stimson Doctrine' of non-recognition of agreements brought about by force.[50] The American Secretary was thus left 'out on a limb'.[51] Second, that after the Japanese attack on Shanghai, Sir John Simon 'preferred to take refuge in the inconspicuousness of . . . action' among a 'flock' of nations rather than to join forces with the United States in a firm line against Japan. The British 'let us down,' were Stimson's famous words. Those charges are complex in detail and clouded with misunderstanding. To comprehend them from the British side it is first important to see clearly who controlled British policy at the time. Unlike the critical juncture a decade earlier, it was not the Cabinet, or even the special Cabinet Committee established to consider Far Eastern affairs.[52] Until mid-February 1932, the Cabinet gave a free hand to Sir John Simon, who guided British

[48] Minute by Vansittart, 1 February 1932, ibid.

[49] See especially Elting E. Morison, *Turmoil and Tradition: A Study of the Life and Times of Henry L. Stimson* (Cambridge, Mass., 1960), chapter 21; and Rappaport, *Henry L. Stimson and Japan*.

[50] See especially Ferrell, *American Diplomacy in the Great Depression*, chapter 10; also Richard N. Current, 'The Stimson Doctrine and the Hoover Doctrine', *American Historical Review*, 59 (1953–4), 513–42.

[51] See Stimson's own account, *The Far Eastern Crisis* (New York, 1936); and Henry L. Stimson and McGeorge Bundy, *On Active Service in Peace and War* (New York, 1947).

[52] The minutes of this Committee are in CAB. 27/482. One of the few interesting remarks was made by the Secretary of State for Dominion Affairs, J. H. Thomas: 'From the standpoint of the League of Nations any protest was a bluff, since no nation was prepared to implement it.' 15 February 1932.

policy with a grasp of detail, if not a firmness of purpose, reminiscent of Lord Salisbury. Like Salisbury, however, he did rely heavily on his permanent staff, of whom the two key experts in this episode were Sir Robert Vansittart and Sir Victor Wellesley.

Between Vansittart and Wellesley existed an important difference in outlook towards the United States. Vansittart thought it at least possible that the Americans might be roused to action against the Japanese. Wellesley was far more pessimistic. He regarded American policy as mercurial and totally unreliable. Numerous quotations could be given to illustrate Wellesley's mistrust of the United States; perhaps this serves as well as any:

[T]he policy of the United States of America in China (as elsewhere) has been erratic and inconsiderate in the past (e.g.), obstruction at the Peking Tariff Conference (1925), withdrawal of co-operation after Nanking outrages (1927), anticipation of tariff concessions (1928). The United States Government is quite capable of backing out after we had agreed to give our support, leaving us to clear up the resultant mess.[53]

Lest Wellesley's strictures sound cynical, it should be pointed out that he genuinely believed in Great Britain's commitment to the League of Nations. Throughout the entire Manchurian crisis he saw this point as crucial in shaping British policy: Britain was a member of the League, the United States was not. When the 'Stimson Doctrine' arrived at the Foreign Office, Wellesley drafted the reply with that distinction in mind.

Neither Wellesley nor his colleagues doubted Stimson's moral earnestness, his belief in international co-operation, his love of England, and his genuine desire for Anglo-American friendship. At the same time the Foreign Office viewed him as a typical American Secretary of State at the mercy of his President—with this exception: the force of Stimson's personality and the vigour of his leadership gave his diplomacy—to the British at least—an air of unmitigated arrogance. Though the United States was not a member of the League, Stimson tried to manipulate its proceedings; for such an ardent supporter of

[53] Memorandum by Wellesley, 1 February 1932 [F 654/1/10], F.O. 371/16143; *D.B.F.P.*, IX, No. 239.

such instruments as the Nine Power Treaty and the Kellogg-Briand or Pact of Paris agreement, he displayed in Vansittart's phrase, a 'curious ignorance' of international protocol and the workings of the League, not to mention the Japanese national psychology. In retrospect the Foreign Office speculated that Stimson apparently had expected the Foreign Office to fall in line when he issued his famous note to China and Japan on 7 January 1931 stating that the United States did not intend 'to recognize any situation, treaty, or agreement which may be brought about by means contrary to the covenants and obligations of the Pact of Paris.' Instead of endorsing that Stimson *démarche*, Wellesley issued this statement to the press:

H.M.G. stand by the policy of the 'open door' for international trade in Manchuria which was guaranteed by the Nine Power Treaty at Washington. Since the recent events in Manchuria the Japanese representative at the Council of the League of Nations at Geneva stated on October 13th that Japan was the champion in Manchuria of the principal of equal opportunity and the 'open door' for the economic activities of all nations. Further, on December 28th the Japanese Prime Minister stated that Japan would adhere to the 'open door' policy and would welcome foreign participation and cooperation in Manchurian enterprises.

In view of this statement H.M.G. have not considered it necessary to address any formal note to the Japanese Government on the lines of the American Government's note, but the Japanese Ambassador has been requested to obtain confirmation of this assurance from his government.[54]

The press release appeared in the newspapers on 10 January 1932, before the Ambassador delivered a communiqué to the same intent at the State Department. Stimson felt rebuffed, and thus began a chapter in Anglo-American relations filled with recrimination and bitterness. The Foreign Office subsequently maintained that no snub had been intended, and it is certainly true that even Wellesley, with his gruff anti-American bias, had no scheme afoot to alienate the United States. Perhaps the communiqué was a blunder, as has commonly been assumed. On the other hand it was a clear statement of British principles,

[54] See minutes in F.O. 371/16140; the press release is printed in *D.B.F.P.*, IX, No. 66, note 2. An entire article has been written on the subject: Robert A. Hecht, 'Great Britain and the Stimson Note of January 7, 1932', *Pacific Historical Review*, **38**, 2 (May 1969), 177–91.

significant more for what was not said than for what it specified. Wellesley had simply stated indirectly that Great Britain could not act independently of the League, and that Japan should be given opportunity to prove her good faith. Sir John Simon, who also did not anticipate the American reaction, merely noted on Wellesley's draft: 'I quite agree: very good.'

Stimson's chief subsequent grievance was that Great Britain blocked his attempt to make Japan willing 'to sit in a fair conference upon the subject of her controversy with China'. He proposed to invoke the Nine Power Treaty, which of course was designed to protect the integrity of China. After very careful examination of the Foreign Office records, Sir John Pratt and others later judged (when they reconstructed the episode in 1936) that Stimson broached the subject to the British Ambassador in Washington, Sir Ronald Lindsay, on 9 February 1932, little over a week after the Japanese attack on Shanghai. In fact there was no mention of a conference in Lindsay's report of the conversation, which is quite specific in describing the language used by the Secretary. Lindsay telegraphed:

It seemed to him [Stimson] that the moment might be approaching when a very strong indictment should be addressed to Japanese Government. He said that no such shock as events at Shanghai had been administered to the cause of international morality since August 1914. His own individual feelings now were precisely what they had been then but today there was a compact answer; instruments, covenant, pact and nine Power treaty which gave legitimate ground for protest. . . . He was thinking of basing his representation mainly on . . . Nine Power Treaty.

I asked if he contemplated anything further than a note. His answer was that whatever his feelings might be restraint was necessary; but he did not desire to bring into his remonstrance a passage in the sense of his note of January 7th to the Japanese Government, refusing in advance of the recognition of any action or situation arising out of the proceedings at Shanghai. . . .

I asked if he meant to invite the co-operation of other Powers. He said that if absolutely necessary he might go ahead alone. His Majesty's Government was the one Government whose co-operation he was really anxious to secure.[55]

According to the British Ambassador, there thus was no plan at

[55] Lindsay to Simon, No. 99 tel., 9 February 1932 [F 1156/1/10], F.O. 371/ 16147.

this stage to invoke a conference under the Nine Power Treaty, but instead a definite plan of indictment. The Foreign Office responded immediately and negatively. On the day of receipt of Lindsay's telegram, a junior member of the Far Eastern Department, C. E. Whitemore, noted that the Japanese would not be deflected from their purposes in China no matter how strongly worded the protest, and that Stimson's proposed note might well provoke them further. The next official who minuted the telegram, C. W. Orde, wrote that however desirable it might be to work with the United States, Great Britain as a member of the League's Council obviously could not make a strong indictment of Japan while the Council still considered the matter. 'It is one thing to take emergency action outside the League to stop further fighting & quite another to adopt the attitude of a judge & pronounce judgment without waiting to confer with one's colleagues on the same bench.' He submitted that Britain's position as a member of the League's Council made it impossible for the Foreign Office to prejudge the issue in the way proposed by the American Secretary. Sir Victor Wellesley noted: 'I agree. A thoroughly ill-advised & impulsive proposal. Typically American & intended for home consumption.' Sir Robert Vansittart wrote:

We should certainly advise the S. of S. against joining in 'a very strong indictment' of Japan at *this* juncture, whatever may be done later. The chief reason given should be that in Mr. Whitemore's minute because it is easier to give it as the first reason to Mr. Stimson. It may serve to dissuade him, and that, just now, is in the common interests. Indictments must wait till the danger is less acute. We have been trying to keep the League from going off the deep end. The same tactics should be followed in regard to Mr. Stimson.[56]

Sir John Simon proceeded accordingly, without success. Four years later, after the Foreign Office had been 'internationally slandered' by Stimson's book, *The Far Eastern Crisis*, Vansittart wrote again:

Mr. Stimson can be remarkably acid and untruthful for so lovable a man, and remarkably stupid for so intelligent a man. It is, & always has been, hard quite to understand what 'got into him' over this affair. He has gone on with this unfounded rancour despite our

explanations, & now he has gone so far that he shd. not be allowed
to get away with it, for the untruth is damaging to our relations.[57]

Sir John Pratt well expressed the ire of the Foreign Office over
this incident when in 1936 he concluded that Stimson probably
did not realize 'how greatly his own impatience, impulsiveness,
and unfounded suspicions contributed to the difficulties he
describes.'[58]

Part of the trouble arose from trans-Atlantic telephone conversations between Simon and Stimson. They generated so
much misunderstanding that Simon later refused to transact
business by telephone. Static greatly vexed comprehension at
this primitive stage of telephonic communication; conventional
blandishments could be misinterpreted as assurances. The
following excerpts illustrate how Simon might well have un-
intentionally misled Stimson into believing that Great Britain
would go along with the American plan of indicting Japan.
This conversation took place on 12 February 1932, following
several other exchanges in which Simon had reassured the
Secretary that Great Britain would attempt to co-operate. The
Foreign Secretary spoke from Geneva.

Sir John: Hallo, how are you?

Simon here. . . .

As regards a possible statement or declaration, a good deal would
depend both upon the time of it and also upon the contents of it,
because we feel rather more hopeful than you that there still are at
any rate some possible ways of approach. . . .

Stimson: Shall I send it [the draft] very secretly to Geneva?

Sir John: Well, that would be very good.

Stimson: It is only a rough draft. It is only British agreement I chiefly
care about.

Sir John: I quite understand and of course I may be able to help you
about that if we agree. . . . The British Government would very

---

[57] Minute by Vansittart, 10 October 1936, F.O. 371/20275.

[58] 'Memorandum concerning Allegations by Mr. Stimson that His Majesty's
Government failed to co-operate with the United States Government in 1932 in
connexion with the Sino-Japanese Dispute', by Sir John Pratt, 1 October 1936
[F 6358/2412/10], F.O. 371/20275. This is the fullest British record of the incident.
See also evidence in F.O. 371/18156 for the development of the dispute. Cf.
Morison, *Turmoil and Tradition*, p. 393, note 39, and Borg, *Far Eastern Crisis*, p. 565,
note 36. See also Pratt's letter to *The Times*, 10 November 1938, reprinted in *War
and Politics in China*, pp. 281–6.

much like to discuss that with you and we shall do our very best to agree with you. . . .

Stimson: I agree. My document would be moderate in tone. Do you agree?

Sir John: Yes, I do indeed. That is very good. . . .

Stimson: Do you think Japan will hold her hand?

Sir John: Personally I do not. Naturally we have to go carefully because we are in very explosive areas. . . . I should be averse to anything which amounted to an indictment of one side because it would be prejudging and the League would very much object to it. But I quite agree with the importance of affirming the 9-Power Pact and all its implications.[59]

Stimson quickly became convinced that Simon was shilly-shallying. On 24 February 1932 the Secretary threw over the British by publishing his famous letter to Senator Borah, in which he urged other powers to adopt a non-recognition policy and indirectly threatened Japan by suggesting that the United States might not be bound by the Washington Naval Treaty if Japan disregarded the Nine Power Treaty. Simon doggedly continued to mollify Stimson. This telephone conversation took place after the publication of the Borah letter. Simon again spoke from Geneva.

Sir John: Hullo, is that you Mr. Stimson?
This is Simon here. . . .
I thought you would like to know what we are doing. . . . I do hope we may have an opportunity jointly together with the other Powers of offering our good offices to stop this awful business [at Shanghai].

Stimson: Well, Sir John, that will depend in large part upon the concrete attitude of your Government and mine and the French.

Sir John: I quite agree with you.

Stimson: And I have been rather sorry that the apparently good

[59] This account is collated from *D.B.F.P.*, IX, No. 431, and *Foreign Relations* 1932, III, 294–8. The telephone connections at the time were often so bad that Charles Evan Hughes, now Chief Justice, apparently was twice mistaken for a Japanese. *Foreign Relations*, 1931, II; Borg, *Far Eastern Crisis*, p. 564, note 31. Three days after this conversation, on 15 February, the Cabinet made a crucial decision: 'SIR JOHN SIMON said that he would speak to Mr Stimson by telephone at once; would make it clear that we could not associate ourselves with the passage in his document relating to Manchuria; and would make certain criticisms of the draft.' (Cabinet Minutes, Secret, 15 February 1932, CAB. 27/482.) The ambiguity of Simon's language with Stimson, however, persisted. See *D.B.F.P.*, IX, No. 458.

concert that we had in the beginning does not seem to be quite as easy now.

Sir John: Yes, I am very sorry about that too. . . .

Stimson: . . . . I want to make it perfectly clear that I am not . . . pressing now the suggestion which I made to you a week ago. I think the occasion for that has momentarily passed by. In my letter to Senator Borah I have made public my own country's position—the position of the American Government has been made clear in this letter so that so far as we are concerned I have no anxiety about the matter that I spoke to you about ten days ago. Do you understand?

Sir John: I am not quite sure that I follow the point you are referring to.

Stimson: I say that my letter to Senator Borah has taken the place of the suggestion which I made to you about ten days ago for the action of our two Governments. My object then was to make the position of our two Governments clear as to the Nine Power Treaty. That has been done now so far as my Government is concerned by my letter to Senator Borah so that I am not pressing the suggestion I made to you at that time.

Sir John: Yes.

Very well.

You are waiting to watch what Britain does. I quite follow that. . . .[60]

Simon wisely concluded that telephonic communication should be avoided.

The British Ambassador in Washington evaluated Stimson's moral diplomacy in regard to both Britain and Japan. On the one hand, the Borah letter seemed to address 'those sections of the British opinion which have been most hesitant in taking an attitude adverse to Japan'. On the other hand, Stimson, in the tradition of President Wilson, apparently utilized moral strictures when other more forcible means could not be employed. In Sir Ronald Lindsay's view:

[T]here are very decided limitations as to the lengths to which the United States Government will go. I should not care to answer for the feelings of the Secretary of State, as he is rather an emotional man, but I have no doubt that the President would very efficiently check anything he thought likely to lead to more than an exchange of notes, and in spite of strong and nation-wide disapproval of Japanese attitudes, Congress is certainly opposed to anything in the nature of sanctions.

[60] *D.B.F.P.*, IX, No. 560; *Foreign Relations*, 1932, III, 432–6.

There seems to be widespread conviction here that the country is in no single respect in a position to face major complications. The extreme reluctance of recourse to physical measures merely emphasizes the desire of United States Government to utilise to the utmost the moral principle, which they regard as one of great efficacy and importance, and as destined, perhaps, to fill a large place in international law.[61]

Whatever might be said of the high-minded purpose of Stimson's tactics, the British diplomat closest in contact with the State Department judged that American diplomacy towards Japan rested on empty threats and calculated bluff. Like his colleagues in London, Geneva and Tokyo, Lindsay feared that actions of 'moral character' such as the Borah letter would only make the Japanese more recalcitrant.

From the vantage point of the British Embassy in Tokyo, the Borah letter constituted another disaster in the relations of the western powers with Japan. Sir Francis Lindley telegraphed:

Presumably it was intended for home consumption but it is difficult to exaggerate harm done here by these outbursts which are utilised to inflame public opinion already dangerously excited. I do not know whether United States Government realise war psychology now prevailing here or how dangerous it is because of its arrogance. But I sincerely trust that His Majesty's Government will not allow themselves to be dragged in by . . . American rashness. It is not too much to say that American residents here look to His Majesty's Government to save them from their own people.[62]

The Japanese reaction to the Borah letter, Lindley reported, was 'as bitter as can be'. The sudden American intervention had all but destroyed his policy of conciliation. He judged that things were worse than ever. 'We believed that, if this process of appeasement were allowed to continue, public opinion here, which, as far as we could judge, was opposed to far-reaching commitments in China proper, would gain sufficient strength to check the ambitions of the forward military party.'[63] Lindley, who had earlier written that he already felt as if he were 'living

---

[61] Lindsay to Simon, No. 127 tel., 25 February 1932 [F 1784/1/10], F.O. 371/16152, with important minutes in the same file.

[62] Lindley to Simon, No. 42 tel., 26 February 1932 [F 1815/1/10], F.O. 371/16152.

[63] Lindley to Simon, No. 109, Very Confidential, 26 February 1932 [F 2768/1/10], F.O. 371/16159.

in a lunatic asylum',[64] now in late 1932 believed that any further pressure on Japan, moral, economic, or otherwise, could well lead to war.

Times of crisis demand heroic action, and in the meantime Britain's hero in the Far East, Sir Miles Lampson, arrived in Shanghai. During the month of February 1932 he lent his informal good offices to both parties of the dispute. To bring about a cease-fire he proposed that both Chinese and Japanese troops withdraw to create a neutral zone, mainly at Chinese expense. As much as he disliked his own advice, he urged on the Chinese 'a policy of non-resistance and retirement'. Pending the arrival of the League's Commission of Enquiry, he played for time. He advised the Chinese military officers that in their own interest they should withdraw from the International Settlement lest they be smashed by overpowering Japanese force. Reassuring the Chinese, he had far less success with the Japanese. He gained the impression that the Japanese military had their Minister at Shanghai under their thumb. Hostilities continued, and of the worst sort. In Lampson's words: 'Inexcusable atrocities were undoubtedly committed by the Japanese marines, and armed civilians, many of the latter roughs of the lowest class, during the heat of the street fighting.'[65] After arduous negotiations surpassing in intensity even those he conducted in the treaty revision programme, Lampson's mission at first failed. He attributed the collapse of his scheme to the Japanese military, who continued to present ultimata 'in so arrogant a tone and dictatorial a form that it was hardly possible to expect their acceptance by the Chinese.'[66] Had he pressed the Chinese further to accept Japanese dictation, Great Britain would have sold China up the Yangtze River, together with British trade. The Foreign Office entirely concurred in Lampson's judgement. According to Sir Victor Wellesley in late February 1932, it would be 'most dangerous' to capitulate to the Japanese:

Sir M. Lampson has gone as far as it is safe to go in this direction. We should be saddling ourselves with an incalculable responsibility

[64] Lindley to Simon, No. 68 tel. Confidential, 5 February 1932 [F 953/1/10], F.O. 371/16146; *D.B.F.P.*, IX, No. 319.
[65] Lampson to Simon, 21 February 1932 [F 3326/1/10], F.O. 371/16163.
[66] Ibid.

& have to reap the odium of the Chinese for any unfortunate consequences that might ensue both direct & indirect.

What we have got to realise is this. Rightly or wrongly the Japanese cannot & will not stop at a point when agreement will be interpreted by the Chinese as a Japanese defeat. That is the unfortunate situation at the present moment & it is the reason why I believe things will have to take their course until the position is reverse. Therefore even if the Chinese could be got to agree through our intervention the Japanese will still find some pretext for fighting & the responsibility would rest on our shoulders.[67]

Vansittart commented, 'I am afraid this is right.' Simon agreed. The Foreign Office began the almost unthinkable process of preparing for the evacuation of Shanghai. Sir Miles Lampson became philosophical. As he had written to Wellesley earlier, he occasionally questioned whether any one individual could influence events so momentous as were occurring in the Far East. 'Physically I am as fit as a fiddle,' he had written in January. 'But, without knowing it, I fancy one's mental outlook is slightly affected if one stays here too long at a stretch. One is apt to become cynical and almost too philosophical. In other words, to give up trying over hard to help influence events.'[68] Nor was the Foreign Office at all optimistic. Sir John Pratt wrote: 'On February 20 Sir M. Lampson after the most gallant and strenuous efforts to avert [further] hostilities found to his bitter disappointment that he received absolutely no response from the Japanese side.'[69] Nevertheless Lampson persisted. On 15 March he reported that discussions between Japanese and Chinese representatives at Shanghai had 'developed along unexpectedly favourable lines.' Finally in early May the two sides reached an uneasy truce. All parties praised Lampson's patience, ingenuity, and fairness in bringing about the agreement of 5 May 1932 that temporarily restored peace between Japan and China.[70]

In the meantime the League's Commission of Enquiry under the Chairmanship of Lord Lytton arrived in the Far East. In the lull that followed while the Commission toured Manchuria, the permanent officials of the Foreign Office continued to

---

[67] Minute by Wellesley, 19 February 1932 [F 1572], F.O. 371/16150.
[68] Lampson to Wellesley, Personal, 20 January 1932 [F 1162], F.O. 371/16147.
[69] Memorandum by Pratt, 21 February 1932 [F 1547/1/10], F.O. 371/16150.
[70] See for example *D.B.F.P.*, X, No. 327.

pursue a policy of reconciliation. They also attempted to influence the Lytton Commission. In a comprehensive survey of the economic causes of the Sino-Japanese dispute, Sir Victor Wellesley concluded that, while both sides were at fault, Japan had the strongest case. Her position in Manchuria, as distinct from Shanghai, could be compared with various situations in the British Empire, as in Malaya. He thought that a legal solution to the problem would be impossible.

I feel very certain that no permanent solution of the problem is to be found on a purely juridical basis. Along that road lies disaster. We have got to get away from theoretical sovereign rights and deal with realities. It may be difficult to justify on legal grounds the present developments of Japan's treaty rights in Manchuria; but on moral and material grounds I am inclined to question whether, in a former province, which has never been wholly identified with China, a country of the size and the wealth of China is justified in obstructing the economic development of her more active and enterprising neighbour to the general detriment of world interests.[71]

Vansittart commented that Wellesley's observations were 'very interesting and very true', and Sir John Simon initialed the memorandum. Wellesley then sent it to Sir Miles Lampson with this covering statement:

It is obviously undesirable that we should take the risk of this memorandum being distorted into allegations that His Majesty's Government were pro-Japanese, as might well happen if it were communicated to the League of Nations Commission. There is however no objection to its being read by Lord Lytton and you might therefore take some opportunity to let him read it in strict confidence and only for his own personal information.

The sentiment of the Foreign Office thus continued to be strongly pro-Japanese in regard to Manchuria, though of course vehemently anti-Japanese where major British economic interests were at stake, as in Shanghai.

When the Lytton report was published in October 1932, its conclusions were generally in line with Foreign Office views. Integral issues such as the creation of an independent state in Manchuria and the consequences of Japan's withdrawal from the League will be dealt with in the next chapter; here will be

---

[71] Memorandum by Wellesley, 6 February 1932 [F 1033/1/10], F.O. 371/16146.

given the Foreign Office's main observations of the significance of the Lytton report. According to the principal analysis made by Sir John Pratt:

The facts are stated fairly and objectively and for the most part are allowed to speak for themselves, but wherever it is necessary to do so the commission do not hesitate to pronounce judgment in moderate but quite unambiguous terms. These expressions of opinion, if considered by themselves and not in relation to the historical background sketched in the first half of the report, could easily be taken as a severe condemnation of Japan, but the general effect of the report as a whole is to convey the impression that though it may be difficult to defend the methods employed by Japan for remedying her grievances and escaping from her difficulties, if one looks to the substance below the surface, the balance of right inclines to her side.[72]

Quoting from the report itself, Pratt saw this paragraph as the key passage:

The issues involved in this conflict are not so simple as they are represented to be. They are, on the contrary, exceedingly complicated, and only an intimate knowledge of all the facts, as well as of their historical background should entitle anyone to express a definite opinion upon them. This is not a case in which one country has declared war on another without previously exhausting the opportunities of conciliation provided in the Covenant of the League of Nations. Neither is it a simple case of the violation of the frontier of one country by the armed forces of a neighbouring country, because, in Manchuria, there are many features without an exact parallel in other parts of the world.[73]

Pratt went on to observe that the indictment of the Chinese 'is not too severe and might have been made severer,' while, on the other hand, 'many harsh things that might have been said about Japan are left unsaid.' He concluded:

The Lytton Report will . . . not effect a settlement of the dispute. It should, however, greatly ease the strain of the present situation, for there will no longer be any excuse for treating Japan as the criminal in the dock, and there can be no question of sanctions or of driving her from the League.[74]

[72] Memorandum by Pratt, 10 October 1932 [F 7304/1/10], F.O. 371/16179. The Lytton Report was published as *League of Nations: Appeal by the Chinese Government: Report of the Commission of Enquiry.*
[73] Ibid.   [74] Ibid.

On the very day that Pratt and the Far Eastern Department penned those logical but wishful thoughts, the Ambassador in Tokyo reported at great length the reasons why Japanese public opinion unanimously condemned the Lytton report and how it jeopardized Japan's relations with the League.[75] Essentially the explanation boiled down to the recurrent analogy used by the British throughout the crisis: the League had no more business in Manchuria than it would have in India.

Perhaps it is appropriate to conclude this chapter by observing that there is no justification for the vilification traditionally heaped upon Sir John Simon's diplomacy. Critics on all sides have attacked him for weakening the League, for letting down the United States, for failing to stand up to Japan, for serving as a lackey to British trade on the Yangtze, for undermining the system of collective security, for fearing to apply sanctions, for abandoning the remnants of the Anglo-Japanese Alliance, and for many other various and contradictory reasons. In fact his chief defect was his failure to defend himself from the wrath of his opponents. As a Foreign Secretary he lacked the colour of a Curzon and the contentiousness of a Chamberlain—and perhaps the courage of a Cecil. To use A. J. P. Taylor's description, he did not possess 'the air of puzzled rectitude which enabled a Grey or a Halifax to lapse from the highest moral standards without anyone complaining or even noticing'.[76] Simon's initiative, however, did carry the League's resolution of March 1932 on non-recognition of changes brought about by force, thus making the essential element of the Stimson doctrine a League principle; and his efforts lay behind the League's acceptance of the Lytton report. At those two critical times, March and November 1932, he reported to the Cabinet. His remarks illustrate the balanced intricacy of his ideas:

In spite of the attempts which we have been making (a) to support the League and (b) to co-operate with the United States of America, the difficulty of co-ordinating these two efforts has tended to expose the United Kingdom at Geneva, and I daresay elsewhere, to the reproach that we were either (a) working behind the back of the

[75] For the Japanese reaction to the Lytton report in relation to British policy, see especially Kennedy, *Estrangement of Great Britain and Japan*, chapter XVIII.
[76] Taylor, *English History*, p. 76.

League, or (b) failing to show ourselves as vigorous as the United States of America were prepared to be. There is no justification for either of these criticisms but Geneva is a place where the United Kingdom has not only got to take the lead, but to take the blame for everything that is done.[77]

In November 1932 he faced up to the possibility that the Lytton Report might cause Japan to leave the League and attempted to reconcile Britain's principles of loyalty to the League and friendship with Japan.

In these difficult circumstances it seems to me that British policy must keep in mind the following *desiderata*; though it will be difficult to pursue them all at the same time. We ought to act as a loyal member of the League and avoid, as far as possible, bringing down on ourselves the condemnation which would attach to isolated or prominent individual action. It is impossible to abandon loyalty to the League and its principles merely because Japan would prefer this: we must explain to Japan that the course we take is *pro* League and not *anti* Japan. Even if other considerations did not compel this course, we have to remember the serious consequences to our trade of antagonising China. In fact, we must strive to be fair to both sides. But we must not involve ourselves with trouble with Japan.[78]

The Cabinet appreciated the difficulty of Simon's task—and stressed the last sentence.

If Sir John's stance sounds like an attempt to please all sides at the expense of a forward or definite policy, his views should be juxtaposed with those of one of his foremost critics, Lord Robert Cecil. In the middle of the crisis Cecil wrote:

I believe that the Far Eastern peoples are masters of bluff and that military authorities, whether in the Far East or elsewhere, understand only force. If we do not take a vigorous line I am confident that the Japanese will establish themselves as the dominating power in China, and through China in the whole of Asia, with consequences to British interests, the League and world peace which may be of the most extreme seriousness.[79]

Simon—and his principal advisers at the Foreign Office,

---

[77] Memorandum by Simon, 1 March 1932 [F 2021/1/10], F.O. 371/16154.

[78] Cabinet Minutes, Secret, 23 November 1932, CAB. 23/73.

[79] Memorandum by Cecil, 6 February 1932 [F 356/1/10], F.O. 371/16141. The notion of Japanese 'bluff' was popularly believed in the 1930s. See for example Freda Utley, *Japan's Feet of Clay* (London, 1936).

Vansittart and Wellesley—believed the opposite. They judged that Japan's policy rested on dominant power in the western Pacific, not bluff, that sanctions, whether moral or economic, would drive Japan into further aggression and isolation from the international community. In this regard Simon's outlook also diametrically opposed Secretary Stimson's. Stimson felt that he had blown the whistle on Japan and had set a precedent in opposing aggression—or, to use the words of his biographer, that he had forced Japan to be the first in 'the community of the damned'.[80] By contrast, Sir John's last desire was to make Japan an international outlaw. Unless Britain were prepared to go to war with Japan, he thought that sanctions would have the opposite from the intended effect, that without the United States 'collective security' was an empty phrase in the Orient.[81] As he explained to the Cabinet Committee on the Far East, he 'never for one moment favoured the adoption by the League of any kind of sanctions, not even of an economic kind. . . . We might provoke a situation that precipitated Japanese resentment.'[82] Moreover, Britain could not contemplate war simply because the United States could not be depended on. The premise of Simon's diplomacy therefore rested on 'peaceful reconciliation with an avoidance of threats'. From first to last he adhered to the principle that the League, as the great moral force in international affairs, was the agency through which international disputes should be resolved. In sum, the previously inaccessible British records confirm the judgement of the principal scholar of Simon and the Manchurian crisis: 'It is difficult, indeed, to dissent from the view that, in the dilemma confronting this country, no greater measure of success could have been achieved, and that seldom or never has so difficult a problem been handled with greater coolness, clear-sightedness, resolution and indifference to consideration of personal popularity.'[83] One final remark by Simon himself should perhaps be

[80] Morison, *Turmoil and Tradition*, p. 402. Like Cecil, Stimson in time changed his views; paradoxically, Stimson emerges as more humble than Cecil.

[81] The possibility of war against Japan in 1932 was conceived in retrospect, not at the time. The reality of the situation is well discussed by Hudson, *Far East in World Politics*, chapter 13.

[82] Cabinet Committee on the Far East, Minutes, Secret, 15 February 1932, CAB. 27/482.

[83] Bassett, *Democracy and Foreign Policy*, p. 625. The last phrase of the sentence clearly is overstated, but on the whole, in my opinion, the judgement is valid.

added to that assessment in order to take full measure of his—
and Great Britain's—tolerance and perspicacity. When discussing in the Cabinet in 1934, the nature of 'Eastern peoples'
and the meaning of Japan's quitting the League, Simon
reflected: 'It was always difficult to know what was going on
inside the anthill.'[84]

[84] Cabinet Minutes, 261, Secret, 9 November 1933, CAB. 2–6.

VII

IMPERIAL DEFENCE AND THE
ECONOMY OF THE FAR EAST

JAPAN'S notice to withdraw from the League of Nations in
March 1933 ended the era of the concert of nations in the
Pacific and opened the period of drift towards war. The
Washington treaty system remained intact; but the Manchurian crisis had rotted away the foundation upon which any
international agreement must rest, that of mutual good faith.
The consensus of British opinion held that Japan's invasion of
Manchuria patently violated the Nine Power Treaty. Yet a
minority continued to plead for tolerance. Reminding his compatriots of Britain's own recent history, Sir Francis Lindley
drew a moral from the Boer War:

The Jamieson [sic] raid was far more indefensible than was the
Manchurian incident of September 1931, and I think it is true to
say that it would have been universally condemned by all serious
opinion in England had it not been for the Kaiser's telegram congratulating the Transvaal Government. That telegram immediately
rallied the public to the defence of Dr. Jamieson; and so it has been
here. Every gesture and every pronouncement in favour of China
has merely served to strengthen the Military party in Japan, and
will continue to do so until the question is finally settled. . . . [C]on-
demnation of the public world opinion had not the smallest influence
on the policy of His Majesty's Government in continuing the war to
the end.[1]

The analogy was apt in another sense. In the years preceding
the Boer War, Great Britain feared that Germany might align
herself with the South African Republic. After the advent of
Hitler and in the aftermath of the Manchurian affair, British
statesmen seriously began to consider the consequence of a
German-Japanese alliance.

[1] Lindley to Simon, No. 152, 8 March 1933 [F 2259/923/61], C.P. 14348. For
general discussion of Britain's Far Eastern policy in the wake of the Manchurian
crisis, see Friedman, *British Relations with China*, chapter III.

The minutes of the Committee of Imperial Defence give a good indication of the rapidity of developing events and changing mood. The words of the two Chamberlains are perhaps especially illuminating because of their sustained interest in foreign affairs. In 1925 Austen Chamberlain, then Foreign Secretary, had stated that there should be no reason to fear Japan or a Japanese alliance with a potential British enemy such as Germany or Russia.

I cannot conceive of any circumstances in which, singlehanded, we are likely to go to war with Japan. I cannot conceive it possible that Japan, singlehanded, should seek a conflict with us. The only case in which I think Japan (which is an uneasy and rather restless Power, whose action is not always easy to predicate) might become dangerous is after a regrouping of the European Powers. In other words, unless we see signs of a German-Russo-Japanese Alliance or agreement, I should not anticipate war between ourselves and Japan. I should regard the signs of such an agreement, such a new re-grouping of the Powers as being a danger signal which would at once call our attention to the situation. . . . Of that regroupment there is at present no sign. Germany is not yet in a position in which she can enter into engagements of that kind.[2]

Less than a decade later, Neville Chamberlain, as Chancellor of the Exchequer, stated before the same Committee that he increasingly regretted the termination of the Anglo-Japanese Alliance. 'It had,' he said, 'gradually poisoned our relations with Japan, and had led them to regard us with increasing suspicion.' The minutes continue:

Personally, he [Chamberlain] was very impressed with the fact that Japan had given notice to leave the League and that Germany had done the same. He would like to know how to estimate the situation if a position arose when Germany and Japan might come together, and it seemed to him such a situation was conceivable when Germany was sufficiently strong to take a hand against us. He thought that would be a very alarming prospect.[3]

[2] Committee of Imperial Defence Minutes, 193, Secret, 5 January 1925, CAB. 2–4).

[3] Ibid., 261, Secret, 9 November 1933, CAB. 2–6. On Japanese-German relations, see Frank Iklé, *German-Japanese Relations, 1936–1941* (New York, 1956); Ernst L. Presseisen, *Germany and Japan: A Study in Totalitarian Diplomacy, 1933–1941* (The Hague, 1958); Th. Somer, *Deutschland und Japan zwischen den Maechten 1935–1940* (Tuebingen, 1962); K. Drechsler, *Deutschland-China-Japan 1933–1939* (East Berlin, 1964); and Johanna M. Meskill, *Hitler and Japan: The Hollow Alliance* (New York, 1966).

When Chamberlain asked how long it might take Germany to prepare for war, the Chief of the Imperial General Staff answered, 'approximately five years'—in other words, late 1938. Six years before the outbreak of European war, the British thus began to grasp the total significance of a possible war fought against their former arch-enemy combined with their former ally. The worst fears of Prime Minister Hughes at the Imperial Conference of 1921 now seemed to be materializing. In 1933 an Australian again sounded the prime alarm about the dangers of war with Japan and noted that Britain's Asian Empire remained as defenceless as ever. The High Commissioner for Australia, S. M. Bruce, stated to the Committee of Imperial Defence: 'the danger was the possibility of Germany and Japan coming together and that Germany would be ready in five years' time. . . . the Far East was the outstanding danger. It was difficult to see what could prevent Japan obtaining a complete mastery of the Pacific if she chose to go to war between now and the time that Singapore was completed.'[4]

It is far beyond the confines of this chapter to discuss the vacillation of British policy towards Singapore, or to trace the intricate naval negotiations of the 1920s and 1930s, of which the Far East was only a part.[5] But the two problems go hand in hand, and it is important to grasp the essentials in order to see

[4] Committee of Imperial Defence Minutes, 261, Secret, 9 November 1933, CAB. 2–6. This and other quotations from the Cabinet and C.I.D. read awkwardly because they were often transcribed into the passive voice. For the work of the C.I.D., Franklyn Arthur Johnson, *Defence by Committee, the British Committee of Imperial Defence 1880–1959* (1960); there is an incisive essay on the C.I.D.'s and Cabinet's policy in the Far East by D. C. Watt, 'Britain, the United States and Japan in 1934', in his *Personalities and Policies: Studies in the Formulation of British Foreign Policy in the Twentieth Century* (University of Notre Dame Press, 1965).

[5] For British policy, the foremost work is by Roskill, *Naval Policy between the Wars;* for the situation in the Far East at the time of the London Naval Conference, see especially Crowley, *Japan's Quest for Autonomy*, chapter 1; also Raymond G. O'Connor, *Perilous Equilibrium: the United States and the London Naval Conference of 1930* (University of Kansas Press, 1962). For later British policy, D. C. Watt, 'The Anglo-German Naval Agreement of 1935: an interim judgement', *Journal of Modern History*, **27**, 2 (June 1956). For the Singapore problem, S. Woodburn Kirby, *The War Against Japan, I: The Loss of Singapore;* see also Kenneth Attiwill, *The Singapore Story* (London, 1959); Winston S. Churchill, *The Second World War: the Hinge of Fate* (London 1951); Russell Grenfell, *Main Fleet to Singapore* (London, 1951); Eugene H. Miller. *Strategy at Singapore* (New York, 1942); Lord Strabolgi, *Singapore and After: A Study of the Pacific Campaign* (London, 1942); Compton Mackenzie, *Eastern Epic* (London, 1951); James Leasor, *Singapore* (New York, 1968).

Britain's Far Eastern stance in the broader framework of global strategy. In a word, Singapore commanded one of the finest geographical positions in the world: the power holding 'the gate to the Pacific' could, theoretically at least, control the passageway to the Far East. For Britain, Singapore thus ranked along with Suez and the Cape as one of the lynchpins of the Empire; if Singapore fell to a hostile power, communication would be severed between the mother country and Australasia. In the post-war era, Singapore had become vulnerable. As one of the more important Cabinet documents about the subject explained in 1930:

After the War, when the position in the Far East was re-examined, it was clear that many new factors had arisen. The Japanese Fleet had grown enormously and had become the third largest Fleet in the world. The end of the Anglo-Japanese Alliance was in sight. Considerations of economy rendered it impossible to maintain permanently in the Far East a fleet large enough to dominate the Japanese Fleet, as had been contemplated before the War in the event of a termination of the Anglo-Japanese Alliance.[6]

Britain's traditional naval policy rested on the assumption that the fleet would be able to wage war simultaneously in both hemispheres. Technological developments now made this a dubious proposition.

During the War the transition of ships from coal-burners to oil-burners had become almost complete. There was but little oil on the eastern route, and supplies in the Far East were insufficient to maintain the Fleet there on its arrival. There were not enough oil tankers in the world to take the Fleet to the Far East and maintain it there in a mobile state in the absence of local reserves. Further, the advent of the submarine had necessitated the 'bulging' of capital ships, with the result that they had outgrown the dry docks in the Far East.[7]

The British had no dockyards for capital ships east of Malta. Logically Singapore therefore had to be developed as a matter of clear military necessity. But military imperatives do not always dictate policy. In the case of Singapore reasons of economy made even Conservative Governments pause, while belief in disarmament caused Labour circles to view the scheme

[6] Memorandum by the Oversea Defence Sub-Committee of the Committee of Imperial Defence, 'The Singapore Base', Secret, O.D.C., dated May 1930, CAB. 21/335.   [7] Ibid.

with aversion. Thus the history of the project: decision to build, 1923; stopped by the Labour Government the next year; renewed by the Baldwin Government, but at a reduced pace; stopped again by the Labour Government, 1929; further delays by the National Government until 1933. In the 1920s the British, regardless of party, feared that Japan would regard the build-up of Singapore as prelude to British aggression; in the 1930s they anticipated that Singapore's development as a major naval installation might provoke the Japanese military clique. The head of the Far Eastern Department of the Foreign Office, C. W. Orde, summed up the problem in late 1933:

It may indeed be said that, in proportion as we strengthen our position against Japan, our interests in China will stand to gain, and from this point of view, the completion of the Singapore Base and the maintenance of an adequate naval force in the Far East will be to the good. . . .

Inspired by such a spirit, we nevertheless cannot ignore the aggressive instincts of the Japanese, and the plans they cherish for an expansion in Asia which must react to our disadvantage if they realise that we are afraid of them. . . . [B]esides meeting firmly the difficulties with which their industrial efficiency confronts us, we should, so far as we are able, but in no spirit of panic or immoderate haste, not hesitate to proceed with the Singapore Base and the strengthening generally of our naval position in the Far East. For financial reasons such a development can hardly be so rapid or so far-reaching as to induce an explosive reaction in Japan. Such a reaction we must be careful not to court by economic, military or political action, but within the limits of moderation there seems more to be lost than gained by a policy of tameness and timidity.[8]

In a similar way the British pursued a moderate line in naval negotiations: in 1930 Great Britain acquiesced in realistic parity with the United States, thus ending what Captain Roskill calls 'The Period of Anglo-American Antagonism'. They subsequently were inclined to work towards parity with Japan, but were restrained by the Americans. Throughout the entire era of the thirties Britain assured Japan that Singapore would never be used as a jumping off place against her but as a 'link in imperial communication' securing the red line of defence from India to Australasia. In 1941 Singapore served neither purpose,

[8] Memorandum by C. W. Orde, 14 December 1933 [F 7824/128/23], F.O. 371/17152.

and must be ranked along with the Maginot Line as one of the great military miscalculations in history. The fortifications served their purpose only too well. The Japanese merely attacked from a different direction.

'It would be the height of folly to perpetuate Britain's present defenceless state there'—Singapore—concluded an inter-service committee in 1932.[9] The same theme can be traced through the Committee of Imperial Defence reports in sub-sequent years, along with the general scheme for defence in the event of war with Japan.[10] The logic remained more or less the

[9] *B.D.*, Second Series, IX, pp. 677–8.

[10] Parallel with these calculations ran the perennial estimates of what could be done if trouble erupted again in China. The following table was usually attached to reports of the C.I.D. dealing with the subject:

Principal Places containing British Communities in China.

Place	Approximate number of British Subjects	Remarks
Shanghai	9,300 (including Indians)	Contains over 50 per cent of the British population. Can be reached by cruiser at any time.
Hankow	200	Can be reached by *gunboats* at all times. Can be reached by *sloops* 26 March–30 November.* Can be reached by '*Castor*' 15 April–30 November.* Can be reached by '*Kent*' 1 May–25 October.*
Nanking	Under 50	Can be reached by all ships at any time.
Amoy	250	Can be reached by cruiser.
Chefoo	250	Can be reached by cruiser.
Ningpo	100	Cannot be reached by cruiser, but sloops and destroyers can get up.
Chinkiang	100	Can be reached by cruiser.
Kiukiang	100	As for Hankow.
Anking	50	As for Kiukiang.
Swatow	250	'C' or 'D' Class cruiser can get in, after half tide.
Foochow	250	10 miles up river. Hard to reach, even for a gunboat, and difficult to protect.
Shameen (Canton)	700 (Europeans)	'C' or 'D' Class cruiser could at H.W.O.S. reach Canton and could lie off Shameen, secured head and stern.
Ichang	Under 100	Can be reached by a gunboat.
Chungking	50	Can be reached by a gunboat.
Changsha	100	Can be reached by a gunboat.
Tientsin	680	Cannot be reached by a gunboat.
Peking	300	Cannot be reached by a gunboat.

* Dates are approximate.

[CAB. 27/412]

same. Singapore would be the pivot of Britain's defence, an impregnable fortress invulnerable from attack by sea. In case of hostilities with Japan, British troops would withdraw from Shanghai and Tientsin to bolster the forces at Singapore. Submarines would defend Hong Kong for the *forty-eight days* required for the main fleet to reach the Far East. In the first few months of the war, little or no help could be expected from Australia or New Zealand, or from China or the United States because of the speed at which events would probably develop. Whether Singapore itself could be defended against Japanese air attack on the floating dock and fuelling facilities remained an open question. In retrospect the major mistake was the supposition that the Japanese would attack by sea, not from Malaya, and that the fleet would be able to survive without air cover (though by the eve of the war there were in fact extensive air and land defence schemes for both Singapore and up-country Malaya). Even more basically the Singapore defence scheme rested on the assumption that the main fleet could arrive in time from home waters, even in time of war in Europe. When Japanese forces sank the *Prince of Wales* and the *Repulse* on 10 December 1941, and when 60,000 British forces at Singapore surrendered to the Japanese the following February, those miscalculations became abundantly clear to the world at large. In the preceding years Britain's military authorities sufficiently appreciated Singapore's vulnerability and urged friendship with Japan at almost any cost.[11]

The political architects of the pillar of Anglo-Japanese amity were Sir John Simon and Neville Chamberlain. In their own words, they pursued a policy of 'political appeasement' in the Far East. Writing in October 1934, they reminded the Cabinet of the perilous position of the Empire in the event of a hostile Germany combined with a hostile Japan.

At this moment, in the autumn of 1934, there is no immediate threat to our safety. But there is the universal feeling of apprehension about the future, and the near future, that such a threat may materialise, and that the quarter from which it will come is Germany.

[11] See for example a memorandum on 'The Importance of Anglo-Japanese Friendship', by the Chief of the Imperial General Staff (Secret, C.P. 12, 36, 17 January 1936, CAB. 24/259), which summarizes the major arguments developed in preceding years. See also End Note.

Whatever may be the outcome of the present régime in Germany, we need not anticipate that we should have to fight her single-handed, and although the results of any war between civilised peoples must necessarily result in appalling loss and suffering, we might reasonably hope to escape ultimate disaster if the hostilities were confined to European nations.

But if we had to enter upon such a struggle with a hostile instead of a friendly, Japan in the East; if we had to contemplate the division of our forces so as to protect our Far Eastern interests while prosecuting a war in Europe; then not only would India, Hong Kong and Australasia be in dire peril, but we ourselves would stand in far greater danger of destruction by a fully armed and organised Germany.[12]

Probing the possibility of a non-aggression pact with Japan, Simon and Chamberlain viewed it as a plausible keystone of the Empire's security and the world's peace. In regard to the Far East, it would stabilize China:

[A]n undertaking which definitely called a halt to Japanese penetration into China, contained in an instrument signed both by Japan and by ourselves . . . would be of the greatest practical value to China and to the British trade with China, as well as making a material contribution to peace in the Far East.[13]

As regards the United States:

[I]t might be possible . . . to approach the United States with the suggestion that Japanese naval claims (which profess to be based on the fear of aggression) would be materially modified if a non-aggression pact could be entered into by Japan with *both* the United States *and* the British Empire—preferably in a single instrument.[14]

As regards Russia and the League of Nations:

[T]he fact that the relation of Japan and Russia to the League of Nations has now been reversed, Russia coming in and Japan going out, may mean, in the event of a Russo-Japanese war, an increased anxiety for ourselves as a member of the League. . . . There is always the possibility, though it is only a possibility, that once specially friendly relations have been established with Japan, Japan might consider coming back to the League.[15]

---

[12] Memorandum by Simon and Chamberlain, Secret, C.P. 223 (34), 16 October 1934, CAB. 27/596. Cf. Keith Feiling, *The Life of Neville Chamberlain* (London, 1946) pp. 253-4.

[13] Ibid.   [14] Ibid.   [15] Ibid.

And, finally, as regards Japan:

The idea . . . is to use the negotiation of a non-aggression pact as a lever for reducing Japan's naval programme. The Japanese desire to increase their relative naval strength *vis-à-vis* of the United States is dictated mainly by their fear of strained relations developing between their two countries and leading ultimately to war. In the measure that political appeasement can be introduced, Japanese naval pretensions are likely to abate.[16]

Despite the seductiveness of the appeasement argument in the Far East, the scheme of a non-aggression pact had one major and insurmountable political flaw: the Americans would never for a moment consider being a part of it. Unless the Cabinet were willing to reverse the drift of British policy since the war, Britain's 'natural alignment' lay with the United States. General Smuts, perhaps the staunchest opponent of the idea of a tacitly renewed Anglo-Japanese alliance, summed up Britain's position in 1934: 'The ultimate objective of that [British] policy should continue to conform with that American orientation which has distinguished it since our Association with the United States in the Great War. . . . Any other course would mean building our Commonwealth policy on quicksands.'[17]

Powerful economic as well as political forces militated against an Anglo-Japanese rapprochement. Indeed the cloud of the great depression dominated the entire era of the 1930s in the Far East more than many other parts of the world, and economic problems as viewed by the British will be the main theme of the rest of this chapter. In an age when a tendency existed to blame all of the world's ills on the economic crisis, the more optimistic of British officials and businessmen hoped that, if progress could be made in international trade, political and other problems would practically resolve themselves; the more sceptical of them—including most of the experts—saw an interaction between political, racial, and economic difficulties that could well explode into war. Even more fundamentally, were the problems of the Far East essentially economic or political with racial overtones? One could make a good case either way, as did various officials of the time. Perhaps the most

[16] Ibid.

[17] General J. C. Smuts, 'The Present Outlook', *International Affairs*, **14**, 1 (January–February 1935).

notable contrast in analytical approach occurred during the Manchurian crisis, when Sir Victor Wellesley traced the economic causes and Sir Francis Lindley the political. The exchange provides good background for understanding the further economic and political controversies of the thirties.

Wellesley argued that the root of the trouble in the Far East 'will be found to lie (as is the case with most international problems) in economic causes.' Specifically:

The increasing population of Japan; the increasing industrialisation; the need of the China market; the increasing (Chinese) population of Manchuria; the heightened Chinese tariffs; the decrease in Japanese trade with China; the effect of the economic crisis, with the effect of the intensified Chinese boycott super-imposed thereon.[18]

Wellesley gave these and other statistics to indicate the tremendously adverse impact the Manchurian crisis had on Japan's economy:

Japanese trade with Central China (based on Shanghai) will be down in the second half of 1931, as compared with the corresponding period of 1930 (already a depressed year), by *63% in respect of exports* from Japan, and by 43% in respect of imports to Japan. Contracts for between £13 and £15 millions worth of Japanese goods, with date of delivery up to about April 1932, have been repudiated by Chinese merchants (September–November 1931). The effects of the boycott have been no less severe on Japanese mills and factories in China, Japanese shipping, banking, &c.[19]

Focusing on Manchuria, Wellesley gave these trade figures:

	1928	1929	1930
Exports to Japan	47%	44%	46%
Imports from Japan	20%	25%	23%

The proportion of Manchuria's foreign trade to the total trade of China he put in broader historical perspective:

1872	0·5%
1888	4·6%
1898	8·7%
1908	14·5%
1918	11·5%
1926	22·3%

[18] Memorandum by Wellesley, 6 February 1932 [F 1033/1/10], F.O. 371/16146. For the economic issues dealt with in this chapter, the basic secondary work is Gull, *British Economic Interests in the Far East*.   [19] Ibid.

In other words, China had built up an economic centre in Manchuria that rivalled the Yangtze basin's. Noting that this development had been possible only because of Japanese initiative and control, he concluded:

Here, then we get some idea of the realities which underlie the outcry about 'treaty rights' which has been so vociferously raised at Geneva. Two over-populated countries, in desperate economic straits, are struggling for control of this rich colonial area, which each conceives to be essential for its future as a nation.[20]

Since Japanese could not emigrate to Canada, the United States, or Australasia, could they not legitimately look towards Manchuria? 'It is the only possible area into which she can expand.' Wellesley further made the point about the close connection between political and economic problems.

There are already the beginnings of Japanese economic penetration in China. In its train may come the usual causes which in the past have made for war: over-population, markets and clients at all costs, and a possible revival of the imperialistic spirit. Industrialism and imperialism often go hand in hand. Is it not highly probable that if China were to close her doors to Japanese manufacturers and place restrictions on the supply of raw material, *Japan would be forced to fight for her very existence*? I do not say that these things are likely to happen, but none the less it shows how important it is to follow the economic developments from the political angle.[21]

Wellesley then expanded his theory into a basic proposition believed by many analysts of the inter-war years, the relationship between economic pressure and expansionism: 'If any country controlling a large portion of the earth's surface closes her doors economically to her neighbours it is likely to produce an explosion.' He thus saw the causes of the conflict between China and Japan as fundamentally economic, and judged that a solution could only be found by establishing a better economic equilibrium. 'It is in essence the same evil which is affecting Europe.'[22]

Sir Francis Lindley responded to Wellesley's 'fashionable' economic interpretation by emphasizing the political angle, in Europe as in Asia. 'In Europe the rise of tariff barriers is not due primarily to economic considerations. It is due to a desire

[20] Ibid.   [21] Ibid.   [22] Ibid.

on the part of the States concerned to be self-sufficing in order to be more powerful politically.'[23] Specifically in regard to Asia he dwelt on the Japanese military reaction to Russian and Chinese influence.

The Japanese military action in Manchuria last September [1931] was a signal instance of the triumph of political ambition over economic considerations. In the first place the military party here are singularly indifferent to anything affecting trade and commerce. For them, as for practically all the rest of the country, Manchuria represents a political ideal—the ideal of a bulwark against Russian and Chinese influence. The pursuit of this ideal, even at the sacrifice of the great economic interests of Japan in China proper, was deliberately chosen when the Japanese started their present Manchurian enterprise.[24]

To return to Lindley's opening sally, which contained his major point, the problem of the Far East derived in large part from the political and racial attitude of the white Pacific powers. Writing about the necessity for Japan to find an outlet for her population and markets for her goods, he observed that there would be no difficulty 'had not other countries, for political motives, shut out the Japanese people and Japanese products from their territories.' He went on:

For it is idle to pretend that the Japanese are excluded from such places as Australia and the United States for other than political motives. The Australians say quite frankly that they intend to have a white Australia, which is a political conception. It is true that the Americans justify their exclusion by claiming that the Japanese, owing to their lower standard of living, make life difficult for native-born Americans. But the justification is a mere justification. It will not hold water for a moment as a motive; since the Portuguese, against whom there is no special prejudice, have a lower standard of life than the Japanese, and there are, no doubt, other immigrants in the same position. The fact is that the Americans object to the Japanese because they are yellow, but do not like to say so officially.[25]

On the question of race Lindley and Wellesley both agreed. As Wellesley often said—the theme runs through much of his writings—there could be no doubt that bias of racism was closely connected with political and economic problems; the

[23] Lindley to Simon, No. 234, 28 April 1932 [F 4400/1/10], F.O. 371/16170.
[24] Ibid.   [25] Ibid.

difficulty was in getting the proper relationship between the variables. This perplexed the Foreign Office. George Mounsey wrote that he supposed political ambitions predominated at crucial times in the world's history. 'The question remains whether these are not mere aberrations, which cannot withstand the reaction of the underlying economic causes isolated thereby, whenever the time comes for these causes to reassert themselves.' Vansittart noted in typical style:

Novalis affirmed that to philosophise is to generalise; and the older I get the more I mistrust the ancestral pastime, whether applied to nations, sexes 'or any other adversity.'—including this one.[26]

One might deduce from that philosophical insight that the Foreign Office at times dealt better with the details of the Sino-Japanese crisis than in analysing the profounder causes of the impending Pacific war. Still, both Wellesley and Lindley made apt points.

In the years following the Manchurian crisis there developed what Vansittart called Japan's 'exceptionally intense competitive onslaught' in international trade. The Commercial Counsellor to the Embassy in Tokyo, G. E. Sansom, observed in the autumn of 1932 that Japan 'is rapidly passing out of the imitative phase and is developing into a powerful industrial and commercial state.'[27] As the Japanese increasingly began 'to dump' (the Anglo-American phrase) manufactures on the world market, tariff barriers rose in the United States and throughout the Empire. The Indian Government felt vulnerable to Japanese cotton textiles and rubber manufactures, the Australian to textiles and pottery, the South African to textiles, hosiery and celluloid, and the Canadian to rubber goods and tinned salmon. Other items of complaint included shoes, tuna, electric light bulbs, grass and fibre rugs, and safety matches. The British and the Americans charged that the Japanese industries manufacturing those goods were subsidized by their Government. In the view of the Embassy in Tokyo—whose Commercial Counsellor had the reputation as one of the world's authorities on international trade—the charge was unfounded.

---

[26] Minutes by Vansittart and Mounsey, 27 and 28 May 1932 [F 4400/1/10], F.O. 371/16170.

[27] Memorandum by Sansom, enclosed in Lindley to Simon, No. 574, 28 October 1932 [F 8307/39/23], F.O. 371/16242.

Sansom wrote in November 1932: 'It is a serious mistake to suppose that Japanese progress in foreign trade is due to any other causes than cheap but not unskilful labour and direction which is energetic and on the whole efficient.' He judged that false accusations about Japan's exports would cause a further deterioration in international relations.

[T]he Japanese, if they find themselves, as they well may, driven out of one foreign market after another by tariff measures directed against them, are likely to be confirmed in their present mood of hostility. They can argue that the very Powers which reproach them for their conduct in Manchuria are forcing them to desperate measures by closing other markets against them. This argument is not without foundation, for the past few years Japan has had to contend with tariff increases—some of which were aimed specifically at her—in India, Australia, South Africa and the United Kingdom; while she is now confronted with the possibility of further increases in the United States, the Philippines, Java and India, at a time when she is suffering severely from the boycott and depressed condition in China.[28]

The Foreign Office, the Colonial Office, and the Board of Trade carefully evaluated Sansom's measured and intricately detailed reports. The consensus that developed during the years 1932–4 held that the Empire should take 'legitimate defensive action' against 'aggressive Japanese economic expansionism'. At the same time, Great Britain would attempt to recognize Japan's real economic needs and would not obstruct her activity in Manchuria. In other words, the British formula consisted of not opposing Japan's economic development except when it conflicted with the Empire's trade.[29]

The Commonwealth countries suffering most from Japanese competition were India, Ceylon, the African colonies, Iraq, Egypt, and, to a lesser extent, Australia. The Egyptian authorities reacted first. In May 1935 they increased import duties on cotton goods up to 30 per cent. The most important British possession affected was India, where Japanese imports increased by about 50 per cent in 1931–2. The Indian cotton

[28] Memorandum by Sansom, 11 November 1932, enclosed in Lindley to Simon, No. 603, 11 November 1932 [A 8174/53/45].

[29] See for example the memorandum by C. W. Orde, 14 December 1933 [F 7824/128/23], F.O. 371/17152.

industry demanded denunciation of the Indo-Japanese commercial convention, which occurred in October 1933. The
Embassy in Tokyo observed a great indignation in Japan,
where the Indian denunciation appeared as a move in the
direction of economic sanctions. In May 1933 the Foreign
Office denounced the Anglo-Japanese commercial agreement
respecting the West African colonies. The Tokyo Embassy
again warned that this 'drastic tariff action' would be interpreted as Britain's attempt to punish Japan and to take unfair
economic advantage. The Foreign Secretary reassured the
Japanese Ambassador that Britain did not wish to deprive
Japan of her due share of the market place, but reminded him
of the intense commercial pressure within the Empire. The
Tokyo Embassy again admonished the Foreign Office that
trade relations could not be kept separate from politics: 'The
present conflict of interests is not a mere dispute between
manufacturers; it is a symptom of the struggle between two
nations, both of which depend for their existence upon their
foreign trade.'[30]

In December 1933 the Foreign Office extensively reviewed
the entire problem of Anglo-Japanese trade relations. The
author of the report, F. A. Ashton-Gwatkin, concluded that
Japanese exports to China had declined from 1930 to 1932 by
120 million yen but that this loss had been recouped in other
markets—mainly those of the British Empire.

	Million yen [gained, 1930–2]
British India	63
Netherlands East Indies	34
Egypt	12
Australia	11
East Africa	5
	123

Ashton-Gwatkin noted that cotton and silk were of such overwhelming importance among Japanese exports that other items
appeared insignificant; but he also observed the greatly improved quality of such goods as rubber shoes, electric light
bulbs, pottery, safety matches and tinned food-stuffs. As to
imports, Japan depended on:

[30] Snow to Simon, No. 272, 13 May 1933 [F 3757/583/23], F.O. 371/17154.

Iron and steel (including pig-iron) from Great Britain, Germany, United States of America, Manchukuo, British India, Belgium, China, Sweden.

Machinery (not including automobiles) from United States of America, Great Britain, Germany, France, Switzerland and Sweden.

He also listed the following imports:

	From:
Wheat (a growing demand owing to change of taste)	Australia.
Beans and peas	Manchukuo, China.
Mineral oils	United States of America, Netherlands East Indies.
Oil cake	Manchukuo, China.
Timber	United States of America, Canada, Siberia, Siam.
Coal	Manchukuo, French Indo-China, China, Siberia.
Vegetable fibres (other than cotton)	Philippine Islands, China, British India.
Ores	Straits Settlement, China, British India.
Rubber	Straits Settlements, Netherlands East Indies.
Pulp for paper manufacture	Norway, United States of America, Canada, Sweden, Germany.
Automobiles	United States of America.
Oil seeds	China, Manchukuo, Netherlands East Indies, British India.

Japan thus depended on imports as well as exports for her survival. With the decline of the China trade, Japan looked for other markets, to the increasing misgiving of the countries within the Empire. To that evaluation Ashton-Gwatkin added *the central factor of the Far Eastern situation:* 'The continuous increase of the Japanese population—by about 1 million a year. . . . To provide for the growing population, Japan must either reduce her already low standard of living, or develop her industries and her export trade.'[31] Could Great Britain ac-

---

[31] Memorandum by Ashton-Gwatkin 5 December 1933 [F 6674/1571/23], F.O. 371/17166.

commodate this desperate Far Eastern economic and demographic colossus? Or, as asked by the Commercial Counsellor in Tokyo, 'Can Japan give us any economic advantages sufficient to justify our mortgaging our political future in the Far East?'[32]

By mid-1934 the British image of Japan had changed from that of an inscrutable oriental power using underhand trade tactics to that of a seemingly invincible nation destined to control the Far East. Again to use the Commercial Counsellor's words in regard to Japanese economic development, 'in 1933 it was ascribed to unfair methods, sweated labour, subsidies and so on. In 1934 the pendulum seems to have swung, and Japan is now often credited with something like invincibility in every sphere.'[33] In May 1933 the 'aggressive instinct' of Japan had manifested itself by the Tanku truce imposed on the Chinese; in April 1934 the Amau doctrine or 'hands off China' statement declared, to Britain at least, Japan's equivalent of the Monroe Doctrine. A new generation of Japanese was in ascendancy— one that could hardly recall the glorious days of the Anglo-Japanese Alliance. Nevertheless the British held out hope that Japan could be placated politically, that trade competition could be allayed. In the summer of 1934 Lindley's successor, Sir Robert Clive—who was far less of a 'Japophile'—welcomed the statement of the Japanese Foreign Minister, 'that the old spirit of the Anglo-Japanese Alliance remained.'[34]

At the same time that the Cabinet studied the possibility of a non-aggression pact, a mission of the Federation of British Industries toured Manchuria to investigate ways of improving Anglo-Japanese trade relations. Lord Barnby, a former President of the Federation, headed the mission. Three prominent businessmen accompanied him: Sir Guy Locock, Director of the Federation; Mr. Julian Piggot of British Iron and Steel; and Sir Charles Seligman, Senior Director of Seligman Brothers, Ltd., Bankers. They believed that a political agreement with Japan would alleviate rivalry in trade. Though the group spent

---

[32] Memorandum by G. B. Sansom, 29 October 1934, circulated to the Cabinet 11 January 1935, Secret, C.P. 8(35), CAB. 27/596.

[33] Ibid.

[34] Clive to Simon, No. 369 Confidential, 5 July 1934 [F 4798/373/23], F.O. 371/18181.

only a few weeks in Japan and Manchukuo in the autumn of 1934, they had opportunity to meet leading industrialists and politicians. On their return they reported to the Cabinet via the Board of Trade.

The dominant impression which we carried away from the Far East was the important rôle which Japan is now playing in that part of the world, and which, in our opinion, she will increasingly play in the future. . . .

Japan undoubtedly feels that it is essentially her mission to solve the problems of the Far East. The question appears to us whether she is going to attempt to do this alone, or whether she is prepared to work in co-operation with this country. We feel that, from every point of view, such as the security of our position in the Far East, our trade relations in China and elsewhere, or a solution of the problem of Anglo-Japanese trade competition, an understanding between the two countries is essential.[35]

Though not going so far as recommending an alliance, the Trade Mission did urge an agreement defining a common policy towards China. They reaffirmed the importance of the open door. Discussing Manchuria, they explained Japan's motives in setting up the puppet state of Manchukuo (established by Japan in March 1932 but not recognized by Great Britain):

Although there is a definite Manchou Government established at Hsinking, there is no doubt that the real power rests in the hands of the Japanese advisers and military and will continue to do so. We do not consider that Japan aims at annexation. We think the motive which prompted her to extend her influence to Manchoukuo was chiefly the desire for the creation of a strong buffer State against Soviet Russia and the spread of Communist ideas throughout the Far East. Leaving out the question of the legality of her past action, the practical effect cannot in our opinion fail to be of advantage to China as well as to herself. Another reason was that Japan looks to Manchoukuo to become a supplier of raw materials and foodstuffs and an important outlet for her manufactured products.[36]

They judged that large-scale Japanese immigration to Manchuria was improbable, but that there could be no doubt that

---

[35] Locock to Sir Horace Wilson, Confidential, 10 December 1934, circulated to the Cabinet 4 January 1935, Secret, C.P. 9(35), CAB. 27/596.
[36] Ibid.

the region would develop economically and culturally under Japanese tutelage:

We feel bound to record our opinion that the Chinese inhabitants of Manchoukuo are undoubtedly far better off under the present régime than they were before. They now enjoy a sound currency, reasonable taxation, freedom from military exactions, and an increasing degree of law and order. Under Japanese guidance Manchoukuo is being transformed into a modern State. Communications are being developed. The amenities of Western life are being introduced. Although difficulties still lie ahead of Manchoukuo, we consider that they will be overcome and that a gradually increasing level of prosperity may be anticipated.[37]

The general message came through loud and clear: unless Great Britain adopted a more friendly political attitude towards Japan, British trade would be shut out of the Manchurian market.[38]

The Commercial Counsellor in Tokyo blasted the Trade Mission's proposal. His analysis of Japan's economic position gave the death blow to the possibility of an Anglo-Japanese non-aggression pact and ended the loose talk about a trade agreement. When Sir John Simon circulated the Counsellor's report to the Cabinet, he noted that Sansom 'has thirty years' experience of Japan, and is generally acknowledged to be the greatest living authority on that country. I have no hesitation in considering that his opinion must be the authoritative one in this matter.'[39] Sansom stated the problem basically and clearly:

[37] Ibid.

[38] The attitude of the Trade Mission differed considerably from that of the Foreign Office: there the consensus, with notable exceptions, held that Japan should be left alone in Manchuria in the hope that she would find a place to fulfil her 'imperialistic' ambitions. British interests were insignificant, estimated at less than £6 million; Great Britain had little to lose by allowing the Japanese a free hand. 'Unless success in Manchujuo is to be followed by expansionist megalomania, it ought to lead to a definite appeasement of tension in the Far East. The problem of an excess population will have ceased to goad Japan to wild adventures. Nothing, therefore, should be done, such, for example, as an irritating and pedantic insistence on the maintenance of the open door, to thwart Japan's endeavours. On the contrary, everything within reason should be done to encourage success. Japan's gain should, at least indirectly, be ours too.' (Memorandum by W. R. Connor Green, 21 November 1933 [F 7765/33/10], F.O. 371/17081.) The Foreign Office took a different line, however, towards the establishment of a Japanese oil monopoly in Manchukuo. For this episode, see Friedman, *British Relations with China*, pp. 47–9.

[39] Minute by Simon covering Sansom's report circulated to the Cabinet, 11 January 1935, Secret, C.P. 8 (35), CAB. 27/596.

(1) The United Kingdom desires relief from the pressure of Japanese competition.
(2) Japan desires relief from the pressure of world-wide disapproval of her policies.
(3) Can any bargain be made on this basis?

Writing that he could well be ignorant of the reasons why a political arrangement with Japan might be desirable, he addressed himself to the economic side of the problem. He first of all noted that relief from Japanese competition would have to take the form of restrictions enforced by the Japanese Government; he doubted whether the Government could or would limit exports.

I very much doubt whether, even assuming a genuine intention on the part of the Japanese Government to moderate Japanese competition in foreign markets, it would be possible for them in practice to enforce upon their industry and trade restriction which would satisfy us. At any rate, the process would be a slow and difficult one.[40]

The Trade Mission had suggested that if Great Britain would 'co-operate' with Japan in China, Japanese pressure on other markets would diminish and British goods would find an outlet in Manchuria as well as China proper. Sansom criticized the idea:

I by no means wish to suggest that the Japanese authorities, in holding out these prospects of commercial benefit, are deliberately attempting to hoodwink us. I think they would genuinely like to see friendly relations restored and trade rivalry sweetened. But I am sure that their idea of a good bargain is not our idea; and I think we ought to be careful not to make a bargain without being able to assess fairly accurately the value, in terms of trade, of Japan's assurances.

Since 1931 Japan has been a very difficult country to deal with, in matters both of diplomacy and commerce. The attitude, now aggressive, now intractable, of the officials with whom we have to do business made negotiations on large and small matters extremely trying for the members of diplomatic missions in Tokyo.[41]

He went on to state that Japan appeared to be entering a new phase of economic development and that the Japanese were

[40] Memorandum by G. B. Sansom, 29 October 1934, circulated to the Cabinet 11 January 1935, Secret, C.P. 8 (35), CAB. 27/596.
[41] Ibid.

not so confident as they had been previously. 'There are many leading industrialists and bankers who feel misgivings as to Japan's industrial future and think that she may be heading for an economic crisis.' He concluded from the general economic thrust of the country that the Japanese would be more amenable later. 'The lapse of time will, I hope, reveal weaknesses in her economic structure of which we may justly take advantage.'[42] The Cabinet decided to reserve judgement on political and economic relations with Japan until the China situation could be thoroughly reviewed.

The Cabinet's discussion of Anglo-Japanese relations lapsed temporarily in January 1935. The China problem came again to the fore. 1934 had been one of the most economically disastrous years since the birth of the Chinese Republic. Among other things, the American purchase of silver had brought China, in British opinion at least, to the verge of collapse.[43] Responding as most political groups do, the Cabinet requested a study to be made. What could be done? The subsequent report began pessimistically on the usual theme: 'The situation in China is admittedly one of chaos. As a result of seventeen years of Civil War, the control of the so-called Central Government is actual over some three provinces and nominal or non-existent over the remainder.'[44] Neville Chamberlain summarized the main points:

(a) The originating cause of China's economic troubles is the long continued state of civil disorder, amounting almost to anarchy, and complicated by Communism.
(b) The silver policy of the United States of America may bring this to a head, unless it is modified.
(c) The possibility of a complete economic collapse in China, with far-reaching consequences, cannot be ignored.

[42] Ibid.

[43] For the silver question as for most other problems dealt with in this chapter, Borg, *Far Eastern Crisis*, is an invaluable guide.

[44] 'Political and Economic Relations with Japan', Secret, C.P. 35 (35), c. 8 February 1935, CAB. 27/596. It was about this time that the Secretariat began to note on Cabinet documents: 'TO BE KEPT UNDER LOCK AND KEY. IT IS REQUESTED THAT SPECIAL CARE MAY BE TAKEN TO ENSURE THE SECRECY OF THIS DOCUMENT.' This particular document was drawn up by the Permanent Under-Secretary of the Treasury and Head of the Civil Service from 1919 to 1938, Sir Warren Fisher, on whom the best commentary is by D. C. Watt, 'Sir Warren Fisher and British Rearmament against Germany'. *Personalities and Politics*, essay 5.

(d) Unilateral action by any one country of the type and on the scale requisite to avert this is impracticable, alike because of the Consortium Agreement of 1920, and because some form of control of China's budgetary and economic arrangements would be a prerequisite condition of any large-scale assistance, and this must obviously be international in character.

(e) In any event, the participation of the Chinese authorities themselves in any joint endeavour is essential.[45]

Great Britain clearly could not stand by and watch the total economic and political disintegration of China. The Prime Minister appointed a committee composed of himself, the Foreign Secretary, the Chancellor of the Exchequer, the Secretary of State for War, and the President of the Board of Trade. They met only three times, in February, May, and June 1935. Though entitled the 'Committee on Political and Economic Relations with Japan',[46] they dealt in fact almost entirely with China. The discussions meandered. But out of them came two major decisions: a British economic expert should be sent out to investigate the problem on the spot; and the British Legation should be raised to an Embassy and transferred from Peking to the seat of the Nationalist Government in Nanking. Those two measures formed the last strenuous or significant attempt to salvage China's finances and bolster Britain's political prestige in the East.

British commercial concerns exerted strong pressure on the Government, particularly on the Chancellor of the Exchequer, Chamberlain, and the President of the Board of Trade, Walter Runciman. Concurrent with the deterioration of China's economy, British trade continued to decline, not merely for commercial reasons. Chamberlain and Runciman wrote, 'In a word, it is the marked decline of British influence and prestige.' Britain faced increasing competition with Japan; and this had to be fought by immediate economic and political action.

[B]oth of us have been greatly impressed with the emphatic views held by representatives of British companies operating in China that there is still a great potential market for British goods in that country —for the higher grade products of Yorkshire and Lancashire as China recovers and grows richer, and for capital goods such as

---

[45] Chamberlain's covering note to the document cited in the preceding footnote.
[46] The minutes and memoranda are in CAB. 27/596.

locomotives, railway material, ships, etc., which we can supply better than the Japanese.

We are informed that the firms concerned are quite ready to undertake new capital expenditure and long-term commitments to the extent necessary if they can feel sure of a positive attitude of support on the part of the Government and its agents in China.[47]

To state the long and the short of the situation, the leading British China firms believed that the character of Britain's trade was changing from cheaper consumption goods to capital goods; they wanted their share of the expanding China market, but could not acquire it without new capital expenditure and long-term commitments. They would not move ahead without an assurance that the British Government would reject 'the attitude of fatalism' and stop 'the process of Treaty Attrition'. In May 1935 Runciman circulated their petition on the 'Crisis in China' to the Committee on Political and Economic Relations with Japan. The signatures indicate the nature and potential of the China trade in 1935.

Sir Harry McGowan, K.B.E., LL.D.,
Chairman,
Imperial Chemical Industries, Ltd.

Sir Arthur Balfour, Bt., K.B.E., J.P.,
Chairman,
Arthur Balfour & Co. Ltd.
The Eagle & Globe Steel Co. Ltd.

O. J. Barnes, Esq.,
Manager,
Hongkong & Shanghai Banking Corporation.

D. G. M. Bernard, Esq.,
Director,
Matheson & Co. Ltd.

F. D'Arcy Cooper, Esq.,
Chairman,
Chas. E. Tatlow, Esq.
Director,
Unilever Limited.

Sir Hugo Cunliffe-Owen, Bt.,
Chairman,
British-American Tobacco Co.

A. H. Ferguson, Esq.,
Manager,
Chartered Bank of India, Australia and China.

Derek FitzGerald, Esq.,
Manager,
E. D. Sassoon Banking Co. Ltd.

T. W. Greenway, Esq.,
W. A. Kearton, Esq.,
Patons & Baldwins, Ltd.

Sir Richard D. Holt,
Chairman,
Alfred Holt & Co. Ltd.

W. J. Keswick, Esq.,
Jardine Matheson & Co. Ltd.

Lennox B. Lee, Esq.,
Chairman,
Calico Printers' Association, Ltd.

[47] Memorandum by Chamberlain and Runciman, 3 May 1935, Secret, P.E.J. (35)2 CAB. 27/596.

Lt. Gen. Sir George M. W. Mac-
donogh, G.B.E., K.C.B.,
K.C.M.G.,
Asiatic Petroleum Co. Ltd.

H. A. J. Macray, Esq.,
Director,
Dodwell & Co. Ltd.

G. W. Swire, Esq.,
John Swire & Sons, Ltd.

W. F. Turner, Esq.,
Chairman,

Chinese Engineering & Mining
Co. Ltd.

M. Wolfers, Esq.,
Manager,
Arnhold & Co.

Brig.-Gen. C. R. Woodroffe,
C.M.G., C.V.O., C.B.E.,
Director,
Pekin Syndicate Ltd.

Their plea boiled down to an effective affirmation of the traditional British policy of Free Trade: 'they are convinced that the present crisis demands a firm stand in defence of Equality and Treatment. Unless that stand is made, and made without delay, the interests now held by Great Britain will steadily disintegrate.'[48]

The Committee on Political and Economic Relations with Japan favourably received the 'Crisis in China' petition and decided to take definite action, not to make mere declarations. They gave first consideration to the status of the Legation in Peking. Compared with the Embassy's in Tokyo, it seemed to indicate, to British and Chinese alike, that China held the position of a second class or primitive power. Whatever the rank of the delegation, there were disadvantages in moving away from Peking: there the Legations were concentrated together, and worked amiably together. In Nanking they would be scattered; moreover the city was inferior in culture, climate, and comfort. According to the Secretary of State for War, Nanking could not compete with Peking from the point of view of prestige:

The British Mission owed its great position in no small degree to the fact that our Legation was the largest, best and finest in Peking. It was housed in an old Palace and no modern building in Nanking, however expensive, could compare with it or could give us the same prestige in the eyes of natives and foreigners.[49]

---

[48] 'British Interests in the Far East, In Relation to the Crisis in China', Confidential, 9 May 1933, circulated by Runciman to the P.E.J. Committee, Secret, 13 May 1935, P.E.J. (35) 3, CAB. 27/596.

[49] Committee on Political and Economic Relations with Japan, Secret, P.E.J. (35) 2nd Meeting, 14 May 1935, CAB. 27/596.

But he and the other members of the Committee agreed that daily personal contact with the central Chinese Government outweighed any objections to transfer. They were willing to recommend anywhere from £150,000 to £500,000 for the construction of an Embassy in Nanking, and, in order 'not to move the flag', to retain the buildings in Peking.

THE PRESIDENT OF THE BOARD OF TRADE thought that the expenditure of £150,000 or possibly some larger sum would be a very cheap investment as compared with the enormous value of our China trade and interests.

THE PRIME MINISTER observed that he felt more concerned as to the effect which the change would have on the Chinese themselves.

THE CHANCELLOR OF THE EXCHEQUER thought that the Chinese would regard the transfer as a great compliment paid to their Government. . . .

THE SECRETARY OF STATE FOR FOREIGN AFFAIRS added that the present building at Nanking was very small containing only four bedrooms. . . .

THE PRIME MINISTER laid stress upon the great desirability of having an impressive building at Nanking. Prestige depended so much on the appearance of the Embassy building, particularly in the East but also elsewhere.

The discussion continued on the theme of site and prestige:

THE CHANCELLOR OF THE EXCHEQUER agreed that if and when the Embassy were moved to Nanking, the new building must be a worthy one.

THE SECRETARY OF STATE FOR WAR raised the question of the site for the building; a suitable and imposing site was as important as a fine building, and was perhaps of more immediate concern.

THE PRIME MINISTER observed that other countries would probably also wish to follow our example, if we moved our Embassy, there would then be competition for good sites. Consequently we should not start with a small and niggardly basis. . . . The moral effect of a large and important site was also of great value. . . .

THE PRESIDENT OF THE BOARD OF TRADE spoke to the same effect. . . . Every precaution would have to be taken against leakage of information that the British Government were interested in suitable sites in Nanking. If this became known prices would be grossly inflated, and it might become impossible to acquire a suitable site on any reasonable basis.[50]

[50] Ibid.

In the course of the discussion, it became clear that 'the whole matter should be treated as extremely secret.' If Japan or the United States learned that Great Britain contemplated raising the Legation to an Embassy and transferring it to Nanking, they might steal the march by doing it first. Such remarks and lengthy quotations might seem out of proportion to the economic and political crisis in China; but such was one of the main preoccupations of the Committee on Political and Economic Relations with Japan.

To make it more definitely clear that Great Britain did not intend to be pushed out of the Far East, the Cabinet despatched Sir Frederick Leith-Ross to find out what ailed China. Leith-Ross was the Chief Economic Adviser to the British Government and one of the world's foremost economists. Though preeminently a financial technician, he did have certain political as well as economic insights. His mission to the Orient in the autumn of 1935 signified Britain's determination at last to put China's finances on a sound footing and to protect the Empire's trade and prestige—to the alarm of Japan and the United States.[51] According to Leith-Ross himself, he achieved reasonable success on both counts. In September 1936 he described the result of his work:

The primary object of my mission to China was to seek a solution of the acute currency crisis caused by the American silver-purchasing policy. This object was achieved as the result of the abandonment by China of the pure silver standard and the adoption of a managed currency last November [1935]. The currency reform then introduced has up to the present proved unexpectedly successful and no serious difficulty has been experienced in maintaining the exchange at the level fixed . . . if a better understanding could be reached between Japan and China, there would be every reason for feeling confidence in the Chinese currency and for anticipating a definite revival in Chinese trade generally.[52]

The voluminous technical details of Leith-Ross's work demand the attention of an economic historian; it is doubtful whether most members of the Cabinet fully comprehended his complex

[51] See Borg, *Far Eastern Crisis*, chapter IV.
[52] Leith-Ross, 'Financial Mission to China: Recommendations', 4 September 1936, circulated to the Cabinet by Chamberlain and Runciman, Secret, P.E.J., 251 (36), CAB. 27/296.

reports, or were even interested. He dealt with such recondite
topics as Chinese customs, tariffs, export credits, railway loans,
indemnities, bank policies, and bonds. When the Cabinet
received his compressed observations, they shunted them on to
the Committee on Political and Economic Relations with
Japan. The Committee did not meet to consider his analysis,
though of course it was read with care.[53] His recommendations
fell roughly into two categories: working out financial assistance
to China; and making diplomatic representations to Japan. He
wrote about financial assistance:

China . . . needs long-term capital for development purposes, particularly Railway construction. Until recently, any such loans were
out of the question owing to the defaults on many of the existing
loans. During my stay in China, the Chinese Government arrived
at settlements of several of the British Loans in default and made
offers, in the other cases, which in my opinion were reasonable and
should be accepted. The door is therefore open for new financing
and a small loan. . . .

I think that the Consortium Banks should be induced to examine
the possibility of a loan of, say, £10,000,000–£15,000,000 for
financing the import of railway materials for the new construction
which is now being undertaken by the Chinese Government.[54]

The gist of his major recommendation for economic growth
thus was the traditional panacea for China's commercial
problems, long-range railway development. He also wrote
about the necessity to protest to Japan:

[W]e should press tirelessly for the abandonment of the Japanese
campaign for 'autonomy' in North China, which, involving as it
does the wholesale smuggling of Japanese goods, and the disruption
of the Customs service, threatens both our trading and our financial
interests in China, and which, if allowed to continue, will undermine both the political and financial stability of China.[55]

The Foreign Office respected Leith-Ross's economic judgement
but distrusted his speculation on the political relations between
Japan and China. In a word, Leith-Ross may have discerned
the intricacies of Chinese finances, but the Foreign Office

[53] Particularly by the Foreign Secretary and Colonial Secretary, because Leith-
Ross criticized the Foreign and Consular Services, and certain Colonial Office
policies in Hong Kong. See their memoranda in CAB. 27/596.
[54] Leith-Ross's report cited in note 52.
[55] Ibid.

thought he was politically naïve.[56] Nevertheless he made one acute observation that caught the Foreign Office between wind and water. It illustrates the difference between the Lampson era and that of the 1930s, and perhaps indicates what went wrong with British diplomacy and commerce in Asia shortly before the war. Writing about his unofficial contacts with the Consular Officers, Leith-Ross observed: 'Something is wrong. Some of the officers—in particular the Consuls-General at Canton and Tientsin—appeared to me admirable; but in other places there was evidence of staleness, discouragement and indifference.'[57]

The question might well be asked whether British diplomacy in any case could have made any difference. From the point of view of Lampson's successor, Sir Alexander Cadogan, China's troubles originated from internal sources and could not be cured by external aid. In candid and probing conversation in April 1936, Chiang Kai-shek asked him, 'What's wrong with China?' Cadogan, who was much less forthright and forceful than Lampson, was almost too embarrassed to reply. He diffidently deferred to Chiang as a greater authority on China than he; Chiang replied with a Chinese proverb: 'The onlooker sees most of the game.' Cadogan promised he would do his best. The premise of his response revolved on the supposition that the West had no monopoly on virtue. Nevertheless, as the world's economics and politics increasingly drew the Chinese into the modern world, China could not remain isolated. The trouble was that the Chinese refused to adapt.

If China could be left to continue along her old ways, it might be that she would be better off. But she could not remain isolated from the rest of the world. For good or for ill, she had been in ever-increasing contact with other civilizations, and these, whether of the west itself or of her neighbour Japan, which had assimilated western methods, were continually pressing upon her. China could not remain indifferent to or untouched by the great forces of 'progress' and modern invention, and that, in its turn, involved the modification of her social and political system.[58]

[56] See for example the implications in Eden's memorandum, 'Sir Frederick Leith-Ross's Report on his Financial Mission to China', 3 November 1936, Secret, P.E.J. (35) 5, CAB. 27/596.
[57] Leith-Ross's report cited in note 52.
[58] Cadogan to Eden, No. 22A. Tour Series, 5 April 1936 [F 2675/166/10], F.O. 371/20249.

16—B.S.F.E.

Coming to the main point, Cadogan pronounced this judgement: 'What was wrong with China was that there was something wrong with the Chinese—something at least that did not conform to western standards and made them unable properly to adjust western standards.' After dwelling on Chinese corruption and maladministration, he went on:

In the dimension of time, the average Chinese seemed to be unable to accept the idea of being content to work for the future, without hope of getting or seeing results in his lifetime. The Chinese were excessively practical, unfortunately to the exclusion of idealism. I did not wish to ascribe any monopoly of virtue to the western races, but if anything of what they had done had good in it, that would generally be found to have sprung from the generous impulse of some idealist rather than from a calculation of purely material advantages.[59]

He concluded that the answer to China's problems lay in youth, as in England:

The proper education of youth—and by education I meant much more than mere school teaching—was receiving daily more attention in many countries, including England. If the family system was a source of trouble for China was it not best—if it were possible—to remove the youth early from the family influence and put them into schools and academies and colleges where they might be trained, not so much intellectually, to fill posts which did not exist in sufficient numbers in the present stage of China's development, but where they might acquire a corporate spirit and a wider loyalty and a sense of service.[60]

Like his predecessor a decade earlier, Cadogan held that the economic and political problems of China could be solved by an honest and loyal civil service administering in the English spirit of fair play.

If the British continued to judge China by their own standards, they also persisted in seeing the Japanese through European spectacles. 'The Japanese are the most ego-centric race on earth—not even excepting the French,' concluded Sir John Pratt in 1933 when he expressed an attitude that ran throughout the era.[61] Nevertheless the theme of racism and its

---

[59] Ibid.   [60] Ibid.
[61] Memorandum by Pratt, 1 December 1933 [F 7818/5189/61].

concomitant political overtones of such qualities as corruption
or arrogance declined in the 1930s. The theories of 'what's
wrong in the Far East' increasingly dwelt on problems of
industrialization, markets, and excess population. In an age
when men believed that economic forces would probably
prevail, the British looked beyond the political problems of
China and Japan to forecast the future of the Orient by emerging economic trends. Perhaps the most systematic analysis of
this sort came from the pen of the Commercial Counsellor in
Peking, Sir Louis Beale, in April 1937. Beale challenged the
common view that Japan and China travelled different roads
of development. 'If,' he wrote, 'Japan is dreaming of industrial
development for herself, with China supplying agricultural and
mineral raw materials, she will have a rude awakening to an
industrial China treading on her heels.' In brief, he argued that
China eventually would be able to supply her own products,
thus forcing Japan to look for other markets for cheaper goods
and to compete with Great Britain in the provision of heavy
industrial manufactures. Unless the British could change the
basic nature of their trade 'from lower to higher good products',
the situation looked gloomy. Beale wrote:

I anticipate our share of that [China] trade decreasing, as more and
more pressure is put on Japan to maintain the value of her trade
with China by scrambling for a larger share of the better-class trade
as China's purchases of the cheaper qualities decline. Yet if she finds
that China, the principal outlet which she has been looking upon as
dependable, is being gradually closed to her bulk manufacturers
from her factories in Japan, is there not a danger that she will go
berserk? She is suffering to-day from a sense of isolation, of frustration and curbing. Market after market throughout the world is being
closed against her goods. The actions of an animal thrashing about
to find an outlet from a net that is narrowing about her are not
predictable or reasonable, and Japan, is, so to speak, in that position
today.[62]

Like many—but not all—Far Eastern experts, Beale urged a
policy of tolerance towards Japan and the removal of 'irritating
pinpricks'. If Japan could be appeased politically, she would

---

[62] Beale to Knatchbull-Hugessen, No. 134 Confidential, 6 April 1937, enclosed
in Knatchbull-Hugessen to Eden, No. 44, 14 May 1937 [F 3975/14/10], F.O.
371/20965.

have less objection to Britain's commercial role in China. He had no doubt that Britain qualified as the nation suited to help in China's economic growth.

I submit that we of all nations are best fitted to assist China in her industrial development, and that here are two ways in which we can participate in it. The first is the supply of capital and/or equipment for her railways, public utilities and major industries. The second is manufacturing in China. Some of our leading producers in the cotton, woollen, and other trades have already adopted the latter course as an alternative to complete severance of their connexion with China, and it is a process capable of endless expansion.[63]

On the eve of the Sino-Japanese war, the vision of the China market thus remained strong.[64] Had the Far Eastern situation been determined solely by economic factors, British trade in China might have flourished for ever after. The outbreak of hostilities ended such economic speculation. When the Foreign Office received Beale's report, Ashton-Gwatkin noted in a concluding minute, 'the whole situation is now melting, or exploding.'

END NOTE

The Washington Treaties and the Singapore Base. 'The naval agreement of 1922 had two sides to it: the capital ship ratios and the restriction on battleship bases. The former gave, or rather preserved, an advantage for either Britain or the U.S. in a pitched battle of main fleets, but the latter enabled Japan to maintain naval command of the seas between Japan and China without having to fight a main fleet action in those waters, for the U.S.A. had no battleship base nearer than Pearl Harbour and Britain none nearer than Malta. If it had not been for the Washington agreement, the U.S. would have been free to construct a main fleet base in the Philippines and Britain one at Hongkong; for security against this danger it was a very good bargain for Japan to renounce the right to build such a base in Formosa. However, the Treaty still left Britain the right to construct a base at Singapore, which, even if too far off for effective operations in the East China or Yellow Seas, could support a naval defence of Malaya itself, the straits into the Indian Ocean and communications with Australia. It was quite a rational strategy to construct such a base and reasonable before 1940 to suppose that it could only be attacked from the sea, because it could be assumed that in a war with Japan (or

[63] Ibid.
[64] Pratt minuted on Beale's despatch: 'An industrialized China means a more orderly stable and a richer China and surely that would mean an expansion ten or even a hundred fold of her present absurdly small volume of trade. As China's millions grew even richer all sorts of new wants would develop and these would be met by imports from abroad balancing the vastly greater volume of her exports. A wealthy China would mean more wealth for all the world and a higher standard of living in China would be reflected in higher standards in other countries.' Ibid.

with Germany and Italy plus Japan), France would be an ally, or at worst a neutral, and this would mean (a) the French fleet in the Mediterranean to deal with Italy and (b) French air and sea action from Indo-China against a Japanese seaborne expedition to the south, or at worst, no Japanese use of Indo-China territory against Malaya. But this calculation, reasonable enough before 1940, was completely upset by the fall of France, which left Britain to cope with both the German and Italian navies without French aid and led to the Japanese occupation of Indo-China. It is true that much more might have been done for the defence of Malaya in the time between the fall of France and the outbreak of the Pacific war, but that is another story and does not affect the merits of the decisions on the Singapore base at the time they were taken in the 1920s and 1930s.'—G. F. H.

VIII

THE UNDECLARED
SINO-JAPANESE WAR

IF APPEASEMENT means buying off a potential aggressor at the sacrifice of principle, then the British stand acquitted in the case of Japan. They made no 'Munich agreement' in the Far East. Nevertheless they gave full thought to political and economic propitiation that might have won Japan's friendship, or at least her neutrality. Even those most antipathetic to Japan's campaign on the Asian mainland saw the force of the economic and demographic arguments put forward by her leaders; even those Englishmen most sympathetic to Japan stopped short of endorsing the full-blown quest for 'autonomy', a 'co-prosperity sphere', or a 'New Order', which to more indiscriminate British minds implied a bid for the hegemony of Asia, the extinction of British interests in China, and a threat to India and even Australasia. Japan somehow had to be accommodated, but at the same time stopped.

The personalities associated with Britain's Far Eastern strategy varied, on the whole, from the officials connected with her European policy. Pre-occupied with Europe, the Chamberlain Government, with important exceptions, left the problem of the Sino-Japanese war to the Far Eastern Department of the Foreign Office.[1] There the leading personages at this time were Sir Alexander Cadogan (now Permanent Under-Secretary superintending the Department) Sir John Pratt, and Sir John Brenan. A distinguishing fact about them stands out: they were all old China hands, temperamentally more averse to Japan than to China. The governing formula they eventually devised

[1] Sir Antony Eden and Lord Halifax (Foreign Secretaries December 1935–February 1938 and March 1938–January 1941 respectively) sometimes did bring Far Eastern issues before the Cabinet. On the whole, though, neither had the time or devoted the attention to Asia that characterized the regimes of Curzon, Austen Chamberlain, or Simon. The result was that British representatives occasionally were left clamouring for instructions in a way unparalleled since the days of Lord Granville.

for the Far East can be stated: 'Firmness towards Japan, generosity towards China.' Or, in Brenan's judgement, British policy from the outbreak of Sino-Japanese hostilities in July 1937 to the occupation of Poland a little over two years later could be summed up in one word: 'stalemate'. Playing for time, British officials hoped that Japan eventually would become exhausted. They believed that Japanese imperialism ultimately would fail. They regarded China's nationalism as at least as strong as Japan's.

Going beyond preconceptions, the over-all formulation of British Far Eastern policy depended on three major and rapidly changing considerations: the situation in Europe; the attitude of the United States; and the progress in British rearmament.[2] Without sufficient force, Britain obviously could not risk war with Japan; when the Singapore base opened in February 1938, the number of cruisers, or rather lack of them, made painfully clear Britain's dependence on the United States; Germany, not Japan, remained Britain's greatest potential enemy, and British policy in the Far East was largely determined by calculations of the role the United States might or might not play in Europe. Britain obviously had to work to remain as friendly as possible with Japan, pursuing a line of conciliation rather than force, but conciliation tempered by growing American antagonism towards the Japanese. Against all that the British faced the problem of China. Without losing sight of either the United States or China, Britain had to decide whether to attempt to buy off Japan in an effort to weaken the Tokyo–Berlin–Rome triangle and to prevent a Japanese-German military alliance. There were two political arrangements against which those emerging trends had to be judged: the anti-Comintern pact concluded by Japan and Germany on 25 November 1936; and the Chinese-Russian non-aggression pact of 21 August 1937.

Leaving aside for the moment the American and European

---

[2] These are the points accurately described, in my opinion, by E. L. Woodward in the preface to volume XIII, Third Series of *D.B.F.P.* [all subsequent references in this chapter are to volumes of the Third Series]. There is an excellent monograph on the subject, especially good in dealing with the Far East in relation to the United States and Europe: Nicholas R. Clifford, *Retreat from China: British Policy in the Far East 1937–1941* (University of Washington Press, 1967); for important evaluation that touches on some of the themes of this chapter, see the review by Robert Joseph Gowen, *Journal of Modern History*, **42**, 1 (March, 1970) 133–6.

aspects of the problem, the most imponderable Far Eastern enigma consisted of the element on which both those transactions hinged, the movements of the Soviet Union and Communism in China. At a time when the Foreign Office studied proposals for non-aggression pacts in Asia and neutralization schemes for the Pacific that would involve both Russia and Japan, Sir John Pratt and others frequently questioned basic assumptions in order to test the validity of their decisions about the Far East.[3] They often disagreed on such questions as, would Japan eventually be able to live harmoniously with China? With Russia? What of the question of race? The future of Communism? Sir Louis Beale, for example, believed that China and Japan would sort out their troubles and co-exist in a sort of quasi alliance. Pratt disagreed: 'Chinese and Russians might live peaceably together and might even coalesce to produce a new civilization, but apart from a very thin veneer there is nothing in common between China and Japan.'[4]

The Chargé d'Affaires in Tokyo, James Dodds, thought that the question of colour made the Japanese fundamentally hostile to the white races. H. H. Thomas of the Far Eastern Department believed otherwise:

Such hostility is not, I am convinced, fundamental. Indeed, I would go so far as to say that the Japanese are personally far more hostile to the Chinese or to the Coreans than they are to Europeans. The hostility of the Japanese towards the latter arises from the national & collective inferiority complex, which unfortunately for themselves and for the world is tending to become not merely a complex but a mania.[5]

So far as Communism was concerned, most British officials continued to think that it could never succeed in China. When Sir Hughe Knatchbull-Hugessen, the Ambassador who succeeded Cadogan, reviewed the problem in 1937, he concluded:

Sympathy with Communist ideas is practically non-existent in China at present. Communism is generally hated and detested for the havoc which has been wrought in its name during the past decade

[3] For examples of discussions of neutralization and other proposals, see F.O. 371/21025.
[4] Minute by Pratt, 28 July 1937 [F 3975/14/10], F.O. 371/20665.
[5] Dodds to Eden, No. 328, 17 June 1937, F.O. 371/21025; minute by H. H. Thomas (of long experience in the Consular Service in Japan), 16 August 1937, ibid.

and for the trick which it played on Dr. Sun Yat-sen and the Kuomintang in the years culminating in 1937 [sic: 1927]. . . .

To sum up, my conclusions are that Communism in China was moribund until it was galvanized into an appearance of revival by association with the anti-Japanese movement, that even now there is little Communist sentiment in China and that, though the Communists may continue to be a nuisance, there is small danger of their being able to regain a footing in the Government or seriously to affect national policy.[6]

Writing five months before the outbreak of the Sino-Japanese hostilities, Knatchbull-Hugessen made an acute observation: 'So long as Japanese pressure on China continues, so long will the Communists be able to make a specious appeal to the patriotic sentiments of the population, especially among its younger elements.'[7] The Foreign Office shared his view: Japan would give impetus to the cause of Communism as long as she remained on the Asian mainland.

Had the Japanese merely consolidated their position in Manchuria, they might, in the British view, eventually have placated the Chinese by the benefits of economic development and the establishment of law and order. That possibility ended on the night of 7–8 July 1937, when Japanese and Chinese troops collided at the Marco Polo bridge in the Lukouchiao region near Peking. Sir John Pratt noted:

The seizure of Manchuria was bad enough, but had Japan been content to remain on the other side of the Great Wall an uneasy sort of *modus vivendi* might perhaps have been patched up. Now that Japan has intruded into China proper relations between Japan and China can consist of nothing but a series of clashes.[8]

---

[6] Knatchbull-Hugessen to Eden, No. 7, 12 February 1937 [F 1767/223/10], F.O. 371/20991.

[7] Ibid.

[8] Minute by Pratt, 28 July 1937 [F 3975/14/10], F.O. 371/20665. The incident is discussed at length by Crowley, *Japan's Quest for Autonomy*. It should be noted at least in passing that the outbreak of hostilities brought an end to the talks in progress about an Anglo-Japanese *rapprochement*. For a speculative contemporary assessment, see G. E. Hubbard, *Survey of International Affairs, 1937*, p. 165:

'For Japan an undertaking with Great Britain might open a door by which she might be able to re-enter the society of Western nations without having to renounce her objects to the League of Nations system; it might provide a means of improving her economic conditions and her financial prospects; and above all, it might lead to a recognition of her "special position" in North China. In

The skirmish seemed to be a repeat performance of the Manchurian incident; but Japan's action now appeared even less excusable. Sir Alexander Cadogan wrote:

The Japanese haven't got a leg to stand upon. Quite probably the Lukouchiao incident was not deliberately engineered—in fact there is circumstantial evidence to show that it was not—but it was seized upon and exploited for the furtherance of a policy of blatant aggression on which the Japanese have not had the good manners to attempt to conceal. . . .

What cannot be contested for 2 minutes is that it was provocative and unnecessary to hold night manoeuvres in that area, and what is common knowledge to anyone who has resided in North China (or in Shanghai) is that the employment and demeanour of Japanese military is always marked by the maximum possible of provocative offensiveness.[9]

No doubt existed about Japan's guilt; but the British, attempting to learn the historical lesson of the Manchurian crisis, resolved not to put Japan 'in the dock'.[10]

The members of the Cabinet discussed possible collaboration with the United States to curtail the hostilities and to prevent the issue from arising in Geneva. They discovered that, by contrast with the Manchurian incident, the State Department now preferred to take 'parallel, though not identical' action on grounds that a joint representation would exacerbate the situation. British policy seemed adrift.[11] The head of the Far Eastern Department, C. W. Orde, consequently prepared a brief on risk of war with Japan if the League attempted to apply sanctions. He proposed that Japan should be assured that Britain would oppose the League's intervention and would

---

return, Japan could offer to conform to British desires by halting in her encroachment upon China's territorial integrity, by respecting British interests in Central and Southern China and by a pledge of non-interference with Chinese plans for economic reconstruction. Apart from China there was room for concessions on both sides.'

Hubbard wisely concluded that such an agreement would be publicly denounced as an Asian Hoare-Laval deal (for the same analogy, see below note 29). The Anglo-Japanese discussions of 1937 need the kind of attention possible only in a monograph.

[9] Minute by Cadogan, 13 September 1937 [F 6115/9/10], F.O. 371/20955.

[10] The phrase used by Hore-Belisha, Secretary of State for War, Cabinet Minutes, Secret, 13 October 1937, CAB. 23/89.

[11] Ibid. For the American side of the question, see especially Borg, *Far Eastern Crisis*.

'minimise at Geneva the strength of any denunciation of Japan as an aggressor.' He thus raised an important moral issue—British support of Japan and obstruction of sanctions would humiliate the League and diminish its already weakened power. But, if Britain from the beginning took the line that sanctions should not be applied, the danger of war might be removed. Without implying 'anything underhand', as he stated, Orde thus argued that the risks of war with Japan were very real indeed and that the proceedings at Geneva should be made as anodyne as possible. As he summarized the rationale of his case: 'We know from 1931–3 that her [Japan's] recklessness is apt to grow the more when she is threatened.'[12]

British policy fell short of a clear-cut decision between Japan and the League. Instead it wavered between adherence to the League's principles and friendship with the United States. The resolution sponsored by Great Britain at Geneva in October 1937 well indicates this schizophrenic approach: (a) it did not state that Japan was the aggressor, though implying so; and (b) it recommended invoking the Nine Power Treaty, which would involve the United States.[13] The members of the Cabinet had good reason to believe that the Americans might now act. They complained of President Roosevelt's 'quarantine' speech of 5 October as vague and ambiguous, but nevertheless saw it as a warning that the United States would not tolerate further aggression. Chamberlain 'recalled that President Roosevelt had used the expression "quarantine," which had been generally interpreted as a boycott. He himself [Chamberlain] had noticed, however, that the President's speech was so worded that he could escape from that interpretation.' Still, Chamberlain 'did not under-rate the importance of his [Roosevelt's] statement, especially as a warning to the Dictator Powers that there was a point beyond which the United States of America would not permit them to go.'[14]

Chamberlain and the Foreign Secretary, Sir Antony Eden, upheld the idea that a conference might bring about an armistice in the Far East. They put their views before the

[12] Memorandum by Orde, 22 August 1937 [F 5720/9/10], with important critical minute by R. C. Skrine Stevenson, 23 August 1937, F.O. 371/20954.

[13] For Chinese tactics at Geneva and the passing of the Cranborne resolution, see Clifford, *Retreat from China*, chapters I–III.

[14] Cabinet Minutes, Secret, 6 and 13 October 1937, CAB. 23/89.

Cabinet on 13 October 1937. Not only had they learned the lesson of the Manchurian affair, when Britain and the United States had failed to work together, but also that of the Abyssinian crisis, when sanctions had failed against Italy. Chamberlain outlined the following desiderata:

(1) It was impossible to put in force *effective* sanctions without a risk of war.

(2) We could put in force ineffective sanctions, but these would not accomplish their purpose and would result (as in the case of Italy) in prolonged bitterness and ill-will.

(3) He doubted whether, even if a sufficient number of countries could be induced to put economic sanctions in force effectively, they would operate in time to save China, whose collapse appeared possible and might even be imminent. The Japanese armies appeared to be rolling up the Chinese. They might in due course capture Nanking, Hangkow and Canton, in which the conditions of the Chinese would be comparable to that of Abyssinia, Chiang Kai Chek taking the place of the Emperor.

(4) If sanctions proved effective there was no guarantee that Japan, possibly egged on by Germany and Italy, would not make some retaliatory attack, e.g., on some oil supplies in the East Indies, or on Hong-Kong, or the Philippines. If they did so what could we do in present conditions? It would not be safe to send the Fleet to the Far East in the present position in Europe. We could not go into sanctions, therefore, without a guarantee from the United States of America that they would be prepared to face up to all the consequences which might fall on nations with large interests in the Far East. Even then it was impossible to foresee how long public opinion in America would be prepared to maintain the position. His conclusion, therefore, was that economic sanctions were of no use unless backed by overwhelming force.[15]

Eden endorsed the Prime Minister's description of the effect of sanctions. 'He himself would never agree to the imposition of sanctions without the agreement of the United States of America and the other signatories of the China Treaty to support those sanctions by the use of force if need be. He thought that President Roosevelt's speech was a most important new factor in the situation, and that Anglo-American co-operation was vital.' The discussion evolved into a colloquium on dictators

[15] Cabinet Minutes, Secret, 13 October 1937, CAB. 23/89.

and the situation in the Far East—one of the few full reviews the Cabinet gave to the latter problem at this time. Some of the historical parallels are instructive about the influence of history on contemporary affairs:

The Secretary of State for Scotland [Walter Elliot] . . . thought there were some not unhopeful features in the situation. The Chinese representatives at Geneva had expressed the view that the Japanese armies were not attempting to over-run China, but that their object was to push the Chinese across the Yellow River in order to get them out of the way with a view to an eventual attack on the U.S.S.R. in Eastern Siberia. . . . He agreed . . . that we should explore the possibility of close co-operation with the United States. Dictators had a habit of going on until they were stopped, and the example of one might be followed by others, with dangerous results in Europe.

The President of the Board of Education [Lord Stanhope] agreed in the Prime Minister's proposals. As to the military situation, he thought it possible that the Japanese might soon find themselves marching across a vast country in the grip of a hard winter, getting nowhere, like Napoleon in Russia. If the Chinese could hold out until the end of the year and then adopt guerilla warfare, the Japanese might be unable to bring the war to an end. This prospect might incline them to negotiations. . . .

The Secretary of State for Dominion Affairs [Malcolm MacDonald] agreed with the Prime Minister. The situation in Europe was too critical to justify our taking any risks in the Far East. . . .

The Lord President of the Council [Lord Halifax] . . . thought we should be content with stating the situation frankly to the United States of America. Even if America did take a more bellicose line than we, we should have to think carefully before committing to them the defence of our interests in the Far East.

The Secretary of State for Foreign Affairs said that it was important to avoid putting the American Government in a position to say they could have cleared up the situation but for our unwillingness.[16]

The Cabinet thus remained wary but hopeful of the United States; they doubted the value of sanctions unless backed by force. They proceeded with plans for a conference. It opened in Brussels on 4 November 1937 and accomplished nothing save to antagonize the Japanese. It did little or nothing to help the Chinese. The participants resolved: 'Members of the League

16 Ibid

should refrain from taking any action which might have the effect of weakening China's powers of resistance and should also consider how far they can individually extend aid to China.'[17] The Brussels Conference gave the death gasp of the Washington treaty system.

Despite the failure of the concert of nations, a strong strain of belief in international law persisted in British thought—a belief that in the end international law would win out, in the Far East and throughout the world. Numerous examples could be cited in order to demonstrate the sustained hope that the Japanese would regain their rationality and rejoin the family of nations, but one analytical piece in particular deserves attention. It was written by a legal expert, G. G. Fitzmaurice, in the spring after the collapse of the Brussels Conference. He attempted to identify the psychological and ideological reasons why Japan as well as Germany and Italy refused to recognize the legitimacy of international law in certain instances. He demonstrated to the satisfaction of his colleagues that international law, far from being an outworn and out-of-date conception, would probably prove tougher than its critics imagined. He began by examining the Japanese plea that the hostilities between China and Japan did not amount to war, and drew comparisons with similar Italian and German arguments.

It will be recollected that the Italians persistently denied that the hostilities between themselves and Abyssinia constituted a war. They said it was a colonial expedition or a police operation. They also refused to admit that the ordinary rules of international law were applicable as between themselves and Abyssinia. Germany has similarly advanced a plea that the ordinary rules do not obtain as between herself and Austria. . . . Now we have the Japanese denying that the Chinese Government is the true Government of China or that they are at war with China itself or that the hostilities amount to war.[18]

He went on to say that behind the actions of Italy, Germany, and Japan lay psychological motives.

So far as psychology goes, the Italians were never prepared to admit

[17] The Conference is well discussed by Clifford, *Retreat from China*, chapter IV; see also especially Borg, *Far Eastern Crisis*, chapter XIV, and Antony Eden, Earl of Avon, *Facing the Dictators* (London, 1962).

[18] Minute by G. G. Fitzmaurice, 23 March 1938 [F 2832/84/10], F.O. 371/22108.

that Abyssinia was a State having equal rights with other States. In spite of Abyssinia's membership of the League they constantly reiterated that the allegedly barbarous character of her Government placed her outside the pale. Ideological reasons similarly account for the attitude of Germany and Italy towards the Barcelona Government. Racial reasons account for the attitude of Germany where Austria was concerned. Again in China, the Japanese are concerned to deny the status of China as a normal State. They wish to regard it as a congerie of separate elements over which the Nanking Government holds no true sway.[19]

In short, the Japanese regarded the conflict as a *colonial* situation. Thus they held that international law could not apply any more than in India. Whatever the legitimacy of the argument—which most Englishmen of course viewed as debatable— it did not mean that Japan had doomed international law to extinction. International law would endure, 'if for no other reason than that in the long run it is easier to have rules than to have a state of complete chaos. Although there may be periods when the rules of international law are extensively violated, yet in general they persist, because international relations between countries cannot conveniently be carried on on any other basis.'[20]

Japanese flouting of 'the code of civilised nations' continued apace. As prelude and finale to the Brussels Conference, Japanese aircraft on 26 August 1937 gunned down the British Ambassador and on 12 December attacked His Majesty's Ships *Ladybird* and *Bee* and sank the American *Panay*. Sir Hughe Knatchbull-Hugessen gave the following description of his journey from Nanking to Shanghai in a motor car flying a Union Jack. His account portrays the imperturbability of the British community in China and also the British tendency to regard the Sino-Japanese hostilities as somewhat of a bother.

We had not gone far . . . when we heard a burst of machine gun fire from the air. I did not see the aeroplane but was unconcernedly counting the shots when I suddenly became aware of something very hard going very fast through my middle. . . . when I put my hand on my leg and discovered I could feel nothing and was completely paralysed from the waist downwards I realised that something unpleasant had happened to me. I observed . . . that I had been shot.

[19] Ibid.   [20] Ibid.

One of his first visitors in the hospital was the Japanese Ambassador.

I was certainly not looking my best. He came and muttered a sentence to his interpreter. When it was translated I was listening for the word 'regret'. But I only heard 'sympathy'. I could not refrain from saying in somewhat outspoken terms exactly what I thought of the whole business.[21]

With equally warm emotion the Ambassador in Tokyo in December demanded a reprimand of the officer responsible for the *Ladybird* incident. The Japanese Government recalled him, to the satisfaction of the British.[22] When Sir John Brenan six months later surveyed the Far Eastern situation, he judged that the *Ladybird* episode had produced a salutary effect on the Japanese. 'We know that the "Panay and Ladybird" incidents caused the Japanese such alarm that they abandoned the invasion of Kuangtun (Canton) for fear of complications with the western Powers.'[23]

Perhaps the wish fathered the thought, but the Foreign Office believed that a policy at once firm and conciliatory might restrain Japan. From the fall of Nanking on 13 December 1937 to the invasion of south China on 12 October 1938, Foreign Office officials examined proposals that would strengthen Japan's economic and strategic position on the Asian mainland but that would be fair to China. They hoped Japan would recognize that she had embarked on a campaign similar to Napoleon's in Russia, and consequently would be more amenable to peace negotiations; or, as in the anecdote that came to the British via the American Ambassador in China, Japan surely would see that she resembled Uncle Remus's Brer Fox, becoming increasingly stuck in the tar baby of China with Russia as Brer Rabbit contentedly looking on. When Japan continued to refuse to learn such historical and folk-lore lessons, the British gave more and more attention to military

[21] Sir Hughe Knatchbull-Hugessen, *Diplomat in Peace and War* (London, 1949), pp. 120–3. In order to impress on the Japanese 'the value which we set upon an Ambassador' (Chamberlain's words), the Government awarded Knatchbull-Hugessen £5000. Ibid. p. 127; CAB. 23/89.
[22] See Sir Robert Craigie, *Behind the Japanese Mask* (London, 1946), pp. 52–3.
[23] Minute by Brenan, 23 June 1938 [F 6708/84/10], F.O. 371/22109. The Panay crisis is thoroughly discussed by Borg, *Far Eastern Crisis*, chapter XVI.

and financial assistance to China, and to sanctions against Japan.

Sir John Brenan and Sir John Pratt devised two of the more notable peace formulas in January 1938. Writing separately in a new series of highly secret 'Green' papers, both arrived at similar conclusions. Brenan's remarks depict several persistent themes:

[I]t would be foolish not to adopt a realistic attitude towards Japan's undoubted military power and her firm resolve to secure a stronger economic and strategic position in East Asia. No more than the Germans can the Japanese be indefinitely suppressed.

So far as the Chinese are concerned, though militarily weak they are racially strong and endued with an enormous capacity for passive resistance to foreign encroachment both physical and in the realm of ideas. In the long run they will be more than a match for the Japanese and the extent of Japan's military domination on the mainland will be the measure of her difficulties in the years to come.[24]

He recommended that these specific proposals be put forward if Britain were called upon to mediate:

(1) [T]he Recognition by Japan of the sovereignty, the independence and the territorial and administrative integrity of China proper, and the withdrawal of all Japanese forces south of the Great Wall. . . .
(2) The recognition by China of Manchukuo and the granting of facilities for economic cooperation between Manchukuo and North China. . . .
(3) The retention of an international customs administration on present lines with tariff amendments in Japan's favour. . . .
(4) The reorganisation and demilitarisation of the whole Shanghai area under one administration. . . .[25]

He warned of the obstreperous influence of local British traders in China:

[W]e should try and put China on her feet again as a prosperous and independent nation and keep before us as our main objective the China market for our trade, trade between the Empire and China and not local vested interests. The latter are too often *mere*

[24] Memorandum by Brenan, 6 January 1938 [F 335/*G*], with important minutes by Orde and Cadogan, F.O. 371/22053.
[25] Ibid.

excrescences on the extraterritorial system, but they are correspondingly vocal against any change and exercise and influence out of all proportion to their real importance.[26]

Whatever the outcome of the Sino-Japanese conflict, Brenan warned that British political pretensions in the Far East would probably diminish; but he judged that British trade might still expand.

Pratt stated three conditions that the peace terms would have to satisfy: '(1) they should be generous to Japan, (2) they should be fair to China, and (3) whether America is actively co-operating or not, they should be such as to win the approval of American public opinion.' He devoted special attention to Shanghai, which from the British point of view was the crux of the problem: 'The choice before us in Shanghai would seem to lie between perpetuating—and endeavouring to prop up and strengthen—the régime of foreign settlements, extraterritoriality, etc., or wiping the slate clean and making a fresh start.'[27] The objections to the first alternative were formidable. Japan's share in the control of the settlement would probably greatly increase, and the foreign administration would become predominantly Japanese in character. Examining the difficulties of the second choice, Pratt predicted a storm of protest far surpassing that of 1927 over Hankow if Britain handed over Shanghai to the Chinese. Nevertheless he decided that to relinquish Shanghai would be the best course.

[T]he arguments in favour of deliberately adopting a policy of immediate rendition are very strong. . . . It would help to restore a friendly and stable Chinese government and to establish the principles of the open door and equal opportunity. Finally—and this is perhaps the strongest argument of all—it is probably the only policy that would be welcomed in America and that is at all likely to secure American co-operation.[28]

Shifting to the general problem of North China, Pratt observed, like Brenan, that the basis of the settlement would have to be the withdrawal of Japanese troops south of the Great Wall.

---

[26] Ibid. The phrase is italicized because Sir John Pratt called it an apt description and because it well illustrates the Foreign Office's attitude towards the British 'diehards' of Shanghai.

[27] Memorandum by Pratt, 5 January 1938 [F 335/*G*], ibid.

[28] Ibid.

But, in fairness to Japan, he concluded that 'we should still do our best to secure for Japan the economic advantages that she seeks in this [North China] region.'[29]

Sir Alexander Cadogan referred to the Brenan-Pratt formulas as the '"optimum" ideal terms that we could impose if we were in a position to dictate'. The British never achieved that position. Rather they had to decide what attitude to take towards Japan's demands of Great Britain. The Ambassador in Tokyo persistently held out hope that if Britain would go to greater lengths to accommodate or understand the Japanese plight, Japan would redress British grievances. For example, the tone of the British press irritated the Japanese Government. If the Foreign Office would stifle anti-Japanese criticism, Britain might get better treatment in China. Sir John Brenan, for one, responded negatively to that idea. If anything, the Japanese ought to be criticized more:

To damp down criticism of Japan will be to play into their hands. If indeed it is true that the new Japanese Government desire to remove the causes of Anglo-Japanese discord (and they doubtless do, as cheaply as possible) the only way to keep them up to the mark is a campaign of protests, criticism, and publicity. Instead of being pleasant and hoping for the best, when we shall get nothing, we should be as surly and unaccommodating as possible and try to give the impression that a wave of anger is arising in Great Britain against Japan and may prove dangerous.

After all, does not recent European history show that that is the way to get things done? Does anyone imagine that Hitler would obtain better terms from Czechoslovakia by damping down the German press and being ingratiating, or that Italy is not forcing concessions from the democratic Powers by abuse and intimidation?[30]

Cadogan and others thought that Brenan on this occasion overstated his case or drew a misleading parallel with the European situation; but they all held that they should not be

[29] Ibid. Note the important minutes by Orde and Cadogan, who concurred, and Eden, who wrote, 'This is most useful.' The gist of the Brenan–Pratt memoranda was communicated to the State Department and subsequently leaked out into the press as an Asian 'Hoare–Laval deal.'

[30] Minute by Brenan, 23 June 1938 [F 6708/84/10], F.O. 371/22109; in the margin next to the remark about Hitler, someone, apparently Cadogan, noted 'Not quite a parallel', and Cadogan further remarked, 'I don't think we need indulge in a "campaign of protests etc.", but I quite agree we needn't damp down any that justifiably arise.'

gulled into believing that concessions on their part would conciliate the Japanese.

Sir John Brenan emerges from the unpublished British documents as the champion of opposition to Japan.[31] Historians interpret records in different ways and acquire divergent impressions, and it could well be that the definitive account of British Far Eastern policy in 1938–9 will portray Brenan in a less prominent role or will deny that his influence carried any particular weight. What cannot be denied is his expert knowledge of the Far East, the vigour of his thought, and the esteem in which his colleagues held his views. He believed fundamentally that concessions to the Japanese would make them clamour for more. He was not, in short, an appeaser. Appeasement in the pejorative sense did not occur in the Far East because officials such as Brenan observed the failure of conciliation with Germany and Italy and judged that appeasement would also fail with Japan. Of greater importance, Chamberlain did not intervene in Far Eastern policy as he did with European. True, after Lord Halifax succeeded Eden in February 1938, the wave of appeasement sometimes became more perceptible in major decisions; but the undertow of British Far Eastern official opinion usually carried Halifax, and Brenan was usually instrumental in the forming of the consensus.

Any number of Brenan's prolific minutes could be quoted to demonstrate the thrust of his ideas, but perhaps these comments written shortly before the Munich crisis are especially illuminating. His analysis reminds one of the Foreign Office's evaluation of the Federation of British Industries' abortive mission in 1934.

There is no need to attribute conscious dishonesty to those Japanese who assure us that they wish for a resumption of more friendly relations. . . . These people are doubtless sincere in their desire to be on better terms with us, but their ideas of how this shall be brought about and what the terms shall be differ vastly from ours.

Apart from the preservation of our numerous and valuable commercial enterprises we want to retain intact our influence in China; our privileges of an unusual and extraterritorial nature such as the British hold on the Customs Service, our control over the administration of the Shanghai settlement, our personnel in the railways

[31] He might not have, had Sir John Pratt not retired on 1 April 1938.

and the maintenance of our shipping interests along the coasts and waterways of China.[32]

With the lapse of the Extraterritoriality Treaty of 1931, Great Britain continued to cling to the privileges of a nineteenth-century imperial power; by refusing to negotiate with the Japanese, the British appeared to be in pursuit of maintaining the *status quo*. 'Consciously or not,' Brenan wrote, 'we are demanding that the Japanese shall put the clock back and restore to us the position we occupied before the outbreak of the hostilities, or as near thereto as may be possible.'[33] With that awareness of the static nature of Britain's position, Brenan often asked how Britain could move forward. He was quite convinced that the road of progress did not lead to 'co-operation' with Japan. After all, what did the Japanese mean by that term?

If we wish to know what is meant by co-operation we must look at the Japanese complaints of the ways in which we have not co-operated. We have sold arms to China and have kept open the Hongkong channel for the supply of munitions. We have criticised Japan in Parliament and the press, and have given moral and material support to the Chinese Government. The British authorities in China have adopted an unfriendly attitude and are always making protests; and on occasion they have done things to impede the Japanese operations.[34]

If the British reversed their un-cooperative attitude, they would undermine their traditional China policy. Brenan in this way interpreted the meaning of the British Ambassador's conversations with the Japanese Foreign Minister, General Ugaki:

The bargain therefore is that if we will cease our moral and material support of Chiang Kai-shek's administration and recognise Japan's new position on the mainland, if we will abandon the League of Nations attitude and condone the Japanese aggression by helping to finance the development of the occupied areas on Japanese lines, then the Japanese will see what they can do to remove some of our more immediate complaints. Our reward will be, possibly, the

[32] Minute by Brenan, 25 August 1938 [F 8961/*G*], F.O. 371/22181.

[33] Ibid.

[34] Minute by Brenan, 30 August 1938 [F 9256/12/10], F.O. 371/22051. Here is an excellent example of how the published British documents can be misleading by failing to reproduce important minutes: one would hardly guess that such minutes by Brenan usually formed the basis of instructions to Tokyo. Brenan thus comes through historically as a sort of Percy Anderson of the late 1930s.

payment of the railway loans and debts, permission to resume some of our commercial activities in the restricted districts at Shanghai, to continue our shipping trade in a modified form, and fewer insults and pinpricks. We are to make the very great concession of a reversal of our whole attitude towards the Far Eastern conflict in return for minor and probable material advantages of a temporary kind. That is undoubtedly what the Japanese mean by 'co-operation'.[35]

Brenan and his colleagues in the Far Eastern Department after many similar discussions concluded that Britain's wisest course would be to mark time 'until the situation in the Far East or in Europe changes for the better.'[36]

Less than two weeks after the Munich agreement, Japanese troops invaded South China on 12 October 1938. Less than two weeks later they seized Canton and Hankow, thus gaining control of China's coastline and sealing off Hong Kong from the mainland. They controlled most of the railways. On 7 November Prince Konoye proclaimed a 'new Order in Asia'. Most Englishmen vaguely thought that such rapid developments in the Far East must be connected with those in Europe.[37] Precious little systematic analysis, however, went into the problem of the Far East in the context of a global struggle. The Far Eastern Department continued to respond to the China situation more in regard to the role Japan might play in a world war. In early December the Ambassador in Tokyo since September 1937, Sir Robert Craigie, challenged the Foreign Office to take a broader view. Brenan wrote:

Sir Robert Craigie tries to lift the Far Eastern question out of the plane on which it has hitherto been treated by His Majesty's Government: the ineffectual attempt to maintain British trading interests in China by means of impotent protests and recriminations: and to place it where it belongs as an important factor in the general world situation.

He shows that the problem involves much greater issues than the mere preservation of such things as the British shipping services on the Yangtze and commercial investments in China. It affects the safety of the United Kingdom and the Empire in the struggle

[35] Ibid.   [36] Ibid.
[37] See A. J. P. Taylor, *The Origins of the Second World War* (London, 1961), *passim*, for perceptive remarks about the connection between events in Europe and the Far East and the difficulty in relating them.

between the democratic states and the partners of the anti-comintern pact.[38]

In this crucial and *Very Confidential* despatch Craigie argued that Great Britain should either fish with Japan or cut bait with China. The history of the despatch itself illumines Britain's dilemma in January 1939 and explains who made Far Eastern policy.

Craigie forcefully contended that Britain alienated Japan without assisting China. He warned that if the present drift continued, Japan might enter into an alliance with Germany and Italy. At the same time he held out hope that friendly relations with Japan might be restored, thus wooing her away from the 'totalitarian Powers'. Recalling his conversations with General Ugaki, Craigie emphasized the General's frequent use of the word 'co-operation'. In a sense, Craigie restated one of the themes of appeasement.

I have never believed that 'cooperation' need necessarily involve a complete surrender to the wishes of the Japanese extremists or the abandonment of the cause of China—quite the contrary. It would however definitely mean the abandonment of any further scheme to support, or give material assistance to, the régime of General Chiang Kai-shek. It would be recognition of the actual fact of Japan's military and economic predominance in China today, and an effort to win back ultimate Chinese independence through cooperation, both with China and Japan, in establishing that assured market and that source of raw material which represent Japan's primary needs in the economic field.[39]

'Co-operation' might not seem attractive at first sight; but might it not be worth it to keep Japan separated from Germany? Craigie also pointed out that an anti-British military alliance was only part of the danger. Unless Japan were appeased in the positive sense of the word, the Eastern hemisphere would face a veritable Yellow Peril. Though he believed that the Chinese ultimately would oust the Japanese from the mainland, in the short run 'the Chinese spirit' might be sufficiently broken to enable Japan to consolidate a Japan-China-Manchukuo bloc.

[38] Minute by Brenan, 11 January 1939; Craigie to Halifax, No. 981 Very Confidential, 2 December 1938 [F 13894/71/23], F.O. 371/22181; cf. *D.B.F.P.*, VIII, No. 308. Printed without minutes.
[39] Ibid.

Japan would be launched on 'the "Kingly Way" i.e. foreign conquest and domination'. He forewarned:

With a China dominated, equipped, organised, trained and directed by Japan, the Yellow Peril would become not a mere abstract conception but a harsh and pressing reality. Its first manifestation would doubtless take the form of the sweeping of foreign markets by goods produced by Chinese labour under Japanese supervision, but its ultimate aim would be political. . . .

With Hongkong, Indo-China, Burma and even India already threatened, risks may now have to be faced which would not be justifiable merely in the defence of our trade and vested interests in China.[40]

If this argument were rejected, he would urge a more forceful China policy, 'a more determined effort than the somewhat desultory plans now under consideration for keeping General Chiang Kai-Shek in the saddle'. He wanted to avoid the disaster of a middle road muddle: 'This conclusion is inescapable, that neither danger [of military alliance with Germany nor Japan's domination of China] is likely to be averted by continuing along the present lines of alienating one party to this conflict without assisting the other.' He concluded by asking Lord Halifax whether he should make further soundings about 'co-operation'.

The Foreign Office gave very careful attention to Craigie's despatch. In one of the first minutes, Sir John Brenan drew attention to the magnitude and complexity of the issue. To gain perspective, he quoted Neville Chamberlain's public statement of the previous month: 'Events in the Far East are intimately connected with affairs in Europe, so when we consider our position there we must do so in close relation to the position nearer home.' Craigie's grand scheme came through clearly: 'The goal to be aimed at is nothing less than the weakening of the Berlin–Rome–Tokyo Triangle by a shrewd blow at its weakest member.' Brenan doubted, however, that appeasement of Japan could be achieved without sacrifice of principle:

He [Craigie] does not believe that 'co-operation' with the Japanese necessarily involves complete surrender to their extremists or the

[40] Ibid.

abandonment of China's cause. The influence we should gain by it might even be used to win back ultimate Chinese independence. I cannot help thinking that the latter point is in the nature of special pleading to cover what would be, in fact, a betrayal of the Chinese to their enemies.[41]

Brenan did grant that the proposition of 'co-operation' in a positive sense might be worth exploring if the United States could be brought into the scheme. He forwarded the despatch on to the European departments for their appraisal of the connection between Far Eastern, American, and European affairs.

Sir William Strang (now Assistant Under-Secretary) next dealt with the despatch in relation to Germany and the Soviet Union. He took issue with one of Craigie's major points, that Japan must be prevented from contracting an alliance with Germany. He judged that Japan's behaviour would be little altered, and, so far as Hitler was concerned, paper agreements amounted to nothing anyway.

The anti-Comintern Pact is of the greatest danger to us even in its present form; and we have some reason to think that Herr Hitler, with his well-known contempt for paper obligations, is not in favour of establishing precise contractual obligations between the parties, since he holds—and rightly so—that in case of a general conflict the three parties concerned will act in the manner best designed to serve their own interests, whatever their obligations may be.
The conclusion would seem to be that we should not stand to gain very much, if anything, by persuading Japan to refrain from entering into an Anti-Comintern *alliance*; and that it is therefore not worth paying any substantial price in an attempt to achieve this end.[42]

Far from fearing a Japanese-Nazi Alliance, Strang saw distinct advantages:

Had the Munich Agreement led to the improvement in relations with Germany which H.M.G. hoped for, there might have been a case for saying that to draw close to Soviet Russia would be to give the three anti-Comintern Powers a pretext for strengthening their association. But since the sequel to the Munich Agreement has been to demonstrate the extreme difficulty, if not impossibility, of coming to terms with Germany on any reasonable basis, one of the chief

[41] Minute by Brenan, 11 January 1939, ibid.
[42] Minute by Strang, 11 January 1939, ibid.

arguments against strengthening our own contacts with the Soviet Union disappears.[43]

Above all, appeasement or 'co-operation' would mean abandoning the Chinese and antagonizing the Americans:

I do not myself believe (though I am here straying beyond my province) that the Japanese could be bought off by any compromise or concession that we could safely offer them; nor does their present military and economic position seem to be so strong as to warrant our choosing this moment to abandon Chiang Kai-Shek and by so doing nip in the bud a useful form of collaboration with the United States, and thus jeopardize a movement in the United States for collaboration with like-minded Governments in Europe which has already gone far beyond what we could have dared to hope for a few months ago.[44]

Like the writers of the preceding minutes, Strang disfavoured any move towards 'co-operation.'

Seen from a European vantage point, the Far Eastern crisis took on a different perspective. The Southern Department concurred in Strang's judgement:

What Mr. Strang says of Herr Hitler's contempt for paper obligations and of his views that in the case of a general conflict the three parties concerned will act in the manner best designed to serve their own interests, whatever their obligations may be, is of course equally true of Signor Mussolini. This fact seems to reinforce the view that it is not worth paying any substantial price in an attempt to persuade Japan to refrain from entering into an anti-comintern *alliance*. . . .

For the rest the Southern Department would wish to associate themselves strongly with the views expressed at the end of the preceding minute regarding the desirability of avoiding any action likely to jeopardise 'the present movement in the United States in favour of collaboration with like-minded Governments in Europe.' To make sure of the sympathy and, if possible, the support of the U.S.A. must surely remain the cardinal principle in the conduct of our foreign policy.[45]

Sir Laurence Collier, a Counsellor, drew morals from what the British had learned recently in Europe:

The argument that we should compromise with Japan lest she ally

---

[43] Ibid.   [44] Ibid.
[45] Minute by P. Nichols, 12 January 1939, ibid.

herself definitely with Germany and Italy is the same as that which
Mussolini used to persuade us to bring the Anglo-Italian agreement
into force without securing his withdrawal from Spain; and, as Sir
R. Vansittart pointed out on that occasion, it is worthless, since
alliance or no alliance, each member of the Berlin–Rome–Tokyo
triangle will support the others or not according as his own purely
selfish interests demand, so that it matters very little to us whether
they are formally allied or not.[46]

The Foreign Office unanimously agreed that attempts to buy
off Japan would be both unrealistic and unwise. The paramount
concern in the whole problem was the possible American
reaction to a British *démarche* in the Far East. Sir Alexander
Cadogan expressed the consensus: 'I think the overriding
consideration is the danger of alienating the U.S.'[47] Lord
Halifax apparently agreed (though he did not minute the
despatch). But he made one important concession to Craigie's
'co-operation' proposal. The last minute reads:

The Secretary of State feels that all these considerations should be
put to Sir R. Craigie, but that he should be left discreet soundings if
in his opinion he is given a peculiarly propitious opening and can
act without real risk.[48]

Halifax thus left open a crack in the door of appeasement in the
Far East. Craigie, for his part, held to the end that it was madness not to try to stop Japan's further drift into the enemy's
camp and that those who saw the Far Eastern crisis through
European glasses gravely misunderstood the psychological and
racial elements of Japanese nationalism. 'Psychologically the
Japanese have a strong sense of loyalty and would regard their
ties with an ally very much more seriously than their con-
nexions with an ideological colleague. This is an opinion
which is shared by members of my staff and others who know
this country best and is based on psychological and racial
factors which are very apparent to us here.'[49]

[46] Minute by Collier, 13 January 1939, ibid.
[47] Minute by Cadogan, 16 January 1939, ibid.
[48] Minute by N. Ronald, 18 January 1939, ibid. For Craigie's instructions based
on these minutes, see *D.B.F.P.*, VIII, No. 433. For German-Italian-Japanese
relations at this time, see *Documents on German Foreign Policy, 1918–45*, Series D,
volume IV, and the works cited above, chapter VII note 3.

[49] Craigie to Halifax, No. 135 Tel., 12 February 1939 [F 1421/176/23], *D.B.F.P.*,
VIII, No. 484.

The Foreign Office agonized as acutely over the issue of assisting China as that of appeasing Japan. Each argument in favour of stiffening Chinese resistance could be refuted by one demonstrating the adverse impact on Anglo-Japanese relations. Note the opposite views put before the Cabinet's Committee on Foreign Policy when called upon to decide whether to grant a loan to China:

A. It is not suggested that to lend China the little money which is all that is likely to be forthcoming will enable her to win the war in a strategical sense. But to lend her what we can.
  (1) may encourage others to the same. . . .
  (2) will enable us to fulfil our obligations under the League Resolutions; and
  (3) even if it does not help China to secure final victory will render Japan the less likely to be able to give effect to her plans for the elimination of foreign interests and competition in China.

B. On the other hand,
  (1) the United States and other Governments may not be prepared to share in the hazards of the undertaking;
  (2) we run the risk of incurring the resentment of the Japanese, a very vindictive people, and this may result in bringing them more within the German orbit; and
  (3) the amount of assistance which we may find ourselves able to give is likely to be on a very limited scale and would not be calculated to postpone for more than a very short while the financial collapse of China, if that financial collapse is otherwise inevitable.[50]

The reconciling of such extreme opposites escaped even the analytical ability of Sir John Simon. China fought for the cause of all law-abiding states; but what would be the consequences of permanently incurring Japanese resentment? With the completion of the Burma road in the summer of 1938, the Chinese with British supplies might be able to hold out; Japanese resources might crack. On the other hand, who could have faith that the Chinese were able to fight to a stalemate? Who could accurately judge Japanese strength? Such questions

[50] Committee on Foreign Policy, Minutes, Secret, 1 June 1938, CAB. 27/623. The Cabinet refused the loan, but in December 1938 granted export credits. The latter part of these technical discussions can be followed in *D.B.F.P.*, VIII.

led the Cabinet to create an inter-departmental committee to determine what would happen if Britain waged economic warfare against Japan to tip the balance towards China. Representatives from the Treasury, Board of Trade, Department of Overseas Trade, and Colonial Dominions, India, and Foreign Offices discussed the increase of export duties on such items as iron ore and talked about restrictions on Japanese fishing in Malayan waters. The discussions were inconclusive. England was at odds with the Empire; the Imperial Government had no control over the Dominions, some of whom had favourable trade balances with Japan.[51] Moreover, measures that might damage Japan might be even more disastrous for, say, India, if Japan retaliated by placing restrictions on the Indian cotton trade. And who was to say whether economic warfare against Japan might not lead to war itself? The economics of the situation remained as problematical as in the depth of the depression. The dilemmas of appeasement versus assistance persisted.

Scholars have devoted so much attention to appeasement in Europe that the subject is in danger of becoming arid. In a Far Eastern context, however, the subtlety of 'co-operation' or 'conciliation' has by no means been fully illuminated. Appeasement in a positive sense can mean the removal of genuine grievances. Co-operation could mean the recognition of Japan's legitimate political and economic position in Asia. Sir Robert Craigie espoused those views. He also continued to hold that it would be strategically disastrous to permit Japan to form an alliance with Germany. His views were out of line with the Foreign Office's and with those of his colleague in China, Sir Archibald Clark Kerr. The latter believed, above all, in fair play to China. The words 'decency', 'justice', 'honour', 'principle', and 'conscience' recur in his despatches. Both Craigie and Clark Kerr, of course, worked towards a common goal of peace and prosperity of British interests in the Far East. But they differed as profoundly in tactics as had their predecessors during the Manchurian crisis. In the tradition of Sir John Jordan and Sir Miles Lampson, Clark Kerr believed in the vitality of the Chinese nation and in the justice of her cause

[51] For examples of the minutes of this Committee, see F.O. 371/22092.

against Japan. In the tradition of Sir Charles Eliot and Sir Francis Lindley, Craigie regarded the Japanese as a fundamentally honourable people and judged that they had certain legitimate interests on the Asian mainland, at least north of the Great Wall.[52] At no time did the clash between those two grand schools of British thought become more poignant than during the last great episode before the war, the Tientsin crisis. The exposition of the ideas generated by this emergency illuminates the agonizing dilemmas of appeasement in every sense.

The usual British interpretation of the origins of the Tientsin crisis is that the Japanese were looking for a showdown; had they not found it there, they would have elsewhere. Those Englishmen who took an alarmist view saw a Japanese plot to drive Britain out of China, not only at Tientsin, but even Shanghai. At Tientsin, China's second largest port, the British concession was especially vulnerable because, unlike Shanghai, it could not be effectively defended. The issue became as symbolic as that of Hankow twelve years earlier—in a different sense. In 1939 concessions such as Tientsin represented opposition to the advance of the New Order: they harboured Chinese guerrillas who used the concessions as bases for terrorism and anti-Japanese propaganda. In fact the Tientsin controversy was much more complex than such straight-forward ideas might suggest, as might be gathered from the details of the situation: in September 1938 British police arrested a 'Chinese guerrilla of doubtful behaviour',[53] Ssu Ching-wu, head of the 'North China National anti-Japanese Army'. What should be done with him? In April of the following year, British and Japanese police arrested four Chinese terrorists. Should they be handed over to the Japanese authorities, expelled from the concession, or interned? Whichever way Britain moved could be interpreted as anti-Japanese and pro-Chinese, or vice versa.

---

[52] In *Behind the Japanese Mask*, written after internment during the war, Craigie concluded: 'Behind the mask of inscrutability; beneath the courteous reserve; despite the treacheries of politicians, the trickeries of big business, and the revolting cruelties of military and police, I believe the Japanese nation to possess fundamental qualities of kindness, courage, loyalty and self-abnegation which should offer a good basis on which to build the new Japan.' (p. 172). Unfortunately Clark Kerr did not write a memoir.

[53] This is the phrase used by E. L. Woodward in the preface to *D.B.F.P.*, VIII. vi.

British opinion split. Sir Robert Craigie and the Consul-General in Tientsin, E. M. Jamieson, held, eventually, that Ssu should be handed over to the Japanese. Sir Archibald Clark Kerr and the Foreign Office insisted that he be interned. Part of the case hinged on the flimsy nature of the evidence that Ssu used the concession as a base for guerrilla activities, but the British officials also clearly saw that important political and moral as well as legal issues were involved. The following excerpts reveal the dilemmas of the affair as viewed from Tokyo, Tientsin, Shanghai, and London.

Sir Robert Craigie (4 October 1938): an awkward situation had arisen at Tientsin through the failure of the British authorities to hand over to the Japanese authorities a Chinese called Ssu Ching-wu who had been arrested in Tientsin about September 28 on the suggestion of the Japanese military authorities. This man was stated to have admitted to His Majesty's Consul-General that he was head of a band of guerillas (some 25,000 strong) which had been engaged in blowing up railroads, cutting telegraph wires etc. . . .

I earnestly hope that our authorities in Tientsin will either hand over or intern this man if there is a *prima facie* case against him.

Sir Archibald Clark Kerr (4 October 1938): I said [to his Japanese colleague] that under no circumstances could I hand him over to Japanese authorities: that the mere fact that he was fighting against the Japanese was not a crime in English law and that I must have evidence that he had engaged in criminal activities in this Concession before I could consider the question of handing him over to the *de facto* Chinese authorities.

Mr. Jamieson (13 October 1938): Ssu in his own confession admits that he has been engaged in anti-Japanese activities for years. . . . I consider that in the circumstances the statement produced by my Japanese colleague may be considered as *prima facie* evidence that Ssu has in fact been engaged in anti-Japanese activities since his arrival in the British Concession.

Lord Halifax (19 October 1938): I am somewhat puzzled by Mr. Jamieson's suggestions: engaging in anti-Japanese activities is not in itself a criminal act. . . .

Sir A. Clark Kerr (23 October 1938): I hope that we will not allow ourselves to be browbeaten. . . .

Mr. Jamieson (25 October 1938): I beg leave to ask whether we are to jeopardise all that has been done, and is being done, for British trade and residents of British Concession for the sake of a principle involving a self-confessed guerilla leader. . . .

Lord Halifax (1 November 1938): this man ought to be interned.[54]

British justice, morality, and a sense of fair play to China thus triumphed over a policy of 'co-operation' with Japan. Craigie thought that Britain's attitude would be incomprehensible to Japan and would precipitate further crises at Tientsin. Clark Kerr judged that if Ssu were handed over to Japan, Britain would perpetrate an act 'upon which none of us could ever reflect without shame'.

Understandably enough, Craigie and Clark Kerr continued to take diametrically opposed positions. Their individual tasks were not enviable. Both had to guard against the charge of 'Perfidious Albion'. Neither desired a 'Far Eastern Munich'. Clark Kerr was convinced that the Chinese would lose hope if Britain sided with Japan, or, if they eventually triumphed, would feel abandoned in their hour of need. He passionately believed in the justice of China's cause. In the case of Ssu, he wrote: 'This man's real crime is that he has been fighting for his country.' From the vantage point of Tokyo, Craigie judged that the internment of Ssu would strengthen the Japanese belief that Britain was responsible for or was contributing to Chinese resistance. He feared that the Japanese would view Britain's stance as hypocritical. Why should the British protect obvious criminals? These differences of approach and attitude flared up again in the spring of 1939 when the police arrested four Chinese terrorists. The British Consul-General had no doubt that they were gangsters and should be handed over to the Japanese. Clark Kerr, however, had moral qualms. He deferred to the Foreign Office:

I am in a difficulty and I need your fearless guidance. . . . I have been compelled to concentrate upon considerations of justice and fair play which must, in my view, be the overruling consideration of reaching a decent solution of the immediate problem of disposing of present cases. . . .

I confess I flinch. The problem reduces itself to a repugnant simplicity to sacrifice the four or perhaps even more scapegoats in the hope that by this sacrifice Japanese may be persuaded to hold their

[54] *D.B.F.P.*, VIII, appendix II.

hand for a time at any rate and give Concession a breathing space. But it offers little hope of freedom from more and equally repugnant sacrifices in the early future. . . . I should find it difficult if not impossible to explain to Chinese who are well aware of what is going on and are watching in full confidence that we shall see to it that justice is done.[55]

To Craigie that view was misguided. He telegraphed to the Foreign Office: 'It seems to me we are risking our whole position in North China involving ourselves at an inappropriate moment in serious trouble with Japan on account of legal niceties which I frankly find myself unable to appreciate.'[56] Clark Kerr retorted: 'The issue seems to be a nicety of morals rather than of law.'[57] By June 1939 even Clark Kerr admitted that the situation demanded more than moral consideration. The Japanese had blockaded the concession and were subjecting British subjects to the indignity of being stripped in the process of search while entering and leaving the concession. Craigie warned repeatedly that Britain and Japan were on the verge of war. The Foreign Office eventually became convinced that a genuine misunderstanding existed (to which the Consul-General in Tientsin contributed), and that the Japanese had a legitimate grievance. Halifax authorized Craigie to negotiate. He arrived at this formula, as described by Halifax:

[W]e had taken great trouble in drafting our statement, and . . . we hoped it had made our attitude clear. It was intended to deal with a state of fact, namely, that hostilities were now in progress in China and that the Japanese army was therefore obliged to defend its own security. The Concessions in China would have regard to this situation and would not allow themselves to be used for anti-Japanese activities. This did not, however, imply any change in our general policy.[58]

[55] Clark Kerr to Halifax, No. 45 Tour Series Tel., 19 May 1939 [F 4808/1/10], *D.B.F.P.*, IX, No. 86.
[56] Craigie to Halifax, No. 556 Tel., 14 June 1939 [F 5785/1/10], ibid., No. 197.
[57] Clark Kerr to Halifax, No. 555 Tel., 15 June 1939 [F 5881/1/10], ibid., No. 203.
[58] Halifax to Seeds (Moscow), No. 596, 25 July 1939 [F 7951/6457/10], ibid., No. 390. For Halifax's public statement, *Parliamentary Debates* (House of Lords), 5th series, vol. 114, cols. 368–9. The two main themes running through the rather fuzzy discussions of the Foreign Policy Committee as they arrived at this formula were (1) Britain's weakness in the Far East, and (2) the difficulty, in Halifax's phase, of avoiding 'a very humiliating position.' See minutes and memoranda in CAB. 27/625; CAB. 21/569; and CAB. 24/288.

To Clark Kerr this was morally repugnant and the equivalent of a sell-out. He referred to it as a 'Far Eastern Munich'. In the sense that Britain had attempted to meet genuine Japanese complaints and had suffered some humiliation, he was indeed correct in viewing the Foreign Office's formula as an appeasement policy. But it was not a 'Munich agreement'. Britain's line towards Japan by no means can be compared with her policy towards Germany in 1938–9.[59]

The rapidity of events in the months before the outbreak of war in Europe defies succinct treatment in relation to the drift towards war in the Far East. It would require a treatise, perhaps two, merely to sketch such major issues as the rising wave of hostile anti-Japanese opinion in Britain, the Foreign Office's evaluation of internal politics in Japan, the impact on the Far East of the German Soviet non-aggression pact, and the necessity of keeping British moves in line with American policy.[60] In sum, there were two historically significant developments. Less than twenty years from the termination of the Anglo-Japanese Alliance, Japan entered into a military alliance with Germany; less than a decade after the outbreak of the Pacific war, China became a Communist power. Of those politically aware and on the scene at the time, Sir Robert Craigie probably detected the sources of Japanese nationalism— the drive for racial equality and security—better than Sir Archibald Clark Kerr understood the meaning of Communism.

[59] However: 'Though it is true that there was no "Far Eastern Munich"—it could be argued that there was no occasion for one, because there was never any situation similar to that which arose in Europe in 1938, i.e. that France would be involved in war by her treaty with Czechoslovakia unless the Czechs could be made to yield without fighting. In the Far East the British disliked what the Japanese were doing in China from 1937 onwards, but had no treaty obligation to go to war on behalf of China and saw no sufficient reason for doing so—nor did the U.S.; the Chinese fought on by themselves for over four years. But neither Britain nor the U.S. entered into any agreement with Japan assigning to Japan any new rights over China. It was not until 1945 that Britain and the U.S. agreed to cede Chinese sovereign rights to another power, and that power was no longer Japan.'—G. F. H.

[60] Whoever investigates these issues will discover some bizarre stories. For example, in July 1939 Ashton-Gwatkin (who now had an established reputation as an economic expert) hustled off to Switzerland to talk with that 'very good German', Dr. Schacht, about stabilizing Chinese currency. Schacht drafted a document, according to Ashton-Gwatkin, 'phrased so delicately that Hitler himself could read it without any harm'. The gist of Schacht's proposal was that he would try to bring about a military '*Stillhalte*' between Japan and China while he solved the problem of 'puppet currency'. Vansittart described the scheme as 'fantastic and dangerous'. *D.B.F.P.*, IX, No. 317.

Historians will long debate the extent to which the British accurately perceived the mainsprings of Japanese nationalism or the nature of the civil war in China. Scholars will long dispute whether a policy of conciliation towards Japan might have averted the Pacific war, or, on the other hand, whether stronger support of China might have prevented her alienation from the western world. On the whole, a study of the British in the Far East during the inter-war years yields the impression that they felt themselves buffeted by Asian forces beyond their control.

SELECT BIBLIOGRAPHY

THIS bibliography is select in the sense that it focuses almost exclusively on *Britain* and the Far East, mainly in the inter-war years. I have included general works or monographs on Asia or technical topics only if I have found them especially helpful, directly or indirectly, in regard to British policy. For other material (including standard biographies), please see the relevant footnotes in the text.

Anyone who draws up a bibliography of even this restricted sort could go on for hundreds of pages, and, even then, face the sin of omission. The following list merely represents my opinion of the most useful works on Britain and the Far East, 1919–1939, with occasional reference to books valuable as background.

ALLEN, G. C., *Japan: the Hungry Guest* (London, 1938). The author was Professor of Economic Science, University of Liverpool. Note the relatively balanced conclusion, uncharacteristic of the time it was written: 'The lawless acts of Japan as a sovereign State and the prevalence of violence and fanaticism in her internal politics are not to be regarded as symptomatic of the character of the people in their ordinary life. The Japanese differ only in degree from other nations in this association of private virtue and political unscrupulousness' (p. 239).

ANGELL, Norman, *The Defence of the Empire* (London, 1937). Angell's argument about the Far East in world politics can be thus summarized: '"It is plain, therefore", a Martian observer might remark, "that an Empire like the British, as Asiatic as it is European, will be even more disturbed at the growth of the Japanese-Teutonic power than it was at the growth of the Austro-German power in the years preceeding those events which compelled Britain to stake her whole existence as an Empire upon the defeat of that combination. And therein, the Martian, as we have seen, would be entirely wrong. The self-same groups which before 1914 saw in the growth of Austro-German power a menace to the Empire, to Britain's political freedom, to democracy, to western civilisation, look quite benignly upon the growth of Japanese and German power in the year 1937 and resent bitterly any proposals

for political combinations which might hold it in check. . . .
America, Russia and China are all potential allies"' (pp. 196-7).

BARNETT, Robert W., *Economic Shanghai: Hostage to Politics. 1937-1941*
(New York, 1941).

BASSETT, Reginald, *Democracy and Foreign Policy: A Case History, the
Sino-Japanese Dispute. 1931-1933* (London, 1952). This is the definitive book on British press opinion during the Manchurian crisis.
It is a masterly work, though perhaps too unrestrained in praise
of Sir John Simon.

BELOFF, Max, *Britain's Liberal Empire, 1897-1921* (London, 1969).
Chapter 6 touches on the racial issue.

BORG, Dorothy, *American Policy and the Chinese Revolution, 1925-1928*
(New York, 1947).

—— *The United States and the Far Eastern Crisis of 1933-1938* (Cambridge, Mass., 1964). Both books by Miss Borg are models of
scholarship and reveal much about Britain's Far Eastern policy.

BREBNER, J. BARTLET, 'Canada, The Anglo-Japanese Alliance and
the Washington Conference,' *Political Science Quarterly*, **50**, 1
(March, 1935), pp. 45-58. The seminal article on the subject.

BUELL, Raymond Leslie, *The Washington Conference* (New York, 1922).
As in his later writings on international affairs and Africa, Buell
dealt with this subject in considerable detail and perception.

BUTOW, Robert J. C., *Tojo and the Coming of the War* (Princeton, 1961).

CARTER, Gwendolen, *The British Commonwealth and International
Security: the Role of the Dominions. 1919-1939* (Toronto, 1947). A
subject worthy of reappraisal.

CECIL, Viscount, *A Great Experiment* (London, 1941). Cecil's comments on the Manchurian crisis do not always accord with his
views at the time.

CHAMBERLAIN, Sir Austen, *Peace in our Time* (London, 1928). Contains some of his speeches on China.

CHANG KIA-NGAU, *China's Struggle for Railroad Development* (New
York, 1943).

CHATFIELD, Admiral Lord, *It Might Happen Again* (London, 1947).
In January 1939 Chatfield became Minister for the Co-ordination
of Defence and devoted considerable attention to the problem of
Singapore's defence.

CLARK, Grover, *Economic Rivalries in China* (New Haven, 1932).

CLIFFORD, Nicholas R., *Retreat from China: British Policy in the Far
East, 1937-1941* (Seattle, 1967). Closely reasoned, with a sure grip

over secondary material. It is a pity that the author did not have access to the unpublished Foreign Office and Cabinet records.

CRAIGIE, Sir Robert L., *Behind the Japanese Mask* (London, 1946). Craigie's reputation rests better on his despatches to the Foreign Office than on this memoir.

CROWLEY, James B., *Japan's Quest for Autonomy* (Princeton, 1966). Along with the book by Sadako Ogata, essential for understanding the Japanese side of the Manchurian episode.

—— ed., *Modern East Asia: Essays in Interpretation* (New York, 1970).

—— forthcoming book on the origins of the Pacific war.

CURTIS, Lionel, *The Capital Question of China* (London, 1932). Superficial, but not without points of interest. Among others, Curtis, like Sir Francis Lindley, compared the Japanese intrusion into Manchuria with the Jameson Raid.

DIGNAN, Don, 'New Perspectives on British Far Eastern Policy, 1913-19,' *University of Queensland Papers*, I, 5 (January 1969). Emphasizes, among other things, Indian aspects of the problem.

EDEN, Anthony, Earl of Avon, *Facing the Dictators* (London, 1962). There is a rather unilluminating chapter on the Far Eastern crisis, 1936-8.

ELIOT, Sir Charles, *Japanese Buddhism* (New York, 1959 edn.) The introduction by Sir Harold Parlett contains perhaps the best sketch of Eliot's personality.

ETHERTON, Colonel P. T. and Tiltman, H. Hessell, *Japan: Mistress of the Pacific?* (London, 1933 edn). 'National sentiment and self-interest alike have imposed upon British governments, of whatever political colour, the necessity for assuming the role, in matters affecting the Pacific, of "the Great Conservator".' There are other remarkable statements.

FIELD, Frederick V., *American Participation in the Chinese Consortiums* (Chicago, 1931). As Sir John Pratt once remarked, to learn about British policy in China, one must read American books, and this subject is a good example of one on which there is a British scholarly void.

FIFIELD, Russell H., *Woodrow Wilson and the Far East: The Diplomacy of the Shantung Question* (New York, 1952). The same remark about the Field book holds true here. Lloyd George was ignorant of the Far East, but an article dealing with his ideas about China and Japan would make fascinating reading. Curzon's ideas about the Far East would fill a book and would be even more fascinating.

FISHEL, Wesley R., *The End of Extraterritoriality in China* (Berkeley, 1962). The Editor of the *China Quarterly*, David C. Wilson, has begun work on the subject from the British side.

FITZ-GERALD, William George, 'Japan's "Monroe Doctrine",' *Nineteenth Century*, CXV, 688 (June, 1934), 630-42.

Fox, Grace, *Britain and Japan, 1858-1883* (Oxford, 1969). An exhaustive treatment.

FRIEDMAN, Irving S., *British Relations with China: 1931-1939* (New York, 1940). Probably the basic introduction to many problems with which I have not attempted to deal. Considering the time it was written and the sources available, it is a remarkably thorough and sound book.

FRY, M. G. 'The North Atlantic Triangle and the Abrogation of the Anglo-Japanese Alliance', *Journal of Modern History*. **39**, 1 (March 1967), 46-64. Should be read in conjunction with the Brebner article.

GREGORY, T. E., 'Japanese Competition in World Markets', *International Affairs*, **13**, 3 (May-June 1934), 325-42. 'I believe that Japan finds herself at the present moment, both as regards population and as regards the alternatives so far as government policy is concerned, in the same position as that in which we [Great Britain] found ourselves at the beginning of the nineteenth century. We also had open to us exactly the possibilities which Japan has open to her . . . and in the end we solved the problem of the growth of British population by a vast increase in the volume of British overseas trade' (p. 328).

GRISWOLD, A. Whitney, *The Far Eastern Policy of the United States* (New York, 1938). Sir John Pratt commented on this book by a scholar who became President of Yale University: 'The author strives on every possible occasion, even at the cost of distorting or flying in the face of the evidence, to divert blame or criticism from America to England. Like King Charles's head the wrong and selfish policy of Great Britain, whether relevant or not, crops up at every turn. Everything relating to England is represented in an unfavourable light, and discreditable motives are found for simple and straightforward actions. . . . The student who cares to consult the texts of the documents . . . will draw his own conclusions as to the degree of trust to be reposed in Griswold. It is only fair, however, to add that Griswold's work must be regarded as the exception which proves the rule. American historians are eminently fair and objective and the amount of scholarly research they have devoted to the Far East puts us to shame. If occasionally they

indulge in what seems to us to be unfair criticism of England it is to
be attributed to a lack of sympathetic understanding of the way in
which our institutions work and not to any failure in intellectual
integrity' (*War and Politics*, pp. 168-70). Pratt's judgement is too
harsh, for the book proved to be an invaluable guide for both
scholars and students at the time (and it remains the only adequate
survey of the topic); but he is correct in saying that one can fault
it on many counts.

GULL, E. M., *British Economic Interests in the Far East* (London, 1943).
'I affirm, with pardonable emphasis, that administration of
justice in British Colonial territories . . . has been second to none,
and superior to most other judicial administrations. . . . The
picture which is sometimes painted of Chinese nationalism as a
movement *sans peur et sans reproche* battling unitedly against a ruthless lot of foreign Imperialists, is ludicrously unreal. A large proportion of rich Chinese in Shanghai and elsewhere were hand-in-
glove with the so-called Imperialists. . . . Remember, there is a
deep vein of mysticism in the Japanese character. Mysticism and
loyalty have ever been partners in their souls, as they have been in
ours. There is, too, a vein of melancholy in the Japanese nature,
illustrated, I suggest, by their music, and melancholy is no foe
either to loyalty as such, or to loyalty to kings and emperors. Does
not our own Stuart period illustrate that?'

Still, this is one of the basic works on the subject and should be
read together with the books by Remer.

HARCOURT-SMITH, Simon, *Japanese Frenzy* (London, 1942). Harcourt-
Smith served both in China and in the Far Eastern Department of
the Foreign Office. His book is perhaps the most eloquent example
of the feeling engendered by the Second World War. For example:
'Let us make no mistake; our enemies are not only the Japanese
militarists but the Japanese people as well. To the poorest farmer,
the humblest mill-worker of Osaka, we must bring home the consequences of war, if the Pacific is to know peace again. . . . Let us
remember that here is no decent reasonable populace, exploited
by a pack of militaristic gangsters, but seventy-five million mad-
men, all prepared to commit any crime at the behest of the State.'
Nevertheless, the book contains some important historical points.

HASLUCK, Paul, *The Government and the People. 1939-41* (Canberra,
1956 edn.) This is a very important work, but the history of
Australian-Japanese relations prior to and during this time remains to be written. David Sissons of the National University of
Australia has begun work in this field.

HECHT, Robert A., 'Great Britain and the Stimson Note of January 7, 1932,' *Pacific Historical Review*, **38**, 2 (May, 1969), 177-91.

HEWLETT, Sir William Meyrick, *Forty Years in China* (London, 1943). Hewlett was a Consular Officer.

HINDMARSH, Albert Edward, *The Basis of Japanese Foreign Policy* (Cambridge, Mass., 1936). Valuable statistical analysis and bibliography.

HOSOYA, Chihiro, 'Miscalculations in Deterrent Policy: Japanese-U.S. Relations, 1938-1941', *Journal of Peace Research*, offprint from No. 2, 1968, Universitetsforlaget (Oslo). A perceptive Japanese interpretation of American 'revisionist' theories.

HSIA CHIN-LIN, *British Far Eastern Policy, 1937-1940* (Chungking, 1940).

HUBBARD, G. E., *Eastern Industrialization and its Effect on the West, With special reference to Great Britain and Japan* (London, 1935). Should be compared with Gull's interpretation.

—— *British Far Eastern Policy* (London, 1939). Sir John Pratt unkindly referred to this as 'almost the worst book ever written on such a subject,' though he admitted that later versions were an improvement; in fact the 1943 edition is valuable as a succinct survey.

HUDSON, Geoffrey, *The Far East in World Politics* (Oxford, 1937). Should be read together with Pratt's book as introductory to Britain and the Far East.

IRIYE, Akira, *After Imperialism: the Search for a New Order in the Far East, 1921-1931* (Cambridge, Mass., 1965). This is the most important work on the general problems of the 1920s as seen through Japanese as well as western eyes and should be read hand in hand with Miss Borg's work on the Chinese revolution.

—— *Across the Pacific: An Inner History of American-East Asian Relations* (New York, 1967).

—— forthcoming book, *The Limits of Empire: An Interpretation of American-East Asian Relations, 1898-1911.*

ISAACS, Harold, *The Tragedy of the Chinese Revolution* (Stanford, 1961 edn.). The occasional comments—often caustic—on the British community in China are of interest.

ISHIMARU, Tōta, *Japan Must Fight Britain* (London, 1936). 'The truth is that the relative positions of Japan and England today are very closely similar to those of England and Germany before the Great War.'

JOHNSON, F. A., *Defence by Committee: the British Committee of Imperial Defence, 1880-1959* (Oxford University Press, 1960).

JOHNSON, Frank W. F., *George Harvey, a Passionate Patriot* (New York, 1929). The word passionate, as distinct from precise, is accurate.

JONES, F. C., *Japan's New Order in East Asia, 1937–45* (London, 1954).
—— *Shanghai and Tientsin* (New York, 1940).

JOSEPH, Philip, *Foreign Diplomacy in China, 1894–1900* (London, 1928). Sir John Pratt takes Joseph to task in *War and Politics* and accuses the Director of the Far Eastern Center of St. Antony's College of following in Joseph's footsteps.

KEETON, G. W., *The Development of Extraterritoriality in China* (London, 1928).

KENNEDY, Captain Malcolm D., *The Estrangement of Great Britain and Japan, 1917–35* (Manchester, 1969). A most interesting combination of history and memoir.

KIERNAN, E. V., *British Diplomacy in China, 1880 to 1885* (Cambridge, 1939).

KIRBY, S. Woodburn, *The War Against Japan, I: The Loss of Singapore* (London, 1957).

KNATCHBULL-HUGESSEN, Sir Hughe, *Diplomat in Peace and War* (London, 1949). For a sense of humour, Sir Hughe ranks with Sir John (Tilley, not Simon).

LA FARGUE, T. E., *China and the World War* (Stanford, 1937).

LAMONT, Thomas W., *Across World Frontiers* (New York, 1950). In regard to the Consortium, Lamont wrote: 'Sir Charles Addis, of the Hongkong and Shanghai Banking Group . . . had in reality been the heart of the enterprise.' That may be so, but the Foreign Office regarded Addis as devious.

LEE, Bradford A., 'Great Britain and the Sino-Japanese War, July 1937–September 1939', unpublished Yale honours essay based on unpublished Foreign Office and Cabinet records.

LIEU, D. K., *The Growth and Industrialization of Shanghai* (Shanghai, 1936). Interesting statistics.

LOWE, Peter, *Great Britain and Japan, 1911–15: a Study of British Far Eastern Policy* (London, 1969). A meticulous, incisive, and thorough monograph.

LOWER, A. R. M., *Canada and the Far East* (New York, 1940). The section on immigration is of some interest.

LU, David J., *From the Marco Polo Bridge to Pearl Harbor: Japan's Entry into World War II* (Washington, 1961). Slight on the British side; in the foreword, Herbert Feis wrote: 'It has become essential to make an intense effort to understand how wars come about.' One would gather that Great Britain had nothing to do with the origins of the Pacific war.

LUARD, Evan, *Britain and China* (London, 1962).

McCORDOCK, R. Stanley, *British Far Eastern Policy, 1894–1900* (New York, 1931). Compare with Parker T. Moon, *Imperialism and World Politics* (New York, 1926).

MACKENZIE, Compton, *Eastern Epic I* (London, 1951). Despite the chances of taking a quotation out of context: 'Probably the wiseest "scorching" was done when large quantities of liquor were destroyed against a certain amount of local opposition. That may have saved Singapore from the fate of Nanking at the hands of the drink-maddened enemy.'

MAY, Ernest R., forthcoming book on the Washington Conference.

MILLER, Ian F. G., *New Zealand's Interests and Policies in the Far East* (New York, 1940). Useful for economic relations, 1936–9.

MORISON, Elting, *Turmoil and Tradition: A Study of the Life and Times of Henry L. Stimson* (Boston, 1960). Sir John Simon does not emerge entirely favourably from this balanced and sensitive account. After reading the manuscript of my book, Professor Morison commented: 'I have, after reading your unpublished British documents and other sources, far more sympathy for Sir John Simon's dilemma than I had before. But I have no more respect for his achievement. What emerges is the picture of a man desperately trying to keep together the parts of a machine that was working very badly. He did succeed, and the machine continued to work very badly.'

MORSE, Hosea Ballou, *The International Relations of the Chinese Empire*, 3 Vols. (London, 1910).

MURPHEY, Rhoads, *Shanghai: Key to Modern China* (Cambridge, Mass., 1953).

NISH, Ian, *The Anglo-Japanese Alliance* (London, 1966). The basic work on the subject.

—— forthcoming book, *Alliance in Decline*.

O'CONNOR, P. S., 'Keeping New Zealand White, 1908–1920', *New Zealand Journal of History*, **2**, 1 (April, 1968), 41–65.

OGATA, Sadako, *Defiance in Manchuria* (Berkeley, 1964).

O'MALLEY, Sir Owen, *The Phantom Caravan* (London, 1954). Chapter 12 relates the Hankow negotiations.

PETRIE, Sir Charles, *The Life and Letters of the Right Hon. Sir Austen Chamberlain* (2 vols., London, 1939–40). See volume II chapter 8 for a few passing comments on Austen Chamberlain and China. The views of all three Chamberlains on the Far East need investigation.

POLLARD, Robert T., *China's Foreign Relations, 1917–1931* (New York, 1933).

PIGGOTT, F. S. G., *Broken Thread* (Aldershot, 1950). Piggott was Military Attaché in Tokyo. Lord Hankey wrote in the foreword: 'Major-General Piggott was for more than a quarter of a century a pillar of those happy relations between our country and Japan, the severance of which was one of the many tragedies of World War II.'

PRATT, Sir John T., *War and Politics in China* (London, 1943). Though highly opinionated, this book is the point of departure for a study of British policy in the Far East.

PRICE, G. Ward, '"Made in Japan" is Writing on the Wall for British Industry,' *Far Eastern Review*, **30**, 2 (February, 1934), 67–8. The title indicates the British mood in the mid-1930s.

RAPPAPORT, Armin, *Henry L. Stimson and Japan* (Chicago, 1963). In this detailed and valuable study, the attitude towards Stimson and Simon is quite different from that of Elting E. Morison.

REMER, Charles F., *Foreign Investments in China* (New York, 1933).

ROSKILL, Stephen, *Naval Policy between the Wars: the Period of Anglo-American Antagonism, 1919–1929* (London, 1968). The fundamental work on the subject.

RUSSELL, Bertrand, *The Problem of China* (London, 1922). 'After making all necessary deductions for the poverty and the disease, I am inclined to think that Chinese life brings more happiness to the Chinese than English life does to us. At any rate this seemed to me to be true for the men; for the women I do not think it would be true.' (p. 73) Russell made many similar and equally curious speculations about China in this book.

SANSOM, G. B., *Japan: A Short Cultural History* (London, 1932). In his day, Sir George Sansom was recognized as one of the foremost western authorities on Japan.

SELLE, Earl A., *Donald of China* (New York, 1948).

SHEPHERD, Jack, *Australia's Interests and Policies in the Far East,* (New York, 1940). As with the companion volumes on New Zealand and Canadian policy, the most interesting sections are on immigration and trade.

SHIGEMITSU Mamoru, *Japan and Her Destiny: My struggle for Peace* (London, 1958). General Piggott edited the book.

SMITH, Sara R., *The Manchurian Crisis 1931–1932: A Tragedy in International Relations* (New York, 1948). The role of Great Britain, in my opinion, is misinterpreted, but this is a very readable work.

SOOTHILL, William Edward, *China and England* (London, 1928). A series of lectures by the Professor of Chinese at Oxford. 'Whatever has been said in them has been said with a sincere affection for China and its toiling and tolerant masses.'

SPROUT, Harold and Margaret, *Toward a New Order of Sea Power* (Princeton, 1940). Why does not the Princeton University Press issue a paperback edition of this classic work?

STEED, Wickham, 'After the Lytton Report', *Contemporary Review* (December 1932). Typical of criticism of Sir John Simon.

STEINER, Zara S., *The Foreign Office and Foreign Policy, 1898–1914* (Cambridge, 1970). Indispensable to anyone dealing with the Foreign Office. God help anyone who attempts the same project for the inter-war years.

STEWART, John R., *Manchuria Since 1931* (New York, 1936).

STORRY, Richard, *The Double Patriots: A Study in Japanese Nationalism* (Boston, 1957).

SUN, E-tu Zen, *Chinese Railways and British Interests* (New York, 1954).

TAKEUCHI, Tatsuji, *War and Diplomacy in the Japanese Empire* (New York, 1935).

TAYLOR, George E., *The Struggle for North China* (New York, 1940). Great Britain's position in China is marginal to the author's argument, but when he does touch on the subject he occasionally repeats well-worn and mistaken themes. For example, 'The Anglo-Japanese talks which the war of 1937 cut short went along on the assumption that Japanese control of North China might be recognized in return for British control of South China' (p. 15). What is meant by 'control'?

TEICHMAN, Sir Eric, *Affairs of China: A Survey of the Recent History and Present Circumstances of the Republic of China* (London, 1938). This is one of the most important British memoirs on China. As Chinese Secretary, Teichman was Sir Miles Lampson's right hand man.

THOMSON, James C., Jr., *While China Faced West: American Reformers in Nationalist China, 1928–1937* (Harvard University Press, 1969). Especially interesting for the role of the missionaries; there is no British equivalent.

THORNE, Christopher, forthcoming book, *The Limits of Foreign Policy*, which deals extensively with the Manchurian crisis from the western vantage point.

TILLEY, Sir John, *London to Tokyo* (London, 1942). 'I cannot say that I think our position very brilliant,' Tilley once wrote. He referred to Africa (specifically to Mfumbiro), but probably, if asked, would have included the Far East.

UTLEY, Freda, *Japan's Feet of Clay* (London, 1936). 'Japan is putting on a big bluff to the world' is a statement typical of Miss Utley's tracts. Her writings deserve attention because they were popularly received. See also *Japan's Gamble in China* (London, 1938) and *China at War* (London, 1939).

WATT, D. C., *Personalities and Policies* (London, 1965).

WEMYSS, Lord Webster, 'And After Washington', *Nineteenth Century* (March, 1922). The most important published statement of the attitude of the Admiralty.

WHYTE, Sir Frederick, *China and the Foreign Powers* (London, 1927).

WILLERT, Sir Arthur, *Aspects of British Foreign Policy* (London, 1928). Willert was Chief of the Foreign Office's Press Bureau and in this book devotes two chapters to the question of China.

WOOD, F. L. W., *The New Zealand People at War: Political and External Affairs* (Wellington, 1958). Chapter IV, 'The Working of Imperialism', is important for the subject of this book. For example, 'It was with justice that Lord Milner in 1925 hailed Massey as both "the true interpreter of New Zealand" and "the most staunch, the most steady, and the most consistent of Imperial Statesmen".' Perhaps the statement explains an important part of New Zealand's history.

WRIGHT, Stanley F., *China's Struggle for Tariff Autonomy, 1843–1938* (Shanghai, 1938).

YOUNG, C. Walter, *The International Relations of Manchuria* (Chicago, 1929).

YOUNG, L. K., *British Policy in China* (Oxford, 1970). An exhaustive treatment of Salisbury's China policy. Taken together, Young's and Fox's bibliographies provide most of the material necessary to comprehend the background of many of the prominent themes of the inter-war years.

Addendum: William Reynolds Braisted, *The United States Navy in the Pacific, 1909–1922* (University of Texas Press, 1971). A comprehensive account of 741 pages that exhaustively and effectively utilizes American unpublished sources.

INDEX

Federation of British Industries, mission to Manchuria, 222–4

Feng Yu-hsiang, 117–18

Fengtien, *see* Mukden

Fitzmaurice, G. G., on international law, 246

Foochow, 14, 24, 211 note 10

Foreign Office, Committee on the Anglo-Japanese Alliance, 19, 43–4, 49; sketch of general problem of the Far East, 38; and the Chinese revolution, 109 ff.; and the Special Tariff Conference, 141 ff.; summary of progress in treaty revision, 161–2; and the Stimson controversy, 189 ff.; and trade relations with Japan, 215 ff.; and appeasement in the Far East, 238 ff.; *see also* entries for individual officials

Formosa, 4, 46, 95

Four Power Treaty, 104

France, and the question of naval disarmament, 100 ff.; *also* 8, 52

Free Trade, defined, 17–18; problems of and the Special Tariff Conference, 142 ff.; *also* 24, 28, 32, 93, 229

Galen, Marshal, biographical description, 119; *also* 109, 138

Geddes, Sir Auckland, 89, 93

Germany, possible alliances, 41, 49, 61, 64, 206–8, 239, 256–9; *also* 8, 31, 52–53, 65, 112, 246

Greene, Sir Conyngham, 43

Halifax, Lord, advocates cautious policy in the Far East, 245; leaves room open for appeasement, 259; and the Tientsin crisis of 1938, 263 ff.; *also* 252

Hankow, incident of 3 January 1927, 130–1, 154 ff.; *also* 162, 167, 211

Harding, President, issues invitations for conference on naval disarmament, 85–7, 91

Harvey, George, 89–90

Hobart Hampden, E. M., 36–7

Hong Kong, trade disrupted by Cantonese boycott, 120, 127–8; defence of, 212; sealed off from mainland in 1938, 254; *also* 162, 256

Hong Kong & Shanghai Banking Corporation, 163

Hughes, Charles Evans, 90, 92, 96, 104

Hughes, William M., and the Anglo-Japanese Alliance, 51 ff.; fears realized, 208

Hurst, Sir Cecil, 57

Ichang, 14, 211 note 10

India, 59, 219, 256

International Export Company, 160

Italy, 52, 100, 258

Jamieson, J. W., and the Canton incident, 126–7; about war with China, 129; on the sterling qualities of the Chinese, 137; and the Tientsin crisis of 1938, 263–5

Japan, and the question of 'race', 2–3, 10–12, 58 ff.; history summarized, 4–6; trade statistics, 8–10, 215; and Manchukuo, 12, 223, 249; and trade rivalry in China, 17 ff.; discussed at Imperial Conference, 52 ff.; and the Washington Conference, 79 ff.; and the Special Tariff Conference, 148, 151; and the Manchurian crisis, 171 ff.; policy shifts in 1930s, 206 ff.; trade relations, 215 ff.; and war with China, 238 ff.

Joffe, Adolph, 112

Jordan, Sir John, his classic definition of China, 20; views on Shantung and the railway question, 21, 24–7, 34, 43; death of, 146; *also* 20 note 5, 261

Kiukiang, 14, 159, 162, 211 note 10

Knatchbull-Hugessen, Sir Hughe, reviews problem of Communism in China, 240–41; shot, 247–8

Konoye, Prince, proclaims 'new order', 254

Korea, compared with Ireland, 30; *also* 4, 24, 33, 46

Kuomintang, British evaluations of during revolution, 109 ff.; and the Nanking incident, 133–4; and the Communists, 136–9; and treaty revision, 167 ff.

Ladybird incident, 248

Lamont, Thomas, threatens Japan, 32; disillusioned with Japanese business, 34

Lampson, Sir Miles, attitude towards Hankow incident, 131; on Chinese

Lampson—*cont.*
Communists, 136; differs with Foreign Office on Hankow issue, 156–7; and reform of unequal treaties, 158 ff.; and the issue of Shanghai, 164 ff.; summarizes situation in China in 1930, 172; and the Manchurian crisis, 179 ff.; *also* 261
League of Nations, and the Anglo-Japanese Alliance, 57 ff.; Commission of Enquiry, 198–9; report of, 200–1; adopts Stimson doctrine, 202; and Japan's withdrawal from Geneva, 203, 206, 213; *also* 44, 177–8, 184–5, 193, 242
Lee, Lord, 46–7
Leith-Ross, Sir Frederick, mission to Far East, 231–3
Li Chai-Sum, 120–1
Lindley, Sir Francis, summarizes situation in Japan in 1931, 172–3; and the Manchurian crisis, 180–4, 197–8; compares Manchurian crisis with Boer War, 206; and possible political causes of war, 216–17; *also* 262
Lindsay, Sir Robert, 192, 196–7
Lloyd George, David, ideas about the China trade, 26–7; and the Anglo-Japanese Alliance, 45–7, 51 ff.; on issues relating to Japan, the United States, and disarmament, 84 ff.; *also* 110
Locock, Sir Guy, 222
Lytton, Lord, 199–201

MacDonald, Malcolm, 245
Macleay, Sir Ronald, and the question of intervention in China, 129–30; defines Chinese character, 139; speech on eve of Special Tariff Conference, 147–8; participates in Special Tariff Conference, 149 ff.
Malaya, and defence of Singapore, 212; *also* 162
Manchuria (Manchukuo), crisis of 172 ff.; British refuse to recognize as Manchukuo, 223; reconsideration of recognition, 249; *also* 12, 24, 28–31, 33–4, 46
Marco Polo bridge incident, 241 ff.
Massey, William F., and the Anglo-Japanese Alliance, 55 ff.; *also* 51
Matheson and Company, 163

Meighen, Arthur, and the Anglo-Japanese Alliance, 56 ff., 83–4; *also* 51
Mongolia, strategic importance of, 24–25; *also* 28–31, 33–4
Mounsey, George, discusses Shanghai, 165–6; *also* 218
Mukden, occupation of by Japanese troops, 176–7; *also* 118, 171

Nanking, incident of, 124, 132 ff.; discussed in regard to British mission, 229–31; fall of, 248; *also* 211 note 10
Naval disarmament, 50 ff.; 99 ff.
Newton, Basil C., on Bolshevism, 123–4
New Zealand, and the question of the Anglo-Japanese Alliance, 51 ff.; *also* 2, 37, 46, 105, 212
Nine Power Treaty, 104–5, 191–3, 195–196, 206, 243
Ningpo, 14
Non-Aggression Pact (Russia and China), 239

O'Malley, Owen, 157–9
Open Door, *see* Free Trade
Orde, C. W., sums up problem of Singapore base, 210; and possible sanctions against Japan, 242–3; *also* 193

Parlett, H. G., 36
Parliament, and the Nanking incident 134
Piggot, Julian, 222
Pratt, Sir John, general ideas about China and Japan, 4–9; on Sun Yat-sen, 111–13; and the Manchurian crisis, 187–8, 199; criticizes Stimson, 194; comments on Lytton Report, 201–2; on the Japanese as egocentric, 234; on economic situation in China, 236 note 64; views on the Marco Polo bridge incident, 241; peace formula, 249–51; *also* 238, 240
'Race' and the origins of the war, 1–3, 10, 12, 58 ff., 94–5, 259
Racial equality clause, 11
Reading, Lord, 178
Roosevelt, Franklin D., quarantine speech, 243–4